SWING TRADING

SWING TRADING

Power Strategies to Cut Risk and Boost Profits

JON D. MARKMAN

WILEY

John Wiley & Sons, Inc.

Published by John Wiley & Sons, Inc., Hoboken, New Jersey.
Published simultaneously in Canada.

For general information on our other products and services, or technical support, please contact our Customer Care Department within the United States at 800-762-2974, outside the United States at 317-572-3993 or fax 317-572-4002.

Wiley also publishes its books in a variety of electronic formats. Some content that appears in print may not be available in electronic books.

For more information about Wiley products, visit our web site at www.wiley.com.

Library of Congress Cataloging-in-Publication Data:

Markman, Jon D., 1958–
    Swing trading : power strategies to cut risk and boost profits / Jon Markman.
        p.   cm.
    ISBN 0-471-20678-4 (alk. paper)
    1. Investment analysis.   2. Stocks.   I. Title.
HG4529 .M375   2003
332.63'2042—dc21   2002154059

ISBN: 0-471-20678-4

Printed in the United States of America.

10 9 8 7 6 5 4 3 2 1

Contents

Introduction

When hitters face New York Yankees pitcher Roger Clemens in a clutch situation, they often choke up the bat. Taking a shorter swing gives them a better chance of making contact—and avoiding a humiliating whiff.

Likewise, investors who have had a hard time getting hits in today's fast-moving, nerve-wracking market ought to think about taking a tip from the major leagues and shorten up on their swing.

The swing, in trading parlance, refers to the length of time a volatile security position is held, either long or short. Conventional wisdom says that long-term holders are the likeliest to succeed, since they lose the least to such money drains as commissions, bid–ask spreads, and taxes. But conventional wise men have had the owl feathers kicked out of them in recent years, as quick-changing technology, an uncertain economy, and manic consumer tastes have made it harder than ever to figure out which companies have so lasting an edge over competitors that their shares merit long-term holds.

Swing traders oriented toward intermediate-term stock moves, in contrast, measure their commitment to a company's shares in weeks and months, rather than years. After identifying a company for purchase or sale through a combination of fundamental and price/volume analysis, a good swing trader tries to determine the direction of its very next move and to avoid hanging around during inevitable reversals. Swing traders try to take profits quickly after a significant pause in upward momentum, and reinvest them in new opportunities.

While some swing traders try to catch intraday moves in stocks, they are not the focus of this book. Instead, I zero in on methods that will allow busy people to hold positions for as long as a week to many months—not minutes or hours. I also explain how new online tools will help investors play and win at a game once dominated by professionals.

Several books have capably covered some of this ground in the past couple of years for the benefit of fellow professionals. They feature a jungle of jargon that average private investors cannot easily penetrate. In contrast, here you find a set of programmatic, easy-to-master, readable approaches that is filled with examples, illustrations, historical perspective, and practical advice from seasoned traders. Advanced beginning or intermediate-level investors should be able to use this book as a step-by-step guide to intermediate-term swing trading and start to profit before they're halfway through. Most importantly, you should be able to swing-trade without making it a full-time job.

The key is to detach this approach from day trading. Day traders, by definition, play for dozens of tiny moves in a stock or index during a single 9:30 to 4 P.M. market period—and close out all positions before the final bell. They get crazy for nickels and dimes, while week-focused swing traders play strictly for the $100 bills.

For example, a swing trader who identified July 23, 2002, as a tradable bottom in stocks would have initiated long positions in a handful of securities as soon as July 24, and profitably stayed in them for at least the next four weeks. A day trader, meanwhile, could have moved in and out of stocks 200 times or more in that two-week period. And the long-term investors who had been holding on since the slide began in March 2000? They continued to sit tight, glumly getting back 20 percent of their massively large lost value.

There are as many ways to find success as a swing trader as there are window ledges on Wall Street. All require substantial reserves of discipline, conviction, patience, and research time. In this book, I explain six ways to get with the swing—each explained by a leading expert in the field. In each case, you meet the traders, learn about their favorite swing-trade setups, and learn about their approach to trade management. Additionally, I have provided my own views on intermediate-term trading that leverages a stock-rating system I helped to design and build at the web site CNBC on MSN Money.

In the first chapter, you meet Toronto-based hedge fund manager and research publisher Terry Bedford and learn how he focuses on chart patterns to find entries and exits for swing trades. In Chapter 2, you meet Bert Dohmen, a Los Angeles-based private trader and research publisher, who leverages his experience as a child in wartime Germany and as a defense industry analyst in the United States to keep cool when the technical indicators on his charts are flying low and fast. In the third chapter, you meet Cuban-born options trader George Fontanills and learn his

unique approach to finding multimonth short sales of crashing companies. In Chapter 4, you learn about my own method of finding stocks to
hold for a month or more at a time, leveraging the StockScouter rating
system at MSN Money as well as my HiMARQ stock-seasonality metrics. In the fifth chapter, you meet Chicago-based swing trader and research publisher Richard Rhodes, who specializes in formulating a
big-picture fundamental view of the economy before zeroing in on stocks
appropriate for multimonth moves on the basis of their accelerating or
waning weekly momentum. And in Chapter 6, you meet Phil Erlanger, an
expert on sentiment and the big moves that ensue when bears or bulls
overstay their welcome in a stock or market.

We start with Bedford, since his approach to trading patterns gives us
a solid foundation for understanding the rest.

SWING TRADING

Chapter 1

TERRY BEDFORD
"Price Is Everything"

Terry Bedford, a tenacious swing trader for two decades, works out of his home in a high-rise condominium on the windswept outskirts of Toronto, Canada. He has an office downtown, too, but rarely visits. Although he runs a one-man shop, his day is a blur of action and noise: He watches CNBC with the sound off, monitors his stocks on two flat-panel computer screens, listens to alternative rock acts like Bjork or Clash at full volume when things get dull, and doesn't mind intrusions at any time by his energetic three-year-old daughter, Zoë. (Research clients, with whom he communicates largely by e-mail and instant messenger, are accustomed to seeing a smiley face inserted by little hands from time to time.)

Terry trades mostly for his hedge fund, Grayhawke Equity Partners; in 2000 it gained 16 percent, in 2001 it gained 42 percent, and in 2002 through June it was up 25 percent. He grinds out the returns week by week, rather than counting on big wins—making as many as 30 trades a day from both sides of the market. He buys shares of companies he hates and sells shares of companies he loves because they're just ticker symbols to him—not businesses. "When you trade, the easiest way to lose money is to fall in love with what the company does," he says. "If you love KLA Tencor as a semiconductor equipment company, you're going to miss 10 great opportunities to short it. When you swing-trade, a little bit of fundamental knowledge is dangerous; it clouds your judgment. That's the reality. Stocks are just playing cards; you can't get invested in a story—it's just hype."

1

An avid impressionist-style painter in his free time, Terry typically looks to hold his stocks for three to five days—treating them, if you will, like quick but colorful brush strokes. To hunt for instruments to wield, he works from the top down—starting with sectors that his data sources show are under strong money-flow accumulation or disposal by professionals, then zeroing in on four or five stocks in those groups which he believes tend to trend the best. Before making his final decision, he starts by looking at a stock's three-year trend with weekly bars, then looks at its one-year trend with daily bars, then zeroes in on its ten-, five-, and one-day intraday trends with ten-minute bars. When he sees setups that have worked in the past, as you will learn in a minute, he pounces and begins the process of buying or shorting in a series of 2,500-share lots until he's got a 7,500- or 10,000-share position. Trading in such size in a small operation throws into relief the value of swing trading: Recognizing patterns of volume and price lets Terry know immediately when he is wrong so that he can exercise risk management.

Terry was born in Halifax, Nova Scotia—called Canada's Atlantic Playground in the travel press—in 1964. When his father retired from the Navy in 1975, his family moved to Brantford, Ontario, which is best known as the birthplace of both hockey player Wayne Gretzky and the place from which Alexander Graham Bell placed the first documented telephone call.

He was drawn to the stock market at age fifteen when working two summer dishwashing jobs: nights at a Chinese restaurant called Danny's Ho-Ho and days at the Ponderosa Steakhouse. He saved some money and decided to invest, then went downtown and found a broker named Richard Blair at a long-gone firm called Pittfield, McKay Ross. Blair gave him a list of books to read, and soon he made his first purchase: $3,000 worth of Alcan warrants on a bet that the economy would improve. Later that summer an aluminum shortage emerged, and he says he felt like a genius for earning $1,500 in two months. Afterward he spent a lot of time in that small brokerage office, and boosted his stake to $15,000 by throwing the dice a lot and making "a lot of stupid bets." By the time he was eighteen, he had bought himself the first in a long series of BMWs with some gains and thought he was smart, so he enrolled in the business program at McMaster University in Hamilton. Terry says he spent most of his college years rummaging through business magazines looking for trading ideas, and by the time he graduated had accumulated a stake around $100,000. He had originally set his cap to become a corporate lawyer—probably from having watched too much *L.A. Law* at the time—but ultimately decided to become a stock broker.

Terry worked at three firms as a broker before realizing it was making him old, fast. He got tired of holding clients' hands, and wanted to manage his own money not theirs. "It occurred to me that I preferred being on the other end of the phone—placing the orders, not taking them," he says. He quit as a broker in 1992 at age twenty-eight, but it didn't take long to lose most of his trading capital—and that is when he figures he started down the path toward becoming a full-time trader. To build his stake back up, he began to sell technical research on stocks to institutions. He started small, sending reports to a few portfolio managers in the Toronto area, and gradually building his client base up to include large U.S. fund managers. He never slept more than five hours a day, and still doesn't, as he's consumed with watching markets around the world and studying charts.

Terry believes that the key to any type of trading activity—but particularly of swing trading—is to stay in the game. You must preserve capital, you must constantly assess and reassess risk and potential reward, and most importantly, you must focus on *getting the money*: You've got to get your profit out of a trade and get out. "Every day, imagine you are sending an army of soldiers out to capture capital. Like any other general you want your soldiers to perform their tasks and get back safely," he says. "Each time your soldiers return with captured capital, the power of your army grows."

He doesn't worry that trading too much will incur too much in taxes. "There are a lot of people living on the sidewalk," he says. "They don't have to worry about taxes. But then again, they don't have any money. Paying taxes is part of the cost of success. The most important rule of trading is to take your profit when it becomes available."

Terry leans almost exclusively on technical analysis to make his trades; in fact, he thinks knowing too much about a company or the economy gets him into trouble. He believes price is the most important statistic to know about a stock because it is the only accurate measure of investor sentiment—it is the intersection of supply and demand. Technical analysis, in his view, makes the assumption that investor sentiment determines price more than fundamental factors like earnings, revenues, and profit margins. Another way to put it: He believes that all fundamental viewpoints of a stock, and all perceptions of that viewpoint, are encapsulated in a single data point: the price.

The three most important principles that guide his approach to swing trading: First, price is not random. Second, price anticipates perceptions of fundamental change. And third, the relationship between price and time is linear.

With that road map in mind, it's time to begin unfolding Terry's approach to the practice, rather than just the theory, of swing trading. We start with the basics of his views on why stocks trend, then discuss the psychology of support and resistance, move on to his most useful chart patterns for reversal, and end with his favorite patterns for continuation plays. Some of the discussion that follows is adapted, with permission, from his own writing on the subject.

Price Is Not Random

Finance professors would have us believe that price action in stocks and markets is random. But that is nonsense. If it were true, then traders like Terry would be broke. Instead, prices move in regular patterns in concert with the ebb and flow of supply and demand. Price consolidates when supply and demand for a security are in relative equilibrium, and price advances or declines rapidly in a trend when there is an imbalance between supply and demand.

Consider the case of Visx in early 1999 (see Figure 1.1).

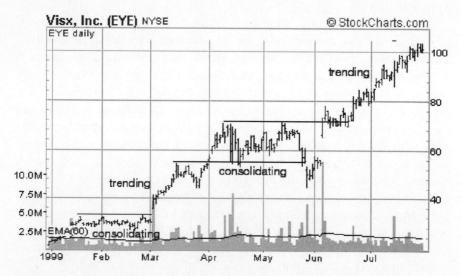

Figure 1.1   Consolidation and trending in Visx, Inc.
Source: StockCharts.com.

In early 1999 Visx, Inc., became a very hot stock. The maker of laser systems used for corrective eye surgery was thought to have unlimited potential. In middle January through late February 1999 the stock began a consolidation phase just below $35 before posting a breakout to $40 at the beginning of March on five times average daily volume. That event sent the stock into a trending phase that lasted through early April. During this phase the stock rallied better than 75 percent as investors began to embrace the idea that laser eye surgery was going to become a multibillion dollar industry. The next consolidation phase began with the April highs and lasted through early June. During this period the stock remained in a relatively tight trading range and volume slowed considerably. In the absence of further fundamental news, the supply and demand for shares was in relative equilibrium. In early June, Visx reported record earnings and revenue growth and once again the stock surged to a new high, this time pushing through $70 on almost 10 times average daily volume. The new trending phase saw the stock appreciate a further 50 percent to $105 in less than two months.

During each of these four phases the share price of Visx moved in distinct patterns of either consolidation or trend. An alert swing trader observing this pattern, anticipating and responding to news, would have initiated purchases at two times: at the breakout in early March or at the breakout in early June. Sales, but not short sales, could have been accomplished at the first return to the consolidation lows of April or May for one- or two-month holds.

Price Anticipates Fundamental Changes

Fundamental change at companies does not happen overnight; it takes time. A new product or service that could make or break a company's financial results could take years to develop in house. When ready, it is presented to the sales force; salespeople present it to clients privately or at trade shows; it then may be improved in house again before being revealed to the public at large. All this time, a company's stock may trade among investors who are unaware of this terrific new offering. Yet it is fair to guess that some buyers and sellers of the company's shares would be better informed than others. They are the "smart money."

Though they are often misdirected, the smart money seeks unbiased, market-moving information not yet in the public domain. In many cases this information is the result of expensive, independent fundamental research—but it may also come from personal contacts deep within public companies. It is this informed buying and/or selling that *anticipates* fundamental changes and initiates early price trends that the swing trader can witness on his or her charts or view on the tape.

It may seem as though the smart money has an unfair advantage over the general public, and to an extent that's true. Information is a commodity like any other, and those with greater resources may have better luck obtaining it. The swing trader needs to keep this in mind when stocks appear to be rising or falling in the absence of information in the public domain.

Consider the case of one-time stock market darling Sun Microsystems in the last quarter of 2000 (see Figure 1.2).

In the first half of 2000, computer workstations manufacturer Sun Microsystems, Inc., and other companies championing the wired world were among the hottest momentum stocks. Despite rising earnings and nothing but good cheer among Wall Street analysts, momentum clearly began to slow by September. After reaching $65 the stock began to move lower, falling all the way to $48 in early October—a level below the August low. Just weeks ahead of the third quarter earnings report in late October, however, several Wall Street firms began announcing their previews of the quarter and issuing bullish recommendations.

Figure 1.2 Price anticipates fundamentals: Sun Microsystems, Inc.
Source: StockCharts.com.

Slowly the stock rallied back to $61 by the end of the month. When the third quarter earnings report was released the news could not have been better. The company reported record revenues and earnings, and executives pronounced themselves wildly optimistic about the future. But after a brief rally, the stock slumped, retreating all the way back to $38 by late November and consolidating there. The alert swing trader observing this stock would keep a close eye on that now-critical level. If broken, a safe short trade could be initiated.

Three weeks later Sun Microsystems executives met at a technology conference and suggested that the outlook was considerably poorer and the stock began a free fall to the high-$20s by year end. As prices consolidated there at the start of the next year, the short trade would have been successfully consummated. (By October 2002, the stock had fallen under $4.)

In the case of Sun, it is important to note that the share price accurately forecast the peak in fundamental prospects long before executives issued bad news. The Sun price chart should be a clue as to the relationship between time and price but in the next example I break it down so it is crystal clear.

The Relationship between Price and Time Is Linear

One of the hardest concepts to grasp is that the relationship between price and time is linear. That is, the longer that price fails to behave as anticipated, the more likely we are to amend our expectations.

The simplest example of this phenomena involves our ability to take losses. Most investors do not like losses. When they buy a stock wrong, they will often attempt to get out of that position without suffering a loss, but as days turn into weeks and weeks turn into months their stubbornness takes a back seat to common sense. A rationalization process begins and slowly the perception of a suitable exit level changes. Obviously, no one wants to sit on a bad stock forever. This is the linear relationship between time and price—the longer the time frame stretches, the more elastic price expectations become.

Consider the case of sports clothing and footwear maker Timberland in the middle of 2001 (see Figure 1.3).

For a long time it seemed that Timberland was a firm doing all the right things. Its clothing and footwear were a prerequisite for outdoorsy Gen-Xers and both sales and profits were advancing at breakneck pace.

Figure 1.3   Buyers' remorse: Timberland Co.
Source: StockCharts.com.

In anticipation of record earnings, the stock surged to a record high at $72 in the middle of January. After it slumped back to $65 just a few sessions later, investors were treated to a strong earnings report and nothing but good news from corporate executives. Expansion of the brand was said to be going well in Europe and the future looked very bright. But despite this rosy backdrop the stock could do no better than a rally to $68 following the earnings release. To make matters worse, the stock closed at the low of the session and gapped a full point lower the following day.

Those who purchased the stock amid all the good news were trapped at the virtual record high price on much stronger than average daily volume. This lead to "buyers' remorse"—characterized by buyers feeling trapped and now motivated to sell for breakeven. Just two weeks later it looked as though those trapped in the stock from the $68 level would have an opportunity to exit without a loss, but after it surged to $66 in a stronger stock market, sellers immediately began to dump the stock and just two weeks later it was changing hands at $52. With hopes of getting out without a loss now fleeting, sellers began to sell every significant rally. They did so in early March, mid-April, and late May.

In each case they were willing to take less for their shares. This "sliding scale" caused the stock to falter all the way to just $37.50 in the middle of July. And the alert swing trader, recognizing this "buyers' remorse" pattern of lower highs and lower lows, could have safely shorted the stock on every rally back to the clearly defined trendline.

Although the case of Timberland involves down-trending price characteristics, the same basic principle applies to stocks moving steadily higher. The longer the price moves away from a predetermined entry level, the more likely investors are to rationalize why they should *chase* the price, and entries for swing traders on the long side emerge at every decline back to a clearly defined uptrend.

Again, it is as important for swing traders to understand *why* chart patterns appear as it is for them to recognize them. Generally speaking, they appear because smart money—successful large fund managers—are better informed than the public. These investors set trends and in this sense, price has a tendency to precede fundamental developments. At the same time, it is human nature for "dumb money" to try to minimize losses when stock positions are purchased at the wrong time. Investors will attempt to exit positions without suffering a loss, but this desire diminishes in a linear fashion with the passage of time, making rallies shorter and declines steeper.

Now that we have a better understanding of price, let's move on to another technical analysis basic for swing traders: support and resistance.

Support and Resistance

Support and resistance are the cornerstones of technical analysis. It's an easy concept: They are simply the areas where buyers and sellers have shown a greater-than-average willingness to either buy (in the case of support) or sell (in the case of resistance).

That may seem a bit simplistic but very often price is ultimately governed by basic human emotions. We have all been in the position where we buy a stock and immediately it begins to decline. Our strongest instinct is to not sell this stock until we can do so without suffering a loss. If enough investors buy at the same price and immediately suffer buyers' remorse, the result is a resistance point. Resistance points often occur after a stock has had a lengthy advance into a key news event. As early investors (the smart money) sell on the news that they anticipated, many unlucky new investors are trapped. The absence of new buyers leads to weakness, and the stock begins to fall. And every time the stock rallies to this level, those who bought poorly will sell.

Support is a more difficult concept, usually the result of buyers being rewarded for purchasing a stock at a specific price. If you buy a stock at a certain price level and it immediately rallies, the odds are you'll feel very good about yourself and your purchase price. After selling that stock for a profit, you are likely to consider buying the stock on any retreat to this level (if it worked once, it could work again). If enough investors are willing to buy at a certain level, it becomes support.

Understanding the nuances of support and resistance is the most important part of technical analysis and must be deeply ingrained in the swing trader's outlook. But there are many nuances to comprehend, so now let's look at support and resistance in some common technical patterns: the flat base, the downtrend, and the uptrend.

Support and Resistance in a Downtrend

Remember, the relationship between price and time is linear, so investors who buy stocks wrong are first motivated to sell the position without suffering a loss. But as days become weeks and weeks become months a rationalization process occurs that allows these same investors ultimately to sell their positions for a loss. Of course, they want to get the best price possible, so they watch the price action very carefully—noting what price points lead to buying and what price points lead to selling. Swing traders must understand that these price points are not random: They are support and resistance.

In the case of Timberland in the middle of 2001, support and resistance price points were obvious. (See Figure 1.4.) After a lengthy run to new highs at the start of the year, Timberland fell out of favor in a weak retailing environment. In January the stock made a new high above $72 but by February the share price was falling fast. In early February, Timberland shares fell to $59.50 and rebounded to $66 just a few days later. This $59.50 level became the first major support level of the new downtrend. By late February the $59.50 support level had been smashed and a relative new low was made at $51.50. This time buyers dug in and the stock rallied smartly only to find sellers at what had been the previous support level at $59.50. Of course, this level was now resistance—and the fact that it was so clearly established would be a boon to swing traders ready to attack from the short side.

Through most of the next three weeks the stock meandered near the support level at $51.50 until that level was broken in early April. After

Figure 1.4 In a downtrend, resistance is futile: Timberland Co.
Source: StockCharts.com.

falling as low as $42, Timberland shares made several attempts to rally back through the $51.50 resistance level but every attempt was rebuffed. This presented another entry for a swing from the short side.

As the series of support and resistance arrows reveal, this stair-step pattern created a very well defined technical downtrend. Note how sellers become willing to sell their shares for successively less as time passes. This may occur due to a change in fundamental factors, but the result is a stair-step pattern of support and resistance that provides well-defined entry points for observant traders.

Now that we have explored support and resistance in a downtrend, let's tackle uptrends.

Support and Resistance in an Uptrend

Although the motivation is not the same, many of the same forces that lead to technical downtrends are also at work in the creation of the technical uptrend. These patterns occur because investors chasing a strong stock rationalize that paying more than their intended purchase price is warranted given its strength. The higher the stock price moves, the more likely it is that investors will rationalize, up to a point, why paying a higher price makes sense. Some will argue this rationalization process is directly related to a perceived change in fundamental factors and very often this is true. Understanding technical analysis does not mean that fundamental factors should be dismissed. Consider the case of SLM Holding, a leading lender to students, in Figure 1.5.

SLM Holding Corporation was one of the few issues to move significantly higher in the latter half of 2000. The stock emerged from a small base pattern in the middle of September at $45 and never really looked back. When this level was penetrated on better than average volume it became important technical support, and buyers were more than willing to step up and buy on every decline to that level. In early October, SLM Holding tested support at $45 on three separate occasions. In each case the stock rallied briskly and after one such test in the middle of October SLM Holding began to trend so strongly that the stock added 30 percent in just two weeks. Each of these declines to support was an excellent entry point for a swing trade on the long side.

That process lifted the stock to a new resistance point at $59. SLM Holding failed to push through the $59 level on two occasions, but in early December volume surged and the share price easily moved beyond $59. Once again the result of the upside breakout was a significant near-term rally. This time the stock rallied to $68.50 before sellers emerged.

Figure 1.5 Support in an uptrend: SLM Holding Corp.
Source: StockCharts.com.

The key support and resistance levels are delineated with arrows. These arrows reveal just how powerful is the role of support and resistance in the formation of a typical technical uptrend. Each time the stock reversed at a prior high or low would make a perfect entry, either long or short—as you will see again later.

The bottom line: Support and resistance are price points where buyers and sellers have shown a greater-than-average willingness to buy and sell stock. When support falters, it becomes resistance. When resistance is eclipsed, it becomes support. This occurs because weak hands (nonbelievers) are replaced with strong hands (believers). Support and resistance play key roles in the determination of major trends, creating "stair-step" levels where both buyers and sellers have shown a willingness to act.

With that out of the way, we're done with two of the three basic building blocks. It's time to pull it all together with the last basic concept—volume.

The Importance of Volume

Let's begin with a common sense theory that is critical for swing traders to grasp: Volume should follow the trend. That is, in a bullish phase, volume should expand on rallies and contract on declines. In a bearish phase, volume should expand on declines and contract on rallies.

That's the theory; now here is the common sense. In an uptrend, an ever-increasing number of buyers are required to soak up pent-up selling pressures. After all, the higher a stock moves in price the more likely it is that investors who bought the stock at lower prices will want to sell. For the rally to continue, these shares need to be absorbed by new buyers. If price advances quickly, buyers may step back—creating temporary weakness. But these periods should be characterized by weak volume if the trend is strong.

When a stock is mired in a bearish trend and the outlook is poor, volume should expand on declines because would-be buyers are overwhelmed by sellers. If the stock sinks quickly, some prospective sellers will refuse to sell, choosing to wait for a small rally in price. This temporary absence of sellers creates a small vacuum that should lead to a light-volume rally. When the stock rallies sufficiently, sellers who failed to exit ahead of the first major decline begin selling and once again volume should expand.

Volume in Trends

Healthy bullish and bearish trends are characterized by rising volume in the direction of the price. But what happens when a stock advances and volume contracts—or a stock falters and volume expands? It is not supposed to happen but when it does the result is almost always a sharp reversal—an ideal setup for swing traders.

Consider this example of a stock that rallied in the face of contracting volume. In the winter of 1999, data-storage stocks were a momentum investors' fantasy. The news flow was positive and analysts were falling over one another to make a name for themselves by finding the next EMC Corporation. Atop the momentum mountain was QLogic (see Figure 1.6).

Shares of QLogic, a designer of high-end switches and software for storage-area networks, had been mired in a consolidation pattern through early January and February 2000 before they had a high-volume breakout at $92. From that point, the stock began a parabolic advance that saw the

Figure 1.6　Rally with contracting volume: QLogic Corp.
Source: StockCharts.com.

issue more than double in just one month. It appeared to be a momentum investors' dream come true. There was just one problem: As the stock rallied to one new high after another amid buy recommendations from analysts and better than expected earnings reports, volume was slowing. In fact, all through the rally, volume did not approach the high made in early January when the initial consolidation began. When stocks rally to new highs amid slow or progressively weak volume, technicians argue that they enter the distribution phase—the phase where the smart money begins selling profitable long positions amid continued good news. By April 15, just another month later, the stock had fallen from $200 per share to just $60. The weak volume rally laid the foundation for a spectacular decline. Of course, there is a moral here for swing traders as position ownership lengthens: Beware weak volume rallies amid good news, and prepare to switch sides of the battle.

Now let's jump ahead one year. We are still looking at QLogic but in the late winter of 2000 the data-storage concern was a very different stock. Ravaged by an ongoing bear market for technology stocks and a steady stream of earnings warnings, QLogic shares had fallen from favor with Wall Street analysts. Those who once had forecast fundamental splendor now talked regularly of impending doom, and the stock fell hard on strong volume, offering traders a chance to short every rally to its trendline. (See Figure 1.7.)

In the winter of 2000, QLogic had fallen far from favor, but the stock did begin the process of consolidating its losses during January 2001 and early February. The stock rallied from $60 to $98 during this time frame on better than average volume only to falter once again in the middle of February after an earnings warning from a peer, EMC Corporation. QLogic, and most other data storage issues collapsed and by early April the stock had fallen to less than $20. It was now a short sellers' dream. . . . And yet there was just one problem: Volume had contracted at each stage of the march to new lows. When stocks decline to new lows amid slow or progressively weak volume, swing traders should note that they enter the "accumulation" phase—the phase where the smart money begins adding new positions for longer-term gains. Over the next six weeks QLogic shares more than tripled on increased volume. The lesson for swing traders: You need to be very careful about shorting into weak volume declines amid bad news.

Now that we know what is supposed to happen to volume in trends—and what to expect when volume doesn't follow the trend—let's take a look at volume in consolidations.

Figure 1.7   Declines with contracting volume: QLogic Corp.
Source: StockCharts.com.

Volume in Consolidations

One of the lessons that all swing traders must take to heart is that large changes in price often follow large declines in volume. This makes good sense. A slowdown in volume (and a narrowly defined trading range) is almost always the result of indecision on the part of investors. When they cannot come to consensus about fair value, volume slows and the trading range narrows as most investors move to the sidelines and await more data. When there are sufficient data to come to a conclusion about future prospects, volume expands and a large price move transpires. In most cases, technicians call the slowdown in volume a consolidation.

On daily price charts, consolidation patterns can last several days, several weeks, or several months. They are most often rectangular in shape, but the geometry is immaterial. The fact is that consolidation patterns are direct results of investor indecision, and they are almost always followed by large price explosions.

Consider the example of Dell Computer. There was a time when Dell was a must-own stock for growth-oriented money managers, but all of this changed in the winter of 2000 when some investors began to doubt that computer makers could turn in strong profits in the face of slowing demand. (See Figure 1.8.)

In November 2000, Dell began a decline that would see the stock almost cut in half over the course of just seven weeks. The stock peaked at $33 and sank to just $16.75 in late December. At the time, very few investors probably guessed that the stock would remain mired in this trading range for most of the next year. In fact, Dell became entangled in a triangular trading range—also called a "wedge"—that saw prices narrow and trading volume collapse as investors tried to make sense of the outlook for computer hardware in a slowing economy. By the middle of April 2001, Dell had rallied to $31 only to falter once again to $22.60 in the middle of June. During this entire consolidation period trading volume slowed progressively.

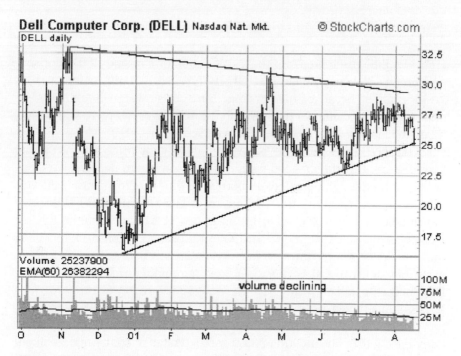

Figure 1.8 Declining volume in consolidation: Dell Computer Corp.
Source: StockCharts.com.

Price consolidation is a necessary stage for all stocks. The period that follows consolidation is a breakout, and this can be the most exciting phase for any stock—and every alert swing trader. Let's examine volume during this phase.

Volume in Breakouts

In its purest form, a "breakout" is the period immediately following a consolidation. It is that point in time when consensus is reached and those who were on one side of the market are overwhelmed by those investors on the other side. For that short moment, investors agree on price direction.

It's fair to say that stocks are mired in some form of consolidation pattern 70 percent of the time. The other 30 percent brings dramatic price breakouts—either up or down—that lead to great trading opportunities. Obviously traders are looking for breakouts because it is during this period that the majority of predictable, successful trades occur.

Upside Breakouts

Consider the upside breakout for Dial Corporation in mid-2001. For several months the soap maker was largely ignored by both traders and investors alike because fundamental prospects were thought to be unexciting. The company was a steady, slow grower but there was no immediate reason to buy or sell its shares. (See Figure 1.9.)

You should recognize the pattern created by the price action for Dial Corporation. It is the dreaded wedge. These long-term patterns are characterized by dramatic declines in both volatility (trading range) and volume. That was certainly true of Dial from late December 2000 through the middle of July 2001. After hitting a low at $10.10 in the middle of December the stock surged to $15.50 in mid-January, fell back to $12 in the middle of March through late April, and rallied toward $15.25 in early June, only to fall back to $13.50 in the middle of July. In late July, Dial began to rally toward $15 on increased volume. Several sessions later volume increased dramatically and the stock had a breakout to a relative new high. Note that both volume and volatility contracted dramatically during the consolidation phase and exploded as the upside breakout occurred. The proper entry method for a swing trader observing the stock's unusual increase in volume was a buy stop at $15.50; the stock ul-

Figure 1.9 Upside breakout. Dial Corp.
Source: StockCharts.com.

timately broke out on volume and went on to rally over the next two weeks to $18.

Understanding the importance of volume in an upside breakout is fairly simple: Volume must expand on the breakout if the move is to be considered valid.

Volume and downside breakouts are more complex because volume is not necessarily required for a sharp decline. This makes sense because unlike rallies, for which increased volume is needed to absorb normal selling pressures, in a decline stockholders become demoralized and that emotion leads to inactivity. Yes, there will be downside breakouts that are characterized by dramatic surges in volume. But these events will always be at the end of the move lower as shareholders capitulate. After all, the longer the decline proceeds, the more volume becomes the ally of buyers, not sellers. As mentioned previously, traders need to be wary of increased volume after a longer-term decline because very often it means the end of that move is near.

Downside Breakouts

Let's consider the downside breakout of onetime energy trading giant Enron. Once considered a broadband play because of its foray into the Internet infrastructure business, Enron fell on hard times in February of 2001. During the span of seven months the stock had two noteworthy downside breakouts. (See Figure 1.10.)

Well before its profound troubles surfaced, from December 2000 through the early part of March 2001, the energy-trading firm Enron was mired in a large wedge formation. The stock hit lows at $65, $66, and $67.50 in December, January, and March, respectively. The top part of the wedge was defined by highs at $83.50, $82.50, and $81.75 in December, January, and February, respectively. The downside breakout occurred in early March at $67.50 amid very subdued volume.

This would have been relatively difficult to capture in a swing trade, but the stock sank to $52 in less than two weeks and it was not until volume increased that the decline subsided. The second wedge began with

Figure 1.10 Downside breakout: Enron Corp.
Source: StockCharts.com.

the $52 low in the middle of March. After several tests of that support level—the second of which was tradable by an alert swing trader, Enron shares fell through $52 in the early part of June. Once again, volume was relatively light but this downside breakout led to a decline that would see the Enron shares sink to less than $35 just a week later. Of course, the stock fell to less than $1 before the year was out, en route to the company's bankruptcy filing.

The lessons? Volume follows price in a healthy trend—swelling on up days and contracting on down days in a rising trend, and the reverse in a falling trend. When volume contracts after an extended rally, or expands sharply after an extended decline, a dramatic reversal will normally transpire. Volume and volatility contract in consolidation patterns because investors cannot reach consensus; they are undecided. Volume should expand significantly for upside breakouts. If volume does not expand, the breakout is considered illegitimate. Volume may not expand for a downside breakout because falling share prices cause demoralization and inactivity among stockholders. During such circumstances, fewer shares are required to drive prices lower.

With an understanding of all the basics under our belts let's get ready to tackle the really fun stuff for active swing traders: reversal chart patterns.

CHART PATTERNS—REVERSAL

Stocks go up and stocks go down. But swing traders can learn with practice that in most cases the reversal is easily detected and capitalized upon.

Although the fundamental and technical factors that lead to reversals may be varied, every stock price reversal is ultimately the result of one of two themes: distribution or accumulation. In this section I explain the way Terry seeks to understand accumulation and distribution patterns and the signs of impending reversal, along with his most trusted patterns.

One-Day Reversal

The one-day reversal is the starting point for most reversal patterns. After an extended rally the stock gaps higher at the open to trade at a new high on a positive news announcement. As the session proceeds, volume expands significantly but by the close the entire rally disappears and the stock closes lower.

Why Does It Happen?

One-day reversals occur because large investors need liquidity to close long positions. They understand that the best way to liquidate a large position is to sell into good news when liquidity is highest—so they are willing sellers on a day when the stock is making a new high and everyone is saying good things. Investors and media wonder how such good news could have resulted in such poor price performance. Indeed, over the next several sessions analysts and traders rationalize that the selling was simply overdue given the strong rally leading into the news, but every subsequent rally fails. Weeks later the stock is well off its recent highs.

How Are Technical Targets Determined?

One-day reversals are by definition one-day events and as such technical targets are not implied. But if you look at every major reversal pattern, you will quickly see that it all began with a one-day reversal that led to good swing trades. (See Figure 1.11.)

With a virtual marketplace Amazon.com was supposed to make tradi-

Figure 1.11　One-day reversal: Amazon.com, Inc.
Source: StockCharts.com.

tional retailing obsolete. The concept was so compelling that Wall Street analysts began devising new data points to make valuations work. This rationalization process saw the stock vault from pennies in 1998 (on an adjusted split basis) to $110 in late April 1999. It was amazing. Then the firm reported record revenues for the first quarter and several Wall Street analysts reiterated their "buy" ratings and raised targets. After closing the previous day at $103.59, the stock opened April 27 at $105.50 and proceeded to rally to $110.63, a record high. Volume swelled and it looked as though the nonbelievers were finally throwing in the towel. But by midday the stock was flat. By the close, it was actually lower for the session. Over the coming weeks new "buy" recommendations and positive comments continued but the stock sank to just $35 in early August.

Vital Signs

- One-day reversals occur because large investors choose to liquidate positions into strength, so it is vital that volume accelerate as the stock begins to work lower.
- The stock must close on the day of the reversal at or very near the session lows.
- Predictable swing trades on the short side are initiated the day after the one-day reversal provided that the stock opens modestly lower (e.g., down 1 percent–2 percent.) If the stock gaps more than 5 percent lower, then you've missed the trade. And if it opens higher, it was not a one-day reversal. Place a stop just above the midpoint of the previous day's trading range.

Wholesale liquidation into good news is an ongoing theme in reversal patterns. Now that we understand the basic premise of the one-day reversal, let's tackle the island reversal.

Island Reversal

Island reversals are isolated data points separated by gaps. After an extended rally the stock "gaps" higher—that is, it proceeds to open outside the most recent trading range. After trading in the new higher range for several sessions, a second gap occurs—only this time the move is lower.

Why Does It Happen?

After an extended rally the stock opens well above the most recent trading range following news. This breakout from the previous consolidation pattern occurs on huge volume and appears legitimate but after several days the stock fails to move significantly higher. New buyers become anxious; sellers should have been removed with the most recent move through resistance; something is wrong. Days later there is fundamental news that contradicts the news that initiated the breakout, and anxious new buyers panic—sending the stock opening lower. Weeks later the stock is well off the recent highs.

How Are Technical Targets Determined?

Like the one-day reversal, island reversals usually occur at the start of larger technical patterns and, as such, technical targets are not implied but these patterns usually lead to much lower prices. (See Figure 1.12.)

The Magna International Island Reversal

Riding a wave of outsourcing, Canadian auto-parts maker Magna International was supposed to have a business model that would smooth the

Figure 1.12 Island reversal: Magna International.
Source: StockCharts.com.

cyclical nature of its industry. On August 13, 2001 the stock zoomed to a relative new high on impressive volume after a Merrill Lynch analyst upgraded the stock from neutral to accumulate. Merrill had been absent in the cheerleading that had helped the stock move from $38 in December 2000 to $66 on August 13, so investors naturally took this recommendation as evidence the coast was clear for new investments. However, in the days immediately following the Merrill recommendation the stock failed to move beyond $69 and to make matters worse, volume increased steadily. On August 17 Ford Motor Company issued an earnings warning and suddenly all the bullish talk about Magna seemed insignificant. Magna shares opened lower and proceeded to work lower for the next several weeks despite a very bullish recommendation by Deutsche Banc's Alex Brown.

Vital Signs

- Island reversals are news driven and usually happen because conflicting news events occur within a short period of time.
- Volume should accelerate on both the initial breakout and the subsequent failure.
- Island reversals are "trend killers" and usually lead to the formation of large patterns that follow the trend.
- Predictable swing trades on the short side are initiated the day after the stock trades below the "island"—usually signified by a 5 percent or greater gap. Place a stop just above the high the stock reached on its down-gap day.

Now let's move on to some of the larger reversal patterns.

Double Top

A double top formation is a distinct pattern characterized by a rally to a new high followed by a moderate pullback and a second rally to test the new high. As the stock rallies to make the second peak, sellers overwhelm buyers and the stock price collapses. Several weeks later the stock moves to test prior support levels.

Why Does It Happen?

Getting caught in a stock at the high is never much fun. The double top pattern occurs because most investors who buy a stock wrong will refuse to exit until they can do so without suffering a loss. Double tops occur af-

ter extended rallies leading to new highs. As the story of the stock becomes more widely accepted, investors are willing to pay increasingly
exorbitant prices. But one day, investors find the price is simply too high,
the stock puts in a top, and prices begin to fall—making top 1. This first
top will normally be sufficient to force many of the more speculative investors from the stock. As they sell, the price of the stock falls further, but
many investors will not sell regardless of how far the price falls because
they refuse to take a loss. After several sessions (sometimes weeks) of
poor price performance, the stock will begin to stabilize until it makes a
"reaction low" and gradually moves higher. In most cases this advance
will occur because of some fundamental factor like an upcoming analysts
meeting, earnings report, or stock split that gives investors hope. As the
stock rises, volume slows and investors who bought at the first top get
ready to exit positions into further strength. As the stock approaches the
prior high, volume surges, and new buyers begin to talk about bright fundamental prospects. It is at that moment that all the skittish investors who
purchased positions at the prior high begin selling. Volume surges and the
stock soon retreats, making top 2. On the chart two equal peaks are created, and the double top is in place. In many cases double top formations
lead to important declines because two separate sets of investors have
been disappointed at a particular level.

How Are Technical Targets Derived?

The technical target for double tops is derived by subtracting the point
difference between top 1 and the reaction low from the breakout level.
After the second top has been created, the breakout level is the reaction
low. No double top formation is complete until the stock falls through
this level, setting up the most predictable short sale for swing traders.
(See Figure 1.13.)

The Emulex Double Top

In the era of momentum stocks, data-storage network device maker
Emulex was one of the favorites. In February 2000 the stock had an upside breakout from a consolidation at $70 and promptly exploded to more
than $112. This rally pushed the stock to one of the richest valuations
anywhere but investors seemed undaunted until the middle of March
when the wheels fell off. The stock skidded from $112.18 to $70.63 amid
rumors that growth rates were slowing. In the following days several
Wall Street analysts made bullish comments and once again momentum
traders piled into the stock. Within days it was very near the first top and

Figure 1.13 Emulex double top.
Source: StockCharts.com.

on March 27 Emulex actually traded at $112.75 before closing at $109.03. The very next day the company warned that growth rates were slowing and Emulex lost $28.57 to close at $80.46. The next day Emulex shares fell through the reaction low at $70.63 and just four days later the stock traded down to $27.00!

Vital Signs

- For a valid double top formation it is important that volume decline significantly as the stock moves toward a test of the first top, and accelerate as price begins to decline.
- No double top is complete until a breakout below the reaction low occurs.
- Downside breakouts often lead to small two to three percent declines followed by an immediate test of the breakout level. If the stock closes above this level (now resistance) for any reason, the pattern becomes invalid.

- Predictable swing trades are made at breakdowns through the reaction low; place a stop just above the reaction low. It's more common, however, to let the stock fall through the reaction low. You will usually get a rally back to the reaction low, and that's where you should initiate the short. Place a stop just above the reaction low. It's also common to sell the first rally back to the first top and place the stop just above that top.

Now let's take a look at the double bottom.

Double Bottom

A double bottom formation is in many ways the mirror image of the double top. After an extended decline to new lows, a stock puts in a bottom on massive volume and a moderate rally ensues. After a few days, or sometimes weeks, the stock drifts back to test the first bottom but this time buying accelerates and another rally occurs.

Why Does It Happen?

Whereas double tops are all about distribution, double bottoms are about accumulation. After an extended decline characterized by aggressive short selling and valuation concerns, value-oriented investors with longer-term time horizons begin to take positions in the stock. They understand that the only way to build a large position in a stock that they like is to do so when selling dominates. It is their willingness to buy the stock when all the news is bad that creates a clear support level, the first bottom (bottom 1). This first part of the pattern will normally be sufficient to force many professional short sellers to cover positions. This coupled with buying from longer-term value investors may be enough to rejuvenate investors who recently purchased the stock at higher levels; they may even rationalize that the market is finally beginning to realize that the current weakness is without merit. A few bullish speculators may be enticed to take new long positions.

Unfortunately, after several sessions of positive price action buying pressures are exhausted and the stock once again begins to falter. The reaction to the decline that formed bottom 1 is complete. Technical traders call this the "reaction high." Sensing easy profits, short sellers return, bullish speculators decide to take profits, and modest selling suddenly becomes a rout. As the stock approaches bottom 1, volume lightens and in many cases the stock will actually fall through the previous low on much lower than average volume.

At this point in time pessimism is greatest; there seems to be no legitimate reason to continue holding the stock. Novice short sellers add new short positions and beleaguered bulls who purchased the stock at much higher levels begin to surrender in anticipation of a new leg lower. However, the expected big decline never materializes since selling pressures have been exhausted. This is when professional short sellers realize the jig is up. It is the new buying by bearish investors to capture profits by covering short positions and the continued accumulation by longer-term investors that help the stock stabilize. As a second bottom (bottom 2) begins to take shape, the pace of short covering accelerates, a new group of bullish speculators take long positions, and the rally explodes. On the chart two equal bottoms are created, and the double bottom is in place. In many cases, double bottoms lead to important rallies because a vital support level has been established.

How Are Technical Targets Derived?

The technical target for a double bottom formation is derived by adding the difference between bottom 1 and the reaction high to the new breakout level. After the second bottom has been created, the new breakout level is the reaction high. No double bottom formation is complete until the stock rallies through this level. (See Figure 1.14.)

The Double Bottom for Mercury Interactive

When momentum stocks shipwreck, it is not a pretty sight. That was certainly the case for software maker Mercury Interactive (MERQ) in 2001. After a parabolic rally that saw the stock reach $160 in October 2000, the stock plunged to $35 by March 12, 2001. That date in March is important because it was then the double bottom pattern for Mercury Interactive began to take shape. Despite a flotilla of bad news, Mercury Interactive stopped going down on March 12 and put in bottom 1. In fact, the stock rallied to a reaction high at $51.68 by March 27 only to fall all the way back to test the March 12 lows a week later. When Mercury Interactive fell through the previous support level at $35 on April 4, there seemed to be few compelling reasons to own the stock. Yet then the most peculiar thing occurred. Despite several Wall Street analyst downgrades, the stock began to move higher on increased volume. Indeed, volume surged to better than 8.9 million shares on that session and the share price slowly began to climb. On April 17 the stock surged through the reaction high at

The implied technical is 64.86. This is the difference between bottom #1 (38.50) and the reaction high (51.68) added to the breakout level (51.68).

Figure 1.14   Double bottom: Mercury Interactive.
Source: StockCharts.com.

$51.68 and that is when the real fun began. Before the start of May, Mercury Interactive had achieved its technical objective.

Vital Signs

- For double bottoms, volume must increase as the stock moves toward the first and second bottoms. In many cases, volume will actually be higher at the first bottom because this is where value-oriented investors first take positions.
- No double bottom pattern is valid until the stock moves through the reaction high.
- Upside breakouts through the reaction high often lead to small two percent to three precent advances followed by an immediate test of the breakout level. If the stock closes below this level (now support) for any reason, the pattern becomes invalid.
- Technical targets are implied but they are by no means assured. Targets are guideposts only.

- To swing-trade, enter after bottom 2 just above the reaction high. Set a stop just below the reaction high.

We have now completed our analysis of the double top and bottom patterns. Now let's move on to the three part patterns, the triple top and bottom.

Triple Top

The triple top is very similar to the double top, only there are three distinctive tops rather than two. A triple top formation is characterized by a rally to a new high followed by a moderate pullback and a second rally to test the new high. As the stock rallies to make the second peak, sellers overwhelm buyers and the stock price falters again. This process is repeated a third time but buyers finally submit, support levels are broken, and a massive decline ensues.

Why Does It Happen?
Like double tops, triple tops occur largely for two reasons. First, those investors who purchased the stock correctly (at lower prices) use good news to liquidate their positions. In this sense the triple top is a distribution pattern because smart buyers are distributing stock. Second, investors who purchased the stock wrongly on the good news refuse to exit their positions until they can do so without suffering a loss. Triple tops occur after extended rallies leading to new highs. As the good-news story becomes more widely accepted, investors are willing to pay increasingly exorbitant prices.

However, at some point those investors who purchased the stock at lower levels feel the urge to take profits. Normally, the bulk of these sellers will use a positive news event such as an earnings report, analyst upgrade, or stock split announcement to begin unwinding long positions. This selling pressure on good news creates resistance and prices begin to fall (top 1). This first top will normally be sufficient to force many of the more speculative investors from the stock. As they sell, the price of the stock falls further but many investors will not sell regardless of how far the price falls because they refuse to take a loss. After several sessions of poor price performance the stock will begin to stabilize, creating what technical traders call a "reaction low" because this move lower was a reaction to the news events of top 1. Slowly the stock begins to move higher. In most cases this advance will occur because the actual fundamental news remains positive. As the stock rises, volume slows and investors who did not sell or bought at the first top get ready to exit positions into renewed strength. As the stock approaches the prior high, volume surges and new buyers begin to talk about the continued bright fundamental prospects—it looks as though new highs are imminent.

At that moment all the investors who want to sell existing positions begin selling. Volume surges and the stock soon retreats (top 2). On the chart two equal peaks are created and recent buyers begin to realize that resistance at these levels is formidable. Selling begins and the stock moves lower on increased volume as recent buyers panic. In most cases the stock will actually fall through the reaction low, setting up a perfect double top pattern, but as this key support level is violated, selling does not intensify. In fact, a rally quickly ensues as short sellers begin to cover positions. Against the backdrop of more positive news and short covering the stock quickly moves toward the old high. Volume is light but there is continued talk of bright fundamental prospects and new highs.

As the stock reaches the prior tops volume accelerates and a distinct third top is created (top 3). The failure to move through formidable resistance helps to reinvigorate bearish investors and for the first time, the stock's valuation is questioned in the media. The stock price begins to plummet and recent buyers begin selling at any cost. The stock falls through the lows set at the trough between top 2 and top 3. The triple top is complete. In many cases these lead to important declines because three separate sets of buyers have been disappointed at distinct levels, the tops and the reaction lows. These levels become formidable resistance.

How Are Technical Targets Derived?

As with double top formations, the technical target for triple tops is derived by subtracting the point difference between top 1 and the reaction low from the breakout level. After the third top has been created, the breakout level is the low created between tops 2 and 3. No triple top formation is complete until the stock falls through this point. (See Figure 1.15.)

The Snap-On Tools Triple Top

When the appetite for technology issues cooled in early 2000 investors began looking for new investment concepts. Snap-On Tools (SNA) was a

Figure 1.15 Triple top: Snap-On Tools.
Source: StockCharts.com.

company with a history of solid growth and great management. In October 2000 the stock rallied from a low of $21 on October 19 to a high of $30.93 on February 2 (top 1) amid rumors of a possible buyout and strong earnings. In fact, on February 2 the company released a press statement saying that it was confident of record earnings despite a softening economy, but investors chose to sell into the good news and by February 23 the stock was trading back at $27.50. This low proved to be significant (a reaction low) because by March 9 Snap-On shares had sprinted back to a high of $30.94 (top 2). On this second rally to resistance, volume slowed and it was not long before the stock was trading back near support and the reaction low at $27.50. From the lows of March 28, Snap-On shares made one final weak-volume rally toward resistance. On April 18 Snap-On shares reached $31.28 intraday but closed at $30.90 and immediately began to work lower (top 3). It would be almost two full months before the triple top pattern was complete but on June 18 Snap-On shares opened below support at $27.50. That downside breakout put Snap-On shares on the path to much lower prices.

Vital Signs

- For a valid triple top, volume should decline on rallies toward tops 2 and 3 and increase into weakness. These volume trends confirm that distribution is taking place into strength.
- Although the lows made during the trough between tops 2 and 3 will often exceed the reaction low, such price action is not necessary during the formation of a triple top.
- No triple top is complete until the stock in question closes below the lows made during the trough between tops 2 and 3.
- Downside breakouts often lead to small two percent to three percent declines followed by an immediate test of the breakout level. If the stock closes above this level (now resistance) for any reason, the pattern becomes invalid.
- To swing-trade, sell on the decline through the reaction low after top 3. Since you may have already stopped out on this stock after the failed double top, this trade requires a little extra courage. Place a stop again just above the reaction low. If there is a price gap just below the reaction low, place the stop above it.

Triple top formations are all about distribution so triple bottoms must be about accumulation. This is our next reversal pattern.

Triple Bottom

A triple bottom formation is the mirror image of the triple top. After an extended decline to new lows a stock puts in a bottom on massive volume and a moderate rally ensues. After several sessions (sometimes weeks) the stock drifts back to test the first bottom and once again buyers push the stock higher. This process is repeated a third time before buyers finally overwhelm sellers and the stock moves significantly higher.

Why Does It Happen?

Whereas triple tops are all about distribution, the triple bottom is about accumulation. After an extended decline characterized by aggressive short-selling and valuation concerns, value-oriented investors with longer-term time horizons begin to take positions in the stock. They understand that the only way to build a large position in a stock that they like is to do so when selling dominates. It is their willingness to buy the stock when all the news is bad that creates a clear support level, the first bottom (bottom 1).

This presence of large buyers in the face of bad fundamental news will normally be sufficient to force many professional short sellers, or bears, to cover positions. This coupled with buying from longer-term value investors may be enough to rejuvenate investors who recently purchased the stock at higher levels—they may even rationalize that the market is finally beginning to realize that the current weakness is without merit, and a few bullish speculators may be enticed to take new long positions. Unfortunately, after several sessions of positive price action buying pressures are exhausted and the stock once again begins to falter. The positive price reaction to the decline that formed bottom 1 is complete. Technical traders call this the *reaction high*. Amid continued negative fundamental news, short sellers return and bullish speculators decide to take profits. What began as modest selling quickly becomes a rout. As the stock approaches bottom 1, volume remains light and in many cases the stock will actually fall through the previous low on very light volume. At this point pessimism is greatest; there seems to be no legitimate reason to continue holding the stock. Novice short sellers add new short positions, and beleaguered bulls who purchased the stock at much higher levels begin to surrender in anticipation of a new leg lower. However, the expected big decline does not materialize because longer-term investors continue to buy the dips in price. A new rally begins as short sellers are forced to buy stock to cover short positions.

As a second bottom (bottom 2) begins to take shape, the pace of short covering accelerates and the stock quickly rallies toward the reaction high. Although the rally is sharp, volume remains light. At this point a new wave of bad news hits the stock price. Bearish investors feel vindicated and the stock slumps back toward bottoms 1 and 2. Now pessimism is greatest; there seems to be no legitimate reason to continue holding the stock. New short sellers add short positions and beleaguered bulls who purchased the stock at much higher levels finally capitulate. Volume swells but oddly support at bottoms 1 and 2 holds. Professional short sellers start to sense that the jig is up; the stock is not going down.

The price begins to stabilize and a third bottom (bottom 3) becomes apparent. Suddenly, the flow of news becomes less pessimistic, short sellers begin to panic, and a massive rally ensues. The stock rallies through the peak set between bottoms 2 and 3. On the chart three equal bottoms are created; the triple bottom is in place. In many cases triple bottoms lead to important rallies because a vital support level has been established at both the bottoms and the reaction high.

How Are Technical Targets Derived?

The technical target for a triple bottom formation is derived by adding the difference between bottom 1 and the reaction high to the new breakout level. After the third bottom has been created, the new breakout level is the peak achieved between bottoms 2 and 3. No double bottom formation is complete until the stock rallies through this level.

Vital Signs

- For triple bottoms, volume must increase as the stock moves toward the bottom of the pattern. Increased volume at the bottom of the pattern suggests that accumulation is taking place.
- No triple bottom pattern is valid until the stock moves above the peak established between bottoms 2 and 3.
- Upside breakouts through the reaction high often lead to small two percent to three percent advances followed by an immediate test of the breakout level. If the stock closes below this level (now support) for any reason, the pattern becomes invalid.
- Technical targets are implied but they are by no means assured. Targets are guideposts only.
- To swing-trade, buy on the rally through the reaction high after bottom 3. Since you may have already stopped out on this stock after the failed double bottom, this trade requires a little extra courage. Place a stop again just under the reaction high. If there is a price gap just above the reaction high, place the stop below it.

MORE COMPLEX REVERSAL PATTERNS

Now that we have some of the basic multiple-phase reversal patterns for swing trading under our belt, let's tackle the more complex reversal patterns. The broadening top is our starting point.

Broadening Top

Technically speaking, a broadening top is a rally to a new high, weakness to an intermediate support level, a second rally to a higher high on increased volume and decline through the intermediate support level, and a third rally to a higher high on strong volume followed by an eventual collapse. (See Figure 1.16.)

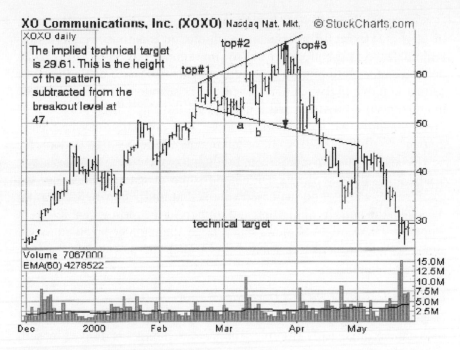

Figure 1.16 Broadening top: XO Communications.
Source: StockCharts.com.

Why Does It Happen?

These patterns always feature indecision and extreme volatility. When you look at the pattern, the resemblance to a megaphone is striking. The stock makes a series of higher highs and lower lows. Normally as time passes and more information is disseminated, investors come to consensus and volatility slows, but just the opposite is true of broadening tops. There are distinct parts of every broadening top formation. The first of three small tops (top 1) occurs after a spectacular run to a new high on increasing volume. Generally, this advance will be the result of better than expected earnings, a new product, or a barrage of Wall Street recommendations. However, as the stock surges to new highs, sellers also step up their efforts and it is not long before the stock settles back to a prior support level (a). After several sessions of slower trade more positive news pushes the stock to yet another new high on increased volume (top 2). The increased volume should be a sign that bullish consensus is building, but once again the stock falters, falling to a relative new low (b) just days after making a new high. Although the news flow is still very positive, rumors might begin to circulate that some institutions and insiders are beginning to liquidate positions. At this time there is a full-scale defense of the stock by bullish investors. Wall Street firms make new recommendations with lofty price targets, and once again the stock begins to move higher. Although volume is strong, it is noticeably less than the prior rallies. The stock moves to a third new high (top 3) in as many attempts. All the news is positive. The company may be raising guidance, setting a stock split, or talking about the positive outlook for new products. The prospects seem bright but even as the stock is making a new high, there is skepticism among some investors. Days later the stock begins to falter on increased volume but no specific news. Several days later the stock is collapsing and support at the most recent low is in jeopardy. There might be news that a large shareholder has filed to sell stock, as bullish investors panic. Weeks later the stock sinks back to long-term support.

How Are Technical Targets Derived?

Because broadening tops are very large reversal patterns, the technical implications are usually extreme. The measured target is derived by subtracting the height of the pattern from the eventual breakout level. (See Figure 1.16.)

Broadening Top for XO Communications

Like so many other telecommunications issues, XO Communications was once afforded a valuation so rich it defied logic. XO Communications was the product of two red-hot telecommunications upstarts, Nextlink Communications and Concentric Networks. Together these firms promised to deliver a wide range of new products that would forever change the telecom industry. Although products needed to facilitate this change did not come cheap, upstart telecom firms found no shortage of willing venture capitalist investors in the winter of 1999 because stock prices were surging and money was cheap. From December 1, 1999 through February 23, 2000, XO Communications surged from $24.40 to $59.50 (top 1), a gain of 107 percent. During that period, the company recorded a loss of $1.57 versus a loss of $1.03 during the prior period. This was offset, psychologically but obviously not fiscally, by a two-for-one stock split announcement.

By March 9 the stock had settled back to $52.93 (a) in light profit taking. The very next day a top Wall Street brokerage analyst upgraded the stock to "top pick" from "buy" in response to the "improved" fundamental outlook. Once again the stock shot higher, reaching a new high at $62.26 by March 13 (top 2) but that rally proved very short lived. By March 16, XO Communications was trading back to $49.48 on no specific news. Once again, the Wall Street analyst community came to the aid of telecommunications issues, making several bullish recommendations in the sector.

Days later XO Communications was pushing higher again, this time reaching a record high on respectable volume at $66.25 on March 24 but just three days later Eagle River Trust, controlled by the firm's founding family, filed to sell 350,000 shares of common stock. The stock began to plummet, falling as low as $47.93 by March 5 (downside breakout). On March 14, XO Communications authorized a boost in common shares from 460 million to 1.12 billion and the stock continued to fall precipitously, reaching $42.50 amid surprisingly slow trade. (By September 2001, it had fallen to less than $1.00, and in the spring of 2002 it was trading at $0.06.)

Vital Signs

- Unlike most other consolidation patterns, broadening tops feature increasing wide ranges and greater volatility as time passes.
- Volume increases as the share price rises. Normally this is bullish but rallies prove very short lived and declines take out previous support levels.
- Broadening formations are only found in topping formations because they are the product of unrealistic expectations on the part of bullish investors.
- Downside breakouts often lead to small two percent to three percent declines followed by an immediate test of the breakout level. If the stock closes above this level (now resistance) for any reason, the pattern becomes invalid.
- To swing-trade, short on a decline through a trendline drawn through the series of reaction lows. Place a stop just above that level. If you are stopped and the pattern repeats as the stock continues to react feebly to good news, try again. If there is a price gap just below the reaction low, place the stop above it.

Head and Shoulders Bottom

Technically speaking, a head and shoulders top pattern is a decline to a new low and rally to intermediate resistance, a second decline to a lower low and rally to resistance, followed by a modest third decline and rally through resistance.

Why Does It Happen?

Head and shoulders patterns are among the most important of reversal patterns because they are both common and reliable. The head and shoulders bottom pattern consists of three declines and a breakout. This reversal pattern, sometimes called the inverted head and shoulders pattern, gets its name because it is the inverse of the head and shoulders top pattern. The *left shoulder* of a head and shoulders bottom pattern will always take shape after an extended decline to new lows. Against the backdrop of increasing unfavorable fundamental developments the stock sinks to one low after another, and investors become decidedly bearish. The first phase of the head and shoulders bottom pattern is usually the product of a particularly negative fundamental development. Although the stock is already well off its recent highs, this new negative development seems to go beyond the pale. The stock immediately sinks to a new low on very strong volume. Despite the bad news, the decline is short lived because serious longer-term investors begin to establish positions.

Just days later, the imbalance between buyers and sellers leads to a brisk rally to an intermediate term resistance level. Technicians call this rally the *reaction high* because it is a reaction to the initial decline to new lows. This price action also completes the *left shoulder* of the pattern. Because all the fundamental news remains bearish, investors and analysts rationalize that the stock had simply fallen too far, and days later the decline resumes. The stock falls to another new low but volume is substantially diminished, as selling pressure is drying up.

The weak volume on the decline and the new lower prices encourage buyers, and very soon a new rally develops and the stock once again moves toward the reaction high—which is now an overhead resistance level. This price action completes the *head* of the pattern. Once again, sellers return amid poor fundamental news. This may be a negative corporate development or an analyst downgrade but the stock starts to drift lower for a third time.

As price falters, volume diminishes substantially again and buyers reassert themselves, forcing a rally back to the overhead resistance level. This price action completes the third and final phase of the pattern, the *right shoulder*. The negative comments from Wall Street analysts continue but this time buyers are more aggressive than sellers and the stock surges through resistance. Weeks later the stock rallies to longer-term resistance.

How Are Technical Targets Derived?

The technical target for a head and shoulders bottom pattern is derived by adding the difference between the neckline and the lowest level achieved in the formation of the "head" to the new breakout level. (See Figure 1.17.)

Head and Shoulders Bottom for Federal National Mortgage

Although Fannie Mae has been one of the few consistently profitable government sponsored enterprises, in the spring of 2000 the firm was the subject of controversy. Richard Baker, a reform-minded Republican from Louisiana, tabled legislation that would have severely limited the firm's ability to raise and lend money. The initial reaction was one of disbelief; investors assumed that such legislation would never really pass because

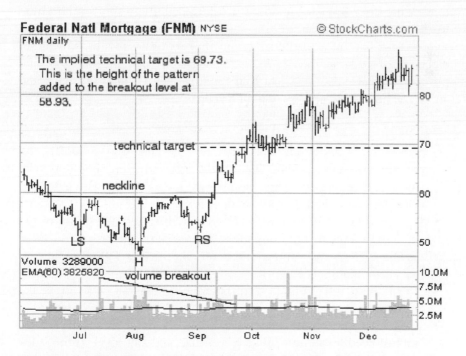

Figure 1.17 Head and shoulders bottom: Federal National Mortgage.
Source: StockCharts.com.

the Clinton administration had expressed opposition to the bill and there did not seem to be the will among Republicans to force the issue.

In June 2000 that all changed when presidential candidate George W. Bush showed an interest in re-examining the issue if he was elected president in the upcoming election. Amid poll results and more wrangling on Capitol Hill, Fannie Mae shares tumbled to a relative new low at $51.30 on June 30. Volume was extremely high as all signs pointed to the fact that Fannie Mae face a tough time under a Bush administration. However, by July 11 cooler heads prevailed and the stock had recovered to $58.93 (reaction high and completion of left shoulder). Just one day later Fannie Mae was on the move lower again. Current monetary policy added to the legislative woes as the Federal Reserve continued to raise short-term interest rates to quell potential inflationary pressures. By April 3 the stock had sunk all the way to $48.13, another new low on lower volume.

Once again buyers returned and the stock began to move higher, reaching the old reaction high at $59.00 by August 22. This move higher completed the head of the pattern but it also energized sellers. By September the stock fell back to $52 in weak trade only to surge a third time to the resistance level at $59 on news that legislative efforts to thwart Fannie Mae had hit a roadblock as lawmakers broke for the November elections. This time the stock soared through resistance at $59 and pushed to greater than $88 just four months later. (It later fell back and stabilized around $65 for more than a year.)

Vital Signs

- Symmetry is important. The most reliable head and shoulders top patterns are symmetrical. That is, the left and right shoulders take shape over roughly the same number of days. Patterns with extended right shoulders should be avoided.
- It is important that volume *decline* on each successive phase of the head and shoulders bottom pattern and *surge* on the break above the neckline. The weak volume and declining price is a good indication that accumulation is at work.
- No pattern is truly complete until there is a breakout close above the neckline of the pattern.
- Upside breakouts often lead to small two percent to three percent rallies followed by an immediate test of the breakout level. If the stock closes below this level (now support) for any reason, the pattern becomes invalid.

- To swing-trade, buy on a three to five percent rally through the neck-line, recognizing that there could be a small decline back to the neck-line before the rally continues. Place a stop below the neckline.

Now let's examine the inverse of the head and shoulders bottom, the head and shoulders top.

Head and Shoulders Top

Technically speaking, a head and shoulders top pattern is a rally to a new high and weakness to intermediate support, a second rally to a higher high and decline to support, followed by a modest third rally and decline through support.

Why Does It Happen?

Head and shoulders tops are among the most useful of reversal patterns because they are common and reliable. The head and shoulders top pattern consists of three rallies and a breakdown. The reversal pattern gets its name because the middle rally reaches the highest point while both the first and third rallies are approximately equal in height, resembling a person's head and shoulders.

The *left shoulder* of a head and shoulders top pattern will always take shape after an extended rally to new highs. Buyers seem willing to pay increasingly higher prices because all the fundamental data, such as earnings releases, are perceived to be improved. After one particularly bullish report the stock surges to a new high on strong volume as analysts pound the table with new "buy" recommendations—but days later, profit taking leads to a modest reactionary pullback (*reaction low*). Bullish investors and analysts rationalize that the weakness is just normal profit taking after a lengthy advance and they are partly correct—the selling is profit taking but it is far from normal.

On this first pullback those investors who bought the stock at lower prices begin distributing their stock into the good news; they have made their money and they want out. As the stock declines, buyers regroup and a torrid rally resumes. Because all the fundamental news remains bullish, the next rally to new highs easily exceeds the first. The stock very quickly rallies to a fresh new high but there is just one problem: Despite the barrage of positive corporate news and Wall Street cheer, volume declines relative to the initial rally. As the stock continues to move higher, selling by investors who purchased the stock at lower prices intensifies and it is not long before the imbalance between buyers and sellers causes a considerable decline. Rumors begin to swirl that institutions and insiders are selling.

Days later the stock drifts back to test the reaction low and volume surges. This price action forms the *head* of the pattern. As the stock tests its reaction lows positive news hits the tape and buyers return. A third rally begins amidst new buy recommendations from Wall Street analysts.

Unfortunately, the third rally is even more feeble than the previous two moves higher. The stock does advance but volume slows to a trickle and it becomes clear that the stock is being distributed. After several more sessions the stock begins to decline yet again and a move back to support at the reaction lows ensues. In keeping with the imagery of the pattern, this key support level is often called the *neckline* of the head and shoulders top pattern.

The third decline to this level completes the *right shoulder* of the pattern. As the stock approaches support for a third time, positive comments from Wall Street analysts continue but this time buyers are overwhelmed by sellers, volume expands, and the stock collapses. Weeks later the stock trades back to longer-term support.

How Are Technical Measures and Targets Derived?

The technical target for head and shoulders top patterns is derived by subtracting the difference between the highest level achieved in the formation of the head and the level of the neckline from the new breakout level. (See Figure 1.18.)

Head and Shoulders Top for Krispy Kreme Doughnuts

Krispy Kreme Doughnuts (KKD) came along at the correct time for frustrated technology investors. In the late winter of 2000 investors had seen technology share prices implode and they were looking for a nontechnology something to sink their teeth into. Krispy Kreme had a well-known and much-loved product and the franchise story seemed like a winner. After making a low on April 5, 2001 at $15.12 the stock soared to a high of $38.53 on May 29. Along the way there were several Wall Street buy recommendations, rumors about a possible merger with Starbucks (SBUX), and a stock split announcement. All things considered, the stock seemed to be climbing the wall of worry nicely but the May 29 high proved short lived.

By June 4 the stock settled back to a low of $33 as some investors began to question the rich valuation. This price action created the *left shoulder*. Just days later the stock began to move higher once again. Although

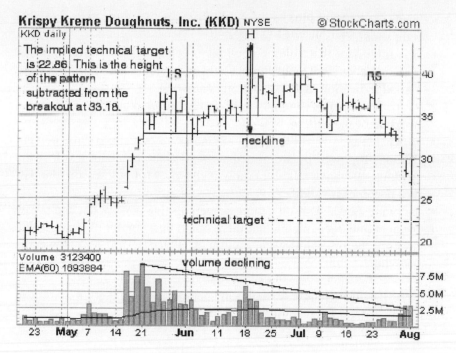

Figure 1.18 Head and shoulders top: Krispy Kreme Doughnuts
Source: StockCharts.com.

volume remained subdued, continued optimism over expansion into new markets and talk about a global brand sent Krispy Kreme shares to a fresh new high at $43.50 on June 19. About that time Securities & Exchange Commission filings revealed that the company's chief executive had petitioned to sell 80,000 shares of Krispy Kreme stock.

The stock immediately began to work lower. By July 11 the stock was back to the $33 support level. This price action created the *head*. On July 12 Krispy Kreme stock once again began to move higher. By July 23 the stock was trading back at $38.38 but volume was even slower than the previous two rallies. It seemed as though it would be only a matter of time before price deteriorated and on July 25 the stock fell back to $33. This price action completed the *right shoulder* of the pattern. Several sessions later the stock traded back to $26.93.

Vital Signs

- Symmetry is important. The most reliable head and shoulders top patterns are symmetrical, that is, the left and right shoulders take shape over roughly the same number of days. Patterns with extended right shoulders should be avoided.

- It is important that volume declines on each successive rally in the head and shoulders top pattern. The weak volume and rising price are a good indication that distribution is at work.
- No pattern is truly complete until there is a breakout close below the neckline of the pattern.
- Downside breakouts often lead to small two percent to three percent declines followed by an immediate test of the breakout level. If the stock closes above this level (now resistance) for any reason, the pattern becomes invalid.
- To swing-trade, short on a three percent to five percent decline below the neckline, recognizing that there could be a small rally back to the neckline before the decline continues. Place a stop just above the neckline.

Now that we're finished with our anatomy lesson, let's move on to the dynamic diamond pattern.

Diamond

Technically speaking, a diamond pattern is a rally to a new high and weakness to an intermediate support level, a second rally to a higher high and a sharp decline through support, followed by a modest third rally and a decline through a longer-term trend.

Why Does It Happen?

At first glance, a diamond pattern may look like little more than head and shoulders top patterns with crooked necklines but this tells only half the story. In reality diamond patterns are more like broadening top formations because they normally reverse only upward trends. In this sense, they are always about distribution. The patterns begin when a very strong stock with stellar growth trends moves to a new high and consolidates after a lengthy advance. For several sessions the stock meanders in a narrow consolidation as pundits discuss the longer-term fundamental merits of the stock, but eventually there is an upside breakout. In many cases, the cause of the upside breakout will be an analyst's preview of an upcoming earnings report or positive comments from the company regarding new products or clients.

As the news breaks the stock surges to new highs on very strong volume. In fact, the upside breakout usually proves legitimate because the stock continues to move higher for several sessions. Then, abruptly the stock begins to fall. Volume is light and there is no corporate news to account for the weakness but as bullish investors rationalize that the stock is merely correcting some of the recent gains, many investors who bought the stock at lower prices are unwinding long positions.

The stock continues to drift lower on relatively light volume until there is an event that raises doubt about the most recent upside breakout. Although all the news from the stock in question has been positive, investors understand that the current share price carries a great deal of risk because it has been priced for perfection. As selling continues volume accelerates and when the stock falls through the previous upside breakout level recent buyers panic leading to further weakness. Analysts continue to reiterate buy recommendations but within days the share price is devastated, moving far below even the most recent consolidation.

As panic subsides steps are taken by the company to reassure investors that all is still well. Very often press releases are issued or leading Wall Street analysts come to the defense of the stock, suggesting that it is a compelling value at current levels. All of this leads to a *reaction low* and slowly the stock begins to move higher. In the days ahead more positive corporate news is disseminated, suddenly investors are reinvigorated, and the share price soars. Investors rationalize that the recent scare was a giant overreaction and the stock offers great opportunity but as the rally progresses, volume is stubbornly average. Finally, the company releases more good news and analysts pound the table with new buy recommendations but despite this, the stock does not come close to reaching the recent new high.

To make matters worse, on the day of the good news the stock opens higher but closes at or near its low on heavy volume. The increase in volume and weaker stock price suggests distribution: Former bulls are selling into the good news. As the stock price falls, puzzled analysts and investors wonder how the stock could be falling on such good news, but investors who bought the stock at much lower prices continue to use every rally to sell. Days later the stock breaks sharply lower. Weeks later news is released suggesting that the fundamental outlook has deteriorated.

How Are Technical Targets Derived?

Because diamonds are very large patterns, the technical implications are often also large. Technical targets are derived by subtracting the difference between the record high and the reaction low from the eventual breakdown level. The breakout level will be determined by a trendline drawn from the reaction low to the first significant low on the right side of the pattern. (See Figure 1.19.)

Diamond Reversal for ADC Telecom

In 2000 ADC Telecom (ADCT) shares rallied to $45.50, then proceeded to consolidate for several sessions. On July 20 ADC announced it had received a three-year contract from German electronics conglomerate Siemens and the future seemed bright. ADC rallied through $45.50 on huge volume and by July 27 the stock had reached a record high at $49. That is when the selling began. The following day Nortel (NT) announced that it would spend billions to purchase Alteon Websystems. The aggressive nature of this transaction meant that competitors would have to get bigger or perish. As investors fretted about dilution, stock prices for the sector plummeted and ADC sank to a reaction low of $33 on August 3. In the aftermath of the Alteon deal analysts once again began to

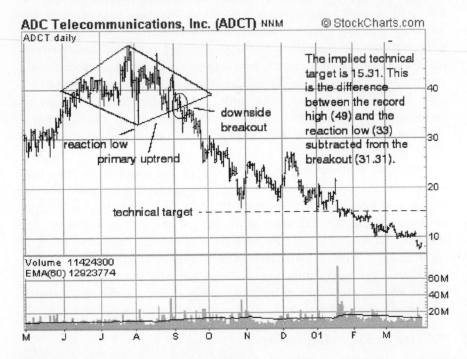

Figure 1.19   Diamond reversal: ADC Telecom.
Source: StockCharts.com.

recommend telecom equipment stocks and it was not long before ADC was moving sharply higher. On August 17 ADC reported third quarter sales rose a remarkable 67 percent and earnings beat estimates by $0.02. On that good news the stock spiked higher and briefly traded at $47.25 before closing near the session low at $42.38.

To make matters worse, competitor Visual Networks tumbled 43 percent on August 23 after warning that sales would be about half of what was expected due to a weakened spending environment. Eight sessions later ADC traded as low as $34.38. On that day, August 29, ADC officials said they were comfortable with Wall Street estimates and vowed not to make dilutive acquisitions. The stock rebounded smartly on a NASDAQ-leading 39.68 million shares but the gains proved short lived—and so, too, was the corporate promise not to make dilutive acquisitions. The stock plummeted $31.31 on September 9 after ADC announced it would acquire money-losing Broadband Access for $2.5 billion in stock. That announcement marked the downside technical breakout for ADC. By late October of that year the stock was changing hands at just $15.88, and a year after that shares were going for around $3.00.

Vital Signs

- Diamonds are complex reversal patterns because volume trends often suggest accumulation. Volume is heaviest at lows and upside break-outs, but moves to new and relative highs are always characterized by one-day reversals.
- Although the spike to the reaction low may be violent, the fact that stockholders are willing to surrender their stock at drastically lower prices without substantive fundamental news portends lower prices.
- Diamonds are large patterns and the technical implications are often dire. It is important to let the pattern reach completion. This means establishing short positions only after the downside breakout.
- Downside breakouts often lead to small two percent to three percent declines followed by an immediate test of the breakout level. If the stock closes above this level (now resistance) for any reason, the pattern becomes invalid.
- To swing-trade, short on a three percent to five percent decline below the upsloping trendline drawn from the first spiked reaction low to succeeding feeble highs, recognizing that there could be a small rally back to that trendline before the decline continues in earnest. Place a stop just above the trendline.

Diamonds are tough patterns because there are many mixed signals. Our understanding of the diamond will definitely help with the rounding top.

Rounding Top

Technically speaking, a rounding top is a rally to a new high on strong volume, several weeks of light trade with limited upside progress, and several more weeks of light trade with a decided downward bias, followed by a sharp move lower on strong volume.

Why Does It Happen?

At first and maybe even second glance, rounding top patterns are going to look very familiar. This is because they have many of the same characteristics of head and shoulders top patterns. Often there will be a very clear head, that is, a rally to a new high in the middle of the pattern. Rounding top patterns differ from garden variety head and shoulders top patterns in that very often there are multiple shoulders. So, why does this happen? As you might expect, rounding top patterns occur for many of the same reasons as do head and shoulders top patterns. The first part of the pattern will always take shape after an extended rally to new highs. The flow of fundamental news is usually positive and buyers seem willing to pay increasingly higher prices—for a while. Following one positive development the stock rallies to a fresh new high on strong volume but to the surprise of bullish investors, sellers are more than willing to liquidate positions.

After a few sessions, the stock begins to move lower on increased volume. Investors and analysts will normally rationalize this development as simple profit taking but the rise in volume and weak price action are clues. Longer-term investors who bought at lower prices are selling; they are using good news to distribute stock. The rally to new highs and pullback to a nearby support level (reaction low) completes the first phase of the pattern.

Because the fundamental news remains positive, bullish investors soon return, sending the stock back to test the recent high but once again they are turned back by sellers and the stock drifts back to the reaction low (now key support). Roused by more positive commentary by either the company or Wall Street analysts, buyers make another run at what has become overhead resistance and to their delight, the stock pushes to a new high. There is just one problem: Volume is even more feeble than the previous two rallies and the move higher stalls. Buyers are beginning to grow anxious because the fundamental news is positive and sentiment excellent, yet sellers continue to exert downside price pressure. A new decline begins but the weakness ends as the stock approaches key support.

Against the backdrop of more good news on the fundamental front, buyers make two further attempts to push the stock through resistance. During each attempt volume slows progressively and ultimately the stock slumps back to support. At this point buyers have reached their limit; they begin to question everything—yes, the fundamental data are currently strong but will that last? Five rallies have failed. At this point of weakness the first piece of bad news is released. Suddenly all the assumptions that led the stock to new highs are called into question, those who had been supporting the stock panic, and key support fails miserably. The stock gaps lower and a huge decline begins. Weeks later the stock trades back to longer-term support.

How Are Technical Measures and Targets Derived?

Unlike head and shoulders top patterns, rounding tops generally do not lend well to price targets because the pattern is meandering. In most cases one can expect a decline back to the longer-term support level following a break below key support. (See Figure 1.20.)

The Rounding Top for International Business Machines

In a world of earnings warnings and unfulfilled promises in the winter of 2001, International Business Machines (IBM) was a refreshing success story. Not only had the firm succeeded where others had failed but by all accounts, it was building market share and becoming the undisputed leader of the new economy. One year after introducing their very successful line of Shark data-storage servers, they began rolling out software applications for mission critical UNIX and LINUX platforms. The stock moved from a low of $87.50 on March 21 to a high of $99.89 on April 16 before releasing first quarter earnings on April 18. The earnings were in line with Wall Street expectations. The revenue numbers were well ahead and the stock spiked higher, trading to $115.87 the next session and as high as $118.93 by May 2. Wall Street analysts were falling over one another to recommend the stock; IBM was seen as the savior for the market. But just two days after all the positive talk the stock settled back to $111.18. Just two days later the stock was moving higher again on a note from UBS Warburg suggesting that IBM would

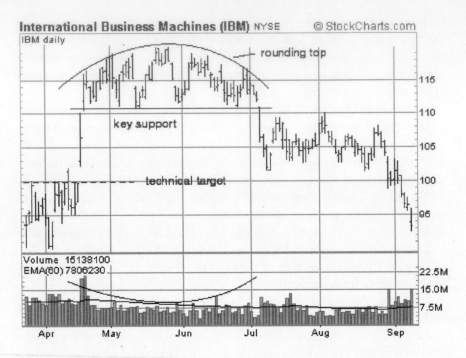

Figure 1.20 Rounding top: IBM.
Source: StockCharts.com.

leapfrog the competition with its UNIX servers. Once again the stock traded back to $118.93 only to decline back to $111 by May 14. Once again Wall Street firms defended the stock and IBM pushed to a new high on May 21 at $119.88 following news releases for several new products and contract wins. The next day IBM chief executive Lou Gerstner filed to sell 250,000 shares and the stock began to move lower again, testing $111 by June 1.

The next session IBM announced a software and hardware deal with the Chinese government. The stock rallied back to $118.93 over the next two sessions but by June 26 shares were back at $111. The final rally came June 29 when IBM announced it had built the "world's fastest transistory." After an initial move to $116.87 IBM shares once again slumped to $111. On July 6 IBM competitor EMC Corporation announced its third earnings warning in as many quarters and IBM shares gapped through support at $111 at the open. A downside breakout became effective; IBM shares traded to $92 just two months later.

Vital Signs

- Symmetry is important. The most reliable rounding top patterns do not stray from the confines of a tight semicircle and usually resemble head and shoulders top patterns with two left shoulders, one head, and two right shoulders. Avoid clearly askew patterns.
- It is important that volume declines on each successive rally in formation of the pattern. The weak volume and rising price are a good indication that distribution is at work.
- Downside breakouts often lead to small two percent to three percent declines followed by an immediate test of the breakout level. If the stock closes above this level (now resistance) for any reason, the pattern becomes invalid.
- To swing-trade, short on a three percent to five percent decline below a line drawn beneath at least three reaction lows. Place a stop just above the trendline.

It makes sense that if we have a rounding top, we can have a rounding bottom. Let's examine that chart pattern.

Rounding Bottom

Technically speaking, a rounding bottom is a decline to a new low on strong volume, several weeks of light trade with limited downward progress, and several more weeks of light trade with a decided upward bias, followed by a sharp move higher on strong volume.

Why Does It Happen?

Like the rounding top pattern, the rounding bottom is often mistaken for its head and shoulders counterpart. This is because the rounding bottom has a lot of the same parts. Both the rounding bottom and head and shoulders bottom have a series of peaks and valleys and declining volume throughout the pattern. Of course the difference is that the rounding bottom has what appears to be multiple "shoulders." So, why does this happen? Like the rounding top, rounding bottom patterns are almost deceptively simple in nature. They are all about the orderly transfer of shares from anxious sellers to serious, value minded longer-term investors. Through a series of peaks and valleys sellers are slowly, painfully removed.

The first part of the pattern will always take shape after an extended decline to new lows. Against the backdrop of very negative fundamental news, sellers become anxious and willing to sell their shares for progressively lower prices. At some point a particularly negative news development such as an earnings warning, product delay, or key executive departure hits the news wires and the stock slumps to a new low on huge volume. One by one Wall Street analysts rush to cut estimates, make disparaging comments, and the free fall in price continues.

However, to the surprise of many, the selling is severe but oddly brief. The reason for the stock strength is that longer-term investors are beginning to accumulate large positions. Days later the stock moves higher on good volume. This brief rally in price affords a new selling opportunity for those who did not exit ahead of the first major decline and the price action reverses, creating a small resistance level (reaction high). Once again the stock moves lower, testing the most recent new low before buyers mysteriously step in and support the stock.

A rally ensues and a move back to the reaction high, (now key resistance) occurs. Normally this type of impressive price action would be enough to make sellers rethink their strategy but the fundamental news is terrible and just days later the stock is rocked by another negative development.

This time the stock moves to a fresh new low but volume is noticeably less than the previous two declines. After a few sessions meandering at the new lower levels, the stock begins to rebound on better volume on the first piece of good fundamental news in several weeks. The rally lasts for a few sessions but it is stopped dead in its tracks at the short-term resistance level. Another decline begins on more bad news but it, too, is short lived and a rally back to resistance occurs.

This process is repeated one more time before sellers get the idea that perhaps the stock is not going to move significantly lower. Anxiety levels grow for short sellers, and longer-term holders who purchased the stock at higher levels begin to feel better about the stock. The idea is that if the stock is not declining amid the current stream of bad news it must be headed higher—and they are unwittingly correct. In the days ahead more good fundamental news hits the news wires and the stock explodes higher. Weeks later the stock trades back to longer-term resistance levels.

How Are Technical Measures and Targets Derived?

Unlike head and shoulders bottom patterns, rounding bottoms generally do not lend well to price targets because the pattern is meandering. In most cases one can expect a decline back to the longer-term support level following a break below key support. (See Figure 1.21.)

Figure 1.21 Rounding bottom: Rite Aid.
Source: StockCharts.com.

Rounding Bottom for Rite Aid

There was a time when Rite Aid (RAD) was among the greatest momentum stocks in the land. Several quarters of strong results coupled with a terrific management team pushed the stock to one new high after another—until it was revealed that the earnings were an illusion and the management team would have to go. By July 11, 2000, investors had slashed the stock from better than $22 to $8.50. That day a new odyssey began with the legitimate real earnings and full disclosure of just how bad previous reports had really been. That day the company reported a staggering loss of $238 million or $.92 per share for the quarter and $1.1 billion or $4.45 per share for the year. Wall Street analysts rushed for the exits with earnings revisions and a slew of negative commentary. The stock slumped to $4.13 by July 27 and $3 by September 21. There was a brief rally to $4.13 by November 2 but by the time Rite Aid reported a wider than expected loss on November 10, the stock was once again on the move lower. The stock traded to $2.46 on November 26. Once again the stock rallied to the $4 level two weeks later but weak same store sales and general weakness in the retail sector sent the stock to a fresh new low at $1.81 on December 29.

The news got better in the new year with Rite Aid reporting smaller losses and stronger pharmacy sales. Rite Aid shares pushed to $4 on January 12, 2000 but sellers quickly returned and a decline back to $3.31 occurred just a week later. Once again, the decline proved short lived as news of a convertible debt offering sent the stock back to the $4 level by February 6. There was more weakness on news that former Rite Aid executives had been named in a fraud suit but buyers proved resilient and the stock began to climb. By March 5 the stock had reached $6.

Vital Signs

- Symmetry is important. The most reliable rounding bottom patterns do not stray from the confines of a tight semicircle and usually resemble head and shoulders top patterns with two left shoulders, one head, and two right shoulders. Obviously askew patterns should be avoided.
- It is important that volume decline on each successive move lower and begin to increase as the stock moves higher. The weak volume on declines and rising volume on rallies are a good indication that accumulation is at work.
- Upside breakouts often lead to small two percent to three percent rallies followed by an immediate test of the breakout level. If the stock falls below this level (now support) for any reason, the pattern becomes invalid.
- To swing-trade, buy on a three percent to five percent decline above a line drawn connecting at least three reaction highs. Place a stop just below this line.

The final two patterns left to examine are wedge formations. Let's take a look at the rising wedge.

Rising Wedge

Technically speaking, a rising wedge in an uptrend is a rally to a new high on strong volume, several weeks of narrowing, range-bound trade characterized by higher highs and higher lows with contracting volume, followed by a sharp break lower on strong volume.

Why Does It Happen?

Like all other reversal patterns, the rising wedge in an uptrend is ultimately about deception. At first glance, the stock may appear to be doing all the right things, making a series of higher highs and higher lows. The flow of news is unanimously positive and Wall Street analysts fall over one another to raise estimates and price targets, yet in reality the stock is being distributed from strong hands (longer-term investors) to weak hands (short-term speculators and less astute investors).

The pattern begins when a much-loved stock moves to a new high after an extended advance on good volume. To be sure, momentum investing and all around euphoria contribute to the surge in stock price but by most accounts the fundamental outlook is solid.

As the stock makes a new high something peculiar occurs. Instead of volume surging, it actually begins to contract and price falters, making a reaction low. Wall Street analysts conclude that the stock is merely having a well-deserved short-term consolidation after a lengthy advance and in the days ahead they reiterate buy ratings. Once again the stock surges to a new high but volume slows even further and very quickly price begins to fade.

At this time the news flow is excellent. The company may be raising guidance, unveiling new products, winning contracts and/or setting stock splits. In short, it is easy to be bullish—especially when most investors share that sentiment.

Nevertheless, beneath the surface something is happening; the stock is being distributed; longer-term investors are using every piece of good news to reduce positions. As the stock falters for a second time the low achieved is well above the reaction low and the chart begins to take on the appearance of a wedge.

After several sessions of consolidation more good news hits the news wires and the stock surges to yet another new high. As was the case during the previous two rallies, volume contracts. Then, abruptly price begins to falter. Wall Street analysts remain steadfast because there have been no fundamental developments to account for the weakness. Several firms reiterate buy ratings, advising clients to use the weakness to build positions but in reality, longer-term investors are continuing to sell.

This time the new bullish talk has little impact and price begins to free-fall. The bullish talk and positive news flow continue but it is just a matter of time before the parameters of the wedge pattern are violated. Soon after, support at the reaction low is violated. Several days after the first negative news item hits the wires and speculators and recent investors begin to panic, price plummets. Several weeks later the stock trades back to intermediate-term resistance.

How Are Technical Targets Derived?

Rising wedges in uptrends are usually part of larger reversal trends so the implications for the pattern are modest. Technical targets are derived by subtracting the height of the pattern from the eventual breakout level. The breakout level is determined by drawing a trendline from the area of initial consolidation through the reaction high. (See Figure 1.22.)

Rising Wedge for Harrah's Entertainment

In the early part of 2001 Harrah's Entertainment (HET) was a terrific stock. Riding a wave of strong earnings reports and rampant bullish fervor for the casino sector, the stock surged to one new high after another on strong volume. On April 18, 2001 Harrah's reported a 43 percent rise in first quarter earnings and just days later the firm agreed to purchase

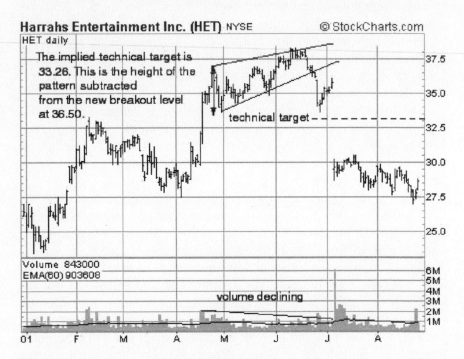

Figure 1.22　Rising wedge: Harrah's Entertainment.
Source: StockCharts.com.

Harvey's Casino Resorts for $625 million. The stock surged to a new high at $36.75. But even as the flow of positive news continued, volume began to contract and by April 30 the stock was trading back at a previous support/resistance level at $33.75.

Two days later Harrah's chief executive filed to sell 101,144 shares in the open market. Through the next three weeks positive news releases continued. On May 15 Harrah's was just one of several gaming firms releasing record revenues and on May 21 the stock reached another new high at $36.88 as news spread that the Nevada Senate was on the verge of passing legislation that would make that state the first to offer Internet gambling.

However, even as the stock surged to new highs, volume contracted. When a competing gaming company announced that it would implement a surcharge because rising energy costs were hurting revenues, Harrah's followed all gaming stocks lower, reaching $34.75 on May 29. Just days later Harrah's signed a long-term deal with energy producer Enron and the stock began working toward new highs. When Merrill Lynch reiterated its buy rating for the stock on June 14, it was trading a fresh new high of $38.20 but volume was very weak. Through the next week the company released several positive news items but the stock price began to falter. By June 25 the stock was trading back to $36. By June 26 the stock was back to the $33.50 level on no specific news.

On July 3 the stock rallied strongly on news that star analyst Jason Ader of Bear Stearns recommended the stock as a recession-resistant top pick with significant upside potential. Three days later on July 6 Harrah's issued an earnings warning, citing the weak economy. The stock opened at $29.50. (It traded down to $22 over the next few months before steadily rising to new highs as investors grew bullish on domestic casinos following the September 11 terrorist attacks.)

Vital Signs

- Rising wedges can be either reversal or continuation patterns. When they occur in an uptrend, they are always reversal patterns.
- Because rising wedges are generally just the starting points for larger reversal patterns, the implied technical targets are modest.
- Volume is key in rising wedge patterns in uptrends. Volume should increase on the initial surge to new highs but dwindle through the remainder of the pattern. As the breakout occurs, volume should surge.
- Downside breakouts often lead to small two percent to three percent declines followed by an immediate test of the breakout level. If the

stock closes above this level (now resistance) for any reason, the pattern becomes invalid.

- To swing-trade, short on a two percent to three percent decline below a line drawn connecting at least three reaction lows. Place a stop just above this line.

A rising wedge in an uptrend is just one half of the wedge reversal family. Now let's take a look at a falling wedge in a downtrend.

Falling Wedge

Technically speaking, a falling wedge in a downtrend is a decline to a new low on strong volume, several weeks of range-bound trade characterized by lower lows and lower highs with contracting volume, followed by a sharp break higher on strong volume. It is important to note, unlike all other chart patterns, valid falling wedge patterns can be either continuation or reversal patterns.

Why Does It Happen?

These patterns, again, are all about deception. When stocks are in a falling wedge, there is every reason to believe they are merely consolidating before making a new leg lower—but a massive rally ensues. Falling wedge patterns always begin when a stock darling has fallen from favor. The initial weakness may be due to an earnings warning, a product delay, lawsuit, or any number of other negative developments but the impact of this news is always sufficient to lead most stockholders to panic.

The result is what technical traders call a watershed decline—a near vertical drop in huge volume. For many sessions after this drop the stock will usually meander in a narrow trading range as investors attempt to catch their breath. Some investors who have been spooked by the big decline feel compelled to exit but their own tendencies will not allow them to sell a position for a loss—so they simply stand aside and hope to sell the stock into strength. Others become so demoralized that they are willing to sell at any price; they just want to get out. Still others look at the recent decline and deluge of poor fundamental news as evidence that the stock is headed much lower and begin adding new short positions. It is this latter group of investors who become most vulnerable in the falling wedge in a downtrend.

It is important to note that the initial spike in volume in the formation of a falling wedge is always about longer-term investors building new positions into the weakness. Days later the stock moves to a new low but volume begins to wane and it becomes very clear that the stock is trying to find a happy balance between buyers and sellers; prices stabilize. Slowly, the stock begins to work higher but volume remains exceptionally light. During this rally the fundamental news is generally quite sparse. As the stock reaches a plateau reaction high, more negative fundamental news hits the wires and the stock begins to move lower yet again, pushing to a second new low. However, this decline is accompanied by very light volume. Those who purchased the stock at higher prices and have not yet sold refuse to liquidate their positions despite the bad news. Days later the lack of new selling leads to price stabilization.

Several days later volume begins to pick up and price rallies. Analysts weigh in with negative comments but the stock continues to move higher on increased volume. As the stock pushes through the reaction high, short sellers panic and a large move higher ensues. Several weeks later the stock trades back to intermediate-term resistance.

How Are Technical Targets Derived?

Falling wedges in downtrends are usually part of larger reversal trends so the implications for the pattern are modest. Technical targets are derived by adding the height of the pattern to the eventual breakout level. The breakout level will be determined by a trendline drawn from the area of initial consolidation through the reaction high. (See Figure 1.23.)

Falling Wedge for Nike

Riding a 58 percent increase in second quarter earnings it appeared as though Nike (NKE) common stock really was touched by the gods but things turned sour very quickly for the maker of athletic shoes and apparel. After reaching a high of $55.88 on December 16, 1999, the stock collapsed over the next two months. It all began on February 8, 2000 when a Nike spokesperson announced that the company expected earnings to fall short of Wall Street expectations due to a decline in the number of retailers carrying Nike products. On that session the stock lost $8.75 to close at $37. In the ensuing sessions both Bank of America and Merrill Lynch joined the ranks of firms cutting estimates and making negative comments.

By February 28 the stock was trading at just $26.81 on very low volume. By March 3 the stock had rebounded modestly to $30.25 on continued light volume. On March 6 the stock began to work lower again after the firm announced that it had reached a deal with American Golf Learn-

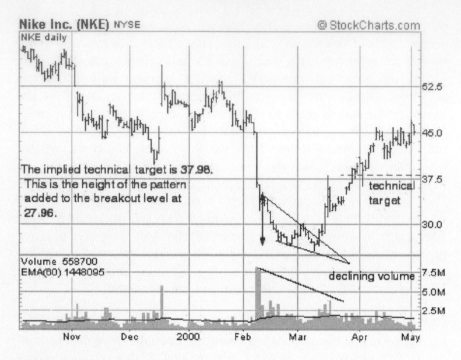

Figure 1.23 Falling wedge: Nike.
Source: StockCharts.com.

ing Centers. By March 9 the stock had reached a new low at $25.81 on very light volume.

Then, unexpectedly the stock began to rally. Despite more negative talk from analysts, Nike shares rallied to $33.88 by March 16. After the close on March 17 Nike reported earnings that were at the high end of Wall Street expectations. By April 11 the stock was trading at $45.75—the start of a long move back in which shares got to the mid-$60s again in March 2002.

Vital Signs

- Falling wedges can be either reversal or continuation patterns. When they occur in downtrends they are always reversal patterns.
- Because falling wedges are generally just the starting points for larger reversal patterns, the implied technical targets are modest.
- Volume is key in falling wedge patterns in a downtrend. Volume should increase on the initial watershed decline but dwindle

through the remainder of the pattern. As the breakout occurs volume should surge.

- Upside breakouts often lead to small two percent to three percent rallies followed by an immediate test of the breakout level. If the stock closes above this level (now support) for any reason, the pattern becomes invalid.
- To swing-trade, buy on a two percent to three percent advance above a line drawn connecting at least three reaction highs. Place a stop just below this line.

That's it for reversal chart patterns. Now let's move on to swing-trading continuation chart patterns.

Cup with Handle

Technically speaking, a cup with handle is a rally to a new high, a decline of 20 percent to 50 percent over 8 to 12 weeks, a rally falling just short of making a new high, a second decline of 8 percent to 20 percent over one to four weeks, followed by a breakout to fresh new highs on strong volume.

Why Does It Happen?

The cup with handle is a variation of the double top pattern. It begins after a well-liked stock rallies to a new high following a positive fundamental development. As the stock surges, investors feel increasingly comfortable paying higher prices but there comes a point when the stock's story fails to convert new believers. Slowly, the stock begins to drift lower as those seeking to lock in profits outnumber those intrigued by the concept. Although most of the fundamental news is still positive, many investors begin to question if the stock really is worth the prevailing market price and over time a substantial decline begins. This process creates an important technical peak (top 1).

As the stock nears a 20 percent decline from the recent highs (this decline could reach 50 percent in bear markets), buyers begin to reassert themselves, the stock stabilizes, and a *reaction low* occurs. From this point forward, the bias begins to tilt gradually higher. During this phase the stock may be the subject of positive Wall Street analyst comments, a new product announcement, or a legal victory. As the rally gains steam, sentiment improves dramatically and new buyers begin to talk about certain new highs but those who purchased the stock at or near top 1 get ready to sell. These investors may have been waiting as long as 12 weeks for an opportunity to sell their positions without incurring a loss and they are not dissuaded by all the newfound bullish talk.

Just short of the old highs at top 1 aggressive selling begins on no specific news but in reality some investors who bought near top 1 have already begun to sell. The stock begins to work significantly lower on increased volume creating a second, well-defined top (top 2). This large U-shaped pattern may look like a typical double top but for the purposes of this pattern, it is called the *cup*.

Noting key resistance at top 1 and top 2, speculators begin to initiate short positions. From a technical perspective, this is a very important part of the pattern. If the stock gains downside momentum and volume continues to increase, this could very easily become a double top but as the price works lower, volume slows; sellers seem to be losing the upper hand.

At this point more positive fundamental news is released and the stock price rallies. With selling pressures satiated and the flow of fundamental news decidedly bullish volume increases dramatically and the stock works toward a fresh new high. This very small U-shaped pullback is called the *handle*. Speculators become frantic; they must cover short positions to cut losses but the supply of stock for sale has been significantly curtailed because investors who bought at top 1 have liquidated positions. The next session Wall Street analysts make positive comments and the stock surges to a new high on dramatically increased volume. Weeks later the stock trades at substantial new highs.

How Are Technical Targets Derived?

The technical target for a cup with handle pattern is derived by adding the height of the cup portion of the pattern to the eventual breakout from the handle portion of the pattern. (See Figure 1.24.)

Vital Signs

- Cup with handle patterns are very similar to double top patterns with the exception being that selling does not accelerate after the formation of the second top. Instead the stock consolidates and eventually pushes beyond overhead resistance on strong volume.
- Generally, most cup with handle patterns are completed over 9 to 16 weeks and involve 2 separate pullbacks of 20 percent to 50 percent (cup) and 8 percent to 20 percent (handle).
- Upside breakout from the handle portion of the pattern should occur on strong volume. This increase in volume verifies that selling pressures have been satiated.

McDonalds Corp. (MCD) NYSE   © StockCharts.com

MCD daily

technical target

The implied technical target is 47.04.
This is the height of the cup
added to the breakout level at 36.63.

handle

cup

Volume 8447600
EMA(60) 4305042

Figure 1.24   Cup with handle for McDonald's Corporation.
Source: StockCharts.com.

- Upside breakouts often lead to small two percent to three percent rallies followed by an immediate test of the breakout level. If the stock closes below this level (now support) for any reason, the pattern becomes invalid.
- To swing-trade, place a buy stop order a fraction above the rim of the cup. You don't know if it is a true cup with handle formation, of course, until this breakout occurs. Place a sell stop approximately 5 percent below the breakout.

Now that we have an understanding of the cup with handle pattern, let's take a closer look at the rectangle.

Rectangle

Technically speaking, a rectangle is a rally to a relative new high, pullback to an intermediate support level, a second rally to test the new high, a second pullback to intermediate support, and a third rally to test the new high level followed by an upside breakout on strong volume.

Why Does It Happen?

At first and perhaps even second glance, a rectangle may seem to be little more than another variation of the double top pattern but while the two technical formations do share some important characteristics, we need to remember that the double top is a reversal pattern while the rectangle is a continuation pattern. Rectangles almost always take shape after a stock has been trending strongly and typically last four to six weeks. Although the fundamental news that gave birth to the strong trend is still valid, investors need an opportunity to digest the recent move.

The stock falls into a holding pattern delineated by near horizontal support and resistance zones. During this phase both support and demand are roughly in equilibrium. Buyers may still like the stock but they are not willing to chase the price significantly higher. Thus, they choose to take profits into strength to a certain level and become aggressive buyers on a pullback to a certain level.

The pattern begins when a well-liked stock moves to a new high on strong volume. As the story of the stock becomes more widely accepted, investors are willing to pay increasingly exorbitant prices. However, one day investors find the price is simply too high, the stock puts in a top, and prices begin to fall (top 1). This first top will normally be sufficient to force many of the more speculative investors from the stock. As they sell, the price of the stock falls further but many investors will not sell regardless of how far the price falls because they refuse to take a loss.

After several sessions (sometimes weeks) of poor price performance the stock will begin to stabilize (*reaction low*) then gradually move higher. In most cases this second advance will occur because of some fundamental factor like a positive fundamental development. As the stock rises, volume slows and investors who bought at the first top get ready to exit positions into further strength.

This selling pressure creates a surge in volume and the stock soon retreats (top 2). As the second top is created, sentiment turns more bearish. Although the flow of news is still positive, pundits begin to talk about rich valuations and buyers step back.

At this time speculators begin to add short positions, sensing that a larger decline is about to unfold. The stock works gradually lower and volume begins to accelerate. In short order the stock is once again testing the reaction low and sentiment is bearish, but somehow the stock manages to hold that key support level and work modestly higher on stronger volume. A subtle rally begins but speculators continue to add short positions because sentiment remains poor.

Days later a positive fundamental development occurs and the stock begins to move toward tops 1 and 2 on heavy volume. During the next session, Wall Street analysts make positive comments and the stock surges through what had been key resistance at the old highs. Speculators begin to panic and their short covering during a period when supply of stock is limited leads to further gains. A new trending phase begins and the stock moves to substantial new highs in the weeks ahead.

How Are Technical Targets Derived?

The technical target for a rectangle is derived by adding the point difference between top 1 and the reaction low to the new breakout level. (See Figure 1.25.)

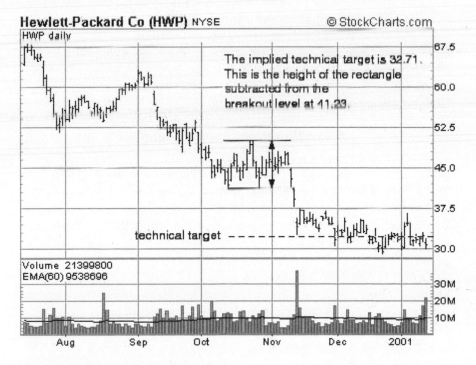

Figure 1.25   Rectangle: Hewlett-Packard.
Source: StockCharts.com.

Vital Signs

- Rectangles are continuation patterns and that means they typically represent little more than a brief period of consolidation in a strong trend. Although I have written about a rectangle in an uptrend, these patterns are just as likely to occur in downtrends.
- Rectangles usually last four to six weeks and always feature very well-defined support and resistance levels characterized by horizontal lines.
- During the rectangle phase, supply and demand are said to be near equilibrium as buyers catch their breath and attempt to digest the most recent trending period.
- Breakouts often lead to two percent to three percent rallies or declines, followed by an immediate test of the breakout level. If a falling stock closes above this level (now resistance) for any reason, the pattern becomes invalid.
- To swing-trade on the short side, place a limit order a fraction below the base of the rectangle. Place a stop loss 5 percent above the base in case you are wrong. To swing-trade on the long side, place a limit order a fraction above the roof of the rectangle. Place a stop loss 5 percent below the roof in case you are wrong.

We now know that rectangles have a great deal in common with the other square patterns. Now let's take a look at technical patterns with different geometry, triangles.

Ascending Right Angle Triangle

Technically speaking, an ascending right angle triangle is a rally to a new high followed by a pull back to an intermediate support level, a second rally to test the first peak followed by a second decline to a level higher than the intermediate-term support level, and finally a rally to fresh new highs on strong volume.

Why Does It Happen?

These patterns typically occur after a stock has had a strong move higher due to a positive fundamental development. Investors come to believe that much higher stock prices are justified given the improved fundamental outlook, but a large portion of investors who were smart enough to have bought the stock at much lower prices disagree. These smart money investors consider the extreme optimism as little more than an opportunity to liquidate positions. Using fundamental metrics, they set a price to sell their large blocks of stock and wait. In effect, they are beginning a distribution process based on their interpretation of fair value.

The first step in the distribution process occurs after one particularly bullish fundamental development. The stock surges to a new high and Wall Street analysts begin pounding the table with new buy recommendations. The increased volume is a perfect opportunity for the smart money to liquidate positions. They begin selling and the rally is stopped in its tracks creating a small top (top 1).

As buyers realize that there is plenty of supply at this level, prices begin to falter and in short order the stock trades back to a previous intermediate-term support level. Because this low is the reaction to the previous rally to new highs, it is often called the *reaction low*. In this very limited sense, ascending right angle triangles are very much like double and triple tops—rising demand meets entrenched supply.

In fact, because the fundamental news is so strong, traders dismiss the weakness as simple profit taking and a new rally soon begins. On strong volume the stock surges toward the recent high where it is once again rebuffed by aggressive sellers (top 2). It is at this point that speculators recognize a trend and they begin adding new short positions just beneath the recent high. This added selling pressure should push the stock significantly lower but bullish enthusiasm is rampant. The stock does move lower but the pull back is subdued. In fact, the stock does not reach the reaction low set in the aftermath of the first move to new highs.

Days later another positive development occurs and the stock begins moving toward the recent high on very strong volume. Speculators step up and add to their short positions but the supply of stock from smart money investors is being satiated. It soon becomes clear that buyers are going to win this battle because sellers are running out of stock to sell.

As the stock pierces what had been strong resistance a strange dynamic occurs: Those traders who had been selling the stock short at the recent high are motivated to cover short positions to cut losses—thereby creating increased demand for the stock at a time when supply has been severely curtailed. Against this backdrop ongoing bullish enthusiasm leads to a spectacular price breakout on strong volume.

Very soon after the breakout several fundamental analysts make positive comments, exacerbating the imbalance between supply and demand. Weeks later the stock surges to a substantial new high. In this rare instance smart money investors are trumped by ongoing bullish fervor and the level that had been resistance becomes important support.

How Are Technical Targets Derived?

The technical target for an ascending right angle triangle is derived by measuring the vertical height of the triangle and applying this length to the new breakout level. (See Figure 1.26.)

Vital Signs

- Ascending triangles are among the most reliable of all technical patterns because both supply and demand are easily defined.
- The defining characteristic of ascending right angle triangles is the pattern of rising lows and a series of equal highs. This combination of points can be connected to form a right angle triangle. If a stock violates any part of the triangle during its formation of the pattern it should be considered void and trading positions should be abandoned.
- Triangles are about indecision and as such volume should slow noticeably as the pattern is being constructed. It is most important that volume surge as the stock rallies through the reaction high. This tells

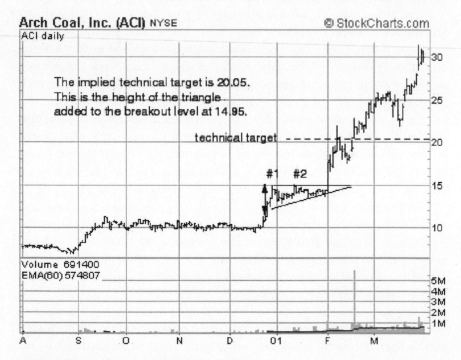

Figure 1.26   Ascending triangle: Arch Coal Inc.
Source: StockCharts.com.

the technical trader that supply has been absorbed, short covering is rampant, and the next leg of the bull phase is about to begin.

- Upside breakouts often lead to small two percent to three percent rallies followed by an immediate test of the breakout level. If the stock closes below this level (now support) for any reason, the pattern becomes invalid.
- To swing-trade, place a buy stop a fraction or two above the top of the triangle. Subsequently, place a stop 5 percent below the top of the triangle in case the trade moves against you.

Descending Triangle

Technically speaking, a descending right angle triangle is a decline to a new low on news followed by a kickback rally to an intermediate resistance level, a second decline to test the recent low followed by a second rally toward but not through intermediate resistance, and finally a decline to fresh new lows on strong volume.

Why Does It Happen?

As you might imagine, the descending right angle triangle is a mirror image of the ascending right angle triangle. Like the ascending triangle, the pattern consists of a right angle triangle formation that follows a lengthy trending period. In the case of the descending right angle triangle, the pattern takes shape after a period in which the stock in question has fallen from favor. This fall from grace may be the result of an earnings warning, product delay, lawsuit, or negative guidance from management but it is fairly certain that the root of the price weakness is poorer fundamentals. For weeks the stock trends lower with no bottom in sight.

Wall Street analysts become extremely bearish and the stock looks like a lost cause but as a fresh new low is created, buyers suddenly emerge. In most cases this initial buying will come from serious long-term investors (smart money) who feel the stock is reasonably priced. These investors have strong hands and all things being equal, they will hold the stock but they are not willing to pay prices in excess of what they feel to be fair value. In short, they look at the position as a work in progress. Since the near-term fundamental outlook is poor they see no need to chase the stock higher. This initial round of buying by longer-term investors creates a short-term bottom (bottom 1).

As days pass some professional traders start to realize that there are

strong bids for the stock at bottom 1 and the technical and emotional selling that had plagued the stock subsides. Slowly the stock begins to move
higher. Although this advance may be aided by positive Wall Street analyst comments or more favorable news flows, volume remains exceptionally light. The stock continues to move higher until there is another
negative fundamental development. At that point sellers return and a reaction high is established. As we will see, this point is vital in the classification of this pattern. The continued negative fundamental news and poor
sentiment for the stock lead to more aggressive selling and once again the
stock drifts back to the bottom 1 level.

Given the negative sentiment a decline through that level seems assured but longer-term buyers renew their efforts, volume increases, and
the stock holds the most recent lows, establishing bottom 2. With two
solid bottoms (support) now in place a new group of buyers enter the picture. Sensing that the buying is entrenched speculators begin to buy new
positions in anticipation of a big move higher—the only problem is the
longer-term buyers are not willing to chase the stock. As the price rallies,
volume slows significantly; in fact, so slow is volume that the stock fails
to move beyond the reaction high. Buyers relent and price begins to falter.

Within a few days the stock is trading back near the level of bottoms
1 and 2. Speculators begin adding new long positions in anticipation of a
rally but the selling continues. Just as longer-term buyers are getting
ready to buy, a new negative fundamental development occurs and the
stock opens dramatically lower, falling well below the levels of bottoms
1 and 2.

This breakout leads speculators to panic and sell existing long positions for a loss. Longer-term investors are also forced to rethink their
strategies in light of the news and some liquidation begins, creating a
huge imbalance between supply and demand. A new leg lower unfolds.
Weeks later the stock trades significantly lower.

How Are Technical Targets Derived?

The technical target for a descending right angle triangle is derived by
measuring the vertical height of the triangle and applying this length to
the new breakout level. (See Figure 1.27.)

Vital Signs

- Descending triangles are among the most reliable of all technical patterns because both supply and demand are easily defined.

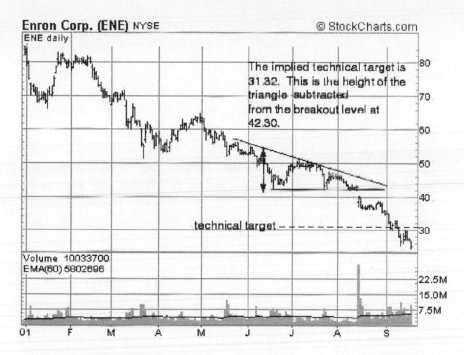

Figure 1.27 Descending triangle for Enron Corporation.
Source: StockCharts.com.

- The defining characteristic of descending right angle triangles is the pattern of declining highs and a series of equal lows. This combination of points can be connected to form a right angle triangle. If a stock violates any part of the triangle during its formation of the pattern, it should be considered void and trading positions should be abandoned.

- Triangles are about indecision and as such volume should slow noticeably as the pattern is being constructed. It is most important that volume surge as the stock declines through the reaction low. This tells the technical trader that demand has been absorbed and the next leg of the bear phase is about to begin.

- Downside breakouts often lead to small two percent to three percent declines followed by an immediate test of the breakout level. If the stock closes above this level (now resistance) for any reason, the pattern becomes invalid.

- To swing-trade, set a sell stop a fraction below the bottom of the triangle. Then set an order to cover 5 percent above the bottom of the
  triangle in case you are wrong.

Symmetrical Triangle

Technically speaking, a symmetrical triangle is a rally to a relative new
high, a pullback to an intermediate-term support level, a second rally that
does not exceed the recent high, and a second decline that falls short of the
intermediate-term support level followed by a breakout on strong volume
above the trendlines created by joining the new high and the secondary high.

Why Does It Happen?

Most consolidation patterns are about indecision—traders are uncertain
about the near-term direction of the stock so they do nothing. Symmetrical triangles are different because when a stock falls into one of these patterns, traders actually behave as though they have reached a consensus
regarding price. We know this because there is a uniform narrowing of
price over time. Symmetrical triangles usually develop after a stock has
had a spectacular move.

After reaching a relative new high, price momentum may begin to
fade modestly and the stock works lower. Because the fundamental news
is so strong, Wall Street analysts will often dismiss this weakness as mere
profit taking following a lengthy advance. The stock slips back to an intermediate-term support level and price stabilizes.

At this point it is common for the stock to begin moving higher on a
positive fundamental development. Perhaps the firm has raised guidance,
announced a stock split, or unveiled a new product but price slowly begins to move higher. There is one problem, however: Volume is noticeably lighter than on previous rallies. The price rally continues but falls
short of the recent new high. This secondary high will be an important
point later in the formation of the pattern.

After several days of strength, momentum once again fades and price
begins to falter. Slowly the stock moves lower on no specific news and
extremely light volume. Sensing that sellers may not have an appetite to
continue selling, buyers reappear and the stock stops short of the intermediate-term support level. This secondary low completes the bottom parameter of a uniform or symmetrical triangle.

Over time the stock begins to trade in an increasingly narrow range characterized by a series of lower highs and higher lows. As time passes traders grow to believe that the current stock price accurately reflects the true value of the stock. Volatility and volume slow dramatically as the stock approaches the apex of the triangle.

Then, abruptly there is a fundamental development that leads to a dramatic upside breakout. Volume swells and Wall Street analysts begin making new buy recommendations and raising their price targets. As price moves beyond the upper parameter created by joining the recent new high and secondary high some investors who had felt the stock was fairly priced at lower levels begin selling but their shares are quickly absorbed by buyers. In fact, the demand for the stock becomes so intense that price very quickly surges beyond the recent new high. Weeks later the stock moves significantly higher.

How Are Technical Targets Derived?

Technical targets for symmetrical triangles are derived by adding the largest vertical height of the triangle to the ultimate breakout level. (See Figure 1.28.)

Figure 1.28 Symmetrical triangle for Transocean Sedco Forex (RIG).
Source: StockCharts.com.

Vital Signs

- Symmetrical triangles are about growing consensus among traders so a breakout from the triangle means that one group of investors, (bulls or bears) have been forced to abandon everything they believed about price. This sudden imbalance between supply and demand always leads to a violent move in price.
- Generally, most issues will record a breakout (either higher or lower) about two-thirds through the pattern. If a stock moves all the way to the apex of the triangle the initial breakout is almost always false and should be avoided.
- Because supply and demand are in equilibrium within the triangle, volume should slow dramatically. Once a breakout has occurred, *volume* must increase significantly.
- Upside breakouts often lead to small two percent to three percent rallies followed by an immediate test of the breakout level. If the stock closes below this level (now support) for any reason, the pattern becomes invalid.
- To swing-trade, place a buy stop a fraction or two above the declining top of the triangle. In case you are wrong, place a sell stop 5 percent or so below the breakout level.

Bull Flags

Technically speaking, a bull flag is a sharp, strong volume rally on a positive fundamental development, and several days of sideways to lower price action on much weaker volume followed by a second, sharp rally to new highs on strong volume.

Why Does It Happen?

Bulls flags are favored among technical traders because they almost always lead to large and predicable price moves. Like all other continuation patterns, bull flags represent little more than a brief lull in a larger move higher. Indeed, in many cases the flag pattern will actually take shape in the middle of the ultimate move higher. Bull flags occur because stocks rarely move higher in a straight line for an extended period. Instead, the move higher is broken up by brief periods where traders catch their breath.

The first part of the flag pattern is often called the *flagpole* or *mast*. During this phase the stock price skyrockets to a reaction high (*a*) on some positive fundamental development. Very often this will be the unveiling of a new product, a favorable legal resolution, or positive earnings surprise but the change in price is near vertical as would-be sellers are overwhelmed by new buyers caught up in the euphoria of the moment. As the stock soars speculators who were smart enough to have purchased the stock at lower levels begin selling.

At this point the second phase or *flag* portion of the bull flag begins. Because the flow of news and investor sentiment is overwhelming positive, most of the stock sold by speculators is easily absorbed in the beginning but as time passes fewer investors seem willing to pay the current price. Slowly, the stock price begins to falter on dramatically reduced volume. The descent is slow because bullish sentiment is still very strong.

After several days of minor weakness, a rally begins and a minor low is set (*b*). Sensing an opportune time to enter new positions buyers begin to return, pushing the stock very near the most recent high but because volume is light this rally is easily rebuffed and a slightly lower high (*c*) is established before the price turns lower. The new round of selling sends the stock modestly lower on reduced volume. After several more sessions the stock moves below the lows made at (*a*) but volume contracts further.

Just as it begins to look as though a real decline is under way there is a new positive fundamental development and the stock begins to move higher (*d*). As the rally accelerates volume increases dramatically; buyers overwhelm those taking profits. Over the next one or two sessions the stock moves through the high set at (*c*) and volume surges further. This triggers an upside breakout point (*e*). During the next session several Wall Street firms either make new buy recommendations or reiterate existing recommendations. The stock opens higher and goes on to make significant new highs in the weeks ahead. (See Figure 1.29.)

How Are Technical Targets Derived?

The technical target for a bull flag pattern is derived by adding the height of the flag pole to the eventual breakout level at (*e*).

Vital Signs

- Bull flag formations involve two distinct parts, a near vertical, high volume flag pole and a parallel, low volume consolidation comprised of four points and an upside breakout.
- The actual flag formation of a bull flag pattern must be less than 20 trading sessions in duration.

Figure 1.29　Bull flag for InfoSpace, Inc.
Source: StockCharts.com.

- Most flag patterns occur at the middle of the larger move higher for a stock.
- Upside breakouts often lead to two percent to three percent rallies followed by an immediate test of the breakout level. If the stock closes below this level (now support) for any reason, the pattern becomes invalid
- To swing-trade, place a buy stop just above the breakout level (*e*). Set a limit order to sell about 5 percent below that level in case you are wrong.

Bullish Pennants

Technically speaking, a bullish pennant is a sharp, strong volume rally on a positive fundamental development, and several days of narrowing price consolidation on much weaker volume followed by a second, sharp rally to new highs on strong volume.

Why Does It Happen?

Bullish pennants are very close cousins to bull flags. In fact, there is only one major difference: The consolidation after the flag pole is triangular (pennant shaped) as opposed to being parallel (flag shaped). Like flags, pennants are favored among technical traders because they almost always lead to large and predicable price moves. Finally, like flags, pennants usually take shape at the midpoint of a major move higher.

The first part of the pennant pattern is often called the *flagpole* or *mast*. During this phase the stock price skyrockets to a reaction high (*a*) on some positive fundamental development. Very often this will be the unveiling of a new product, a favorable legal resolution, or a positive earnings surprise but the change in price is near vertical as would-be sellers are overwhelmed by new buyers caught up in the euphoria of the moment. As the stock soars speculators who were smart enough to have purchased the stock at lower levels begin selling.

At this point the second phase or *pennant* portion of the pattern begins. Because the flow of news and investor sentiment is overwhelming positive, most of the stock sold by speculators is easily absorbed in the beginning but as time passes fewer investors seem willing to pay the current price. Slowly, the stock price begins to falter on dramatically reduced volume. The descent is slow because bullish sentiment is still very strong and after several days of minor weakness, a brief rally begins and a minor low is set (*b*).

Sensing an opportune time to enter new positions buyers begin to return, pushing the stock very near the most recent high but because volume is light this rally is easily rebuffed and a slightly lower high (*c*) is established before the price turns lower. The new round of selling sends the stock modestly lower on reduced volume. After several more sessions the stock approaches the lows made at (*a*) but volume expands and a higher low is set at (*d*). This higher low establishes the parameters of a very small symmetrical triangle pattern.

As the stock begins to move higher from (*d*) volume increases dramatically and buyers overwhelm those taking profits. Over the next one to two sessions the stock moves through the high set at (*c*) and volume surges further. This triggers an upside breakout (*e*). During the next session several Wall Street firms either make new buy recommendations or reiterate existing recommendations. The stock opens higher and goes on to make significant new highs in the weeks ahead.

How Are Technical Targets Derived?

The technical target for a bull flag pattern is derived by adding the height of the flag pole or (*a*) to the eventual breakout level at (*e*). (See Figure 1.30.)

Vital Signs

- Bullish pennants involve two distinct parts, a near vertical, high-volume flagpole and a symmetrical, low-volume triangular consolidation comprised of four points and an upside breakout.
- The triangular consolidation during the formation of the pennant is very much like a symmetrical triangle and this implies that traders feel comfortable with the current price.
- The actual pennant formation of a bullish pennant pattern must be less than 20 trading sessions in duration.
- Most bullish pennant patterns occur at the middle of the larger move higher for a stock.

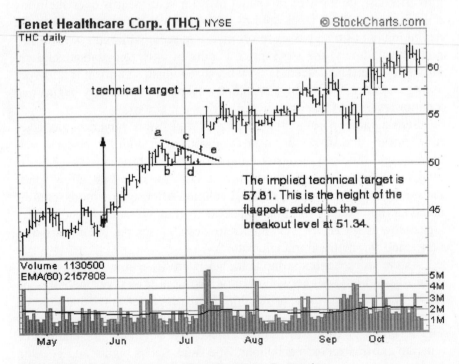

Figure 1.30   Bullish pennant for Tenet Healthcare Corporation.
Source: StockCharts.com.

- Upside breakouts often lead to two percent to three percent rallies followed by an immediate test of the breakout level. If the stock closes below this level (now support) for any reason, the pattern becomes invalid.
- To swing-trade, either wait for that fifth point (*e*) and buy above the pattern—or to be more certain, buy a short pullback to (*e*) after the breakout. In case you're wrong, place a sell limit around 5 percent below the breakout level.

Bear Flags

Technically speaking, a bear flag is a sharp, strong volume decline on a negative fundamental development and several days of sideways to higher price action on much weaker volume followed by a second, sharp decline to new lows on strong volume.

Why Does It Happen?

Bear flags are favored among technical traders because they almost always lead to large and predicable price moves. Like all other continuation patterns, bear flags represent little more than a brief lull in a larger move lower. Indeed, in many cases the flag pattern will actually take shape in the middle of the ultimate move lower. Like bull flags, bear flags occur because stocks rarely move in one direction for an extended period. Instead, the move is broken up by brief periods where traders catch their breath. These periods are flags and pennants.

The first part of the bear flag pattern is often called the *flagpole* or *mast*. During this phase the stock price collapses to a reaction low (*a*) following some negative fundamental development. Very often this will be downward guidance, an unfavorable legal resolution, or a negative earnings surprise but the change in price is near vertical as would-be buyers are overwhelmed by frantic new sellers caught up in the euphoria of the moment. As the stock collapses, some speculators who were smart enough to have sold short stock at higher levels begin buying to cover short positions and some less-informed investors actually begin bargain hunting.

At this point the second phase or *flag* portion of the bear flag begins. Because the flow of news and investor sentiment is overwhelming negative, most of the stock bought by speculators is easily absorbed by nervous sellers in the beginning but as time passes, selling pressures abate and slowly the stock price begins to rise on dramatically reduced volume. It is bargain hunting that pushes the stock off the lows but volume is so weak that the rally soon fizzles and the stock puts-in a short-term top (*b*).

With bearish sentiment still rampant the next decline threatens to push the stock to fresh new lows, but as the decline begins volume slows further and the bargain hunters become more enthusiastic. As the stock approaches the reaction low, price stabilizes and a second short-term bottom is established at slightly higher levels (*c*).

Buoyed by the fact the stock did not make a relative new low, bargain hunters once again begin buying the stock. This time the stock rallies slightly higher than (*b*) but volume is even weaker and the rally soon fails (*d*). During the next three to four sessions the stock trades in a narrow range and volume slows dramatically before the stock begins to slide toward the lows established at (*c*).

Over the next one to two sessions the stock moves through these lows, triggering a downside breakout (*e*). Over the next session several Wall Street firms make negative comments or reduce earnings estimates and a new leg lower begins. The stock opens lower and goes on to make significant new lows in the weeks ahead.

How Are Technical Targets Derived?

The technical target for a bear flag pattern is derived by subtracting the height of the flag pole from the eventual breakout level at (*e*). (See Figure 1.31.)

Vital Signs

- Bear flag formations involve two distinct parts, a near vertical, high-volume flagpole and a parallel, low-volume consolidation comprised of four points and an upside breakout.
- The actual flag formation of a bear flag pattern must be less than 20 trading sessions in duration.
- Most bear flag patterns occur at the middle of the larger move lower for a stock.
- Downside breakouts often lead to small two percent to three percent declines followed by an immediate test of the breakout level. If the stock closes above this level (now resistance) for any reason, the pattern becomes invalid.
- To swing-trade, sell short on the breakout below (*e*), or on a pullback to (*e*). Place stop to cover 5 percent or so above the breakout in case you are wrong.

Figure 1.31 Bear flag for Beazer Homes.
Source: StockCharts.com.

Bearish Pennants

Technically speaking, a bearish pennant is a sharp, strong volume decline on a negative fundamental development and several days of narrowing price consolidation on much weaker volume followed by a second, sharp decline to new lows on strong volume.

Why Does It Happen?

Bearish pennants are very close cousins to bear flags. In fact, there is only one major difference: The consolidation after the flag pole is triangular (pennant shaped) as opposed to being parallel (flag shaped). Like flags, pennants are favored among technical traders because they almost always lead to large and predicable price moves. Finally, like flags, pennants usually take shape at the midpoint of a major move higher.

The first part of the bearish pennant pattern is often called the *flagpole* or *mast*. During this phase the stock price collapses to a reaction low (*a*) following some negative fundamental development. Very often this will be

downward guidance, an unfavorable legal resolution, or a negative earnings surprise but the change in price is near vertical as would-be buyers are
overwhelmed by frantic new sellers caught up in the euphoria of the moment. As the stock collapses some speculators who were smart enough to
have sold stock short at higher levels begin buying to cover short positions
and some less informed investors actually begin bargain hunting.

At this point the second phase or *pennant* portion of the bearish pennant begins. Because the flow of news and investor sentiment is overwhelming negative, most of the stock bought by speculators is easily
absorbed by nervous sellers in the beginning, but as time passes selling
pressures abate and slowly the stock price begins to rise on dramatically
reduced volume. It is bargain hunting that pushes the stock off the lows
but volume is so weak that the rally soon fizzles and the stock puts-in a
short-term top (*b*).

With bearish sentiment still rampant the next decline threatens to
push the stock to fresh new lows but as the decline begins volume slows
further and the bargain hunters become more enthusiastic. As the stock
approaches the reaction low price stabilizes and second short-term bottom is established at slightly higher levels (*c*).

Buoyed by the fact the stock did not make a relative new low, bargain
hunters once again begin buying the stock. This time the stock rallies but
fails to move beyond the highs established at (*b*). This lower high establishes the parameters of a very small symmetrical triangle pattern and becomes (*d*) in the bearish pennant pattern. During the next three to four
sessions the stock trades in a narrow range and volume slows dramatically before the beginning to slide toward the lows established at (*c*).

Over the next one to two sessions the stock moves through these
lows, triggering a downside breakout (*e*). During the next session several
Wall Street firms make negative comments or reduce earnings estimates
and a new leg lower begins. The stock opens lower and goes on to make
significant new lows in the weeks ahead.

How Are Technical Targets Derived?

The technical target for a bearish pennant pattern is derived by subtracting the height of the flagpole from the eventual breakout level at (*e*). (See
Figure 1.32.)

Vital Signs

- Bearish pennant formations involve two distinct parts, a near vertical, high volume flagpole and a symmetrical, low-volume trian-

Figure 1.32   Bearish pennant for Pulte Corporation.
Source: StockCharts.com.

gular consolidation comprised of four points and a downside
breakout.

- The triangular consolidation during the formation of the pennant is
  very much like a symmetrical triangle and this implies that traders
  feel comfortable with the current price.
- The actual flag formation of a bearish pennant pattern must be less
  than 20 trading sessions in duration.
- Most bearish pennant patterns occur at the middle of the larger move
  lower for a stock.
- Downside breakouts often lead to two percent to three percent declines followed by an immediate test of the breakout level. If the
  stock closes above this level (now resistance) for any reason, the pattern becomes invalid.
- To swing-trade, sell short on the breakout below (*e*), or on a pullback
  to (*e*). Place stop to cover 5 percent or so above the breakout in case
  you are wrong.

Rising Wedge

Technically speaking, a rising wedge in a downtrend is a decline to a new low on strong volume and several weeks of narrowing, range-bound trade characterized by higher highs and higher lows with contracting volume, followed by a sharp break lower on strong volume.

Why Does It Happen?

Rising wedge formations in downtrends are very similar to other triangle patterns in that they are characterized by narrowing price ranges and slowing volume. There is one important difference: Unlike symmetrical and right angle triangles, rising wedge formations in downtrends almost always result in large price declines. Many bearish technical patterns are about deception and this is particularly true for the rising wedge. Because this pattern features gradually higher stock prices, many investors will jump to the incorrect conclusion that the stock is acting well from a technical perspective. This is false. Although prices continue to rise, every rally is more feeble than the last and it soon becomes clear that interest in owning the stock at higher prices is waning.

The first point in every rising wedge in a downtrend formation begins with a relative new low. This low is generally in response to a series of negative fundamental developments. The stock may have had an earnings warning, product delay, or litigation setback but the story behind the price weakness is always legitimate and leads to a real change in the way the stock is perceived. What makes the pattern interesting is that like many other reversal patterns, the decline to relative new lows actually leads to what appears to be aggressive buying by large investors. This turn of events creates a short-term bottom (a).

Encouraged by the show of strength at (a), selling pressures begin to wane and over the next several days the stock begins to move higher. Volume is light but it soon becomes clear the panic that led to the recent relative new low has been replaced by more rational thinking. Wall Street brokerages begin to make more positive comments and volume increases modestly. This increase in volume should lead to further gains but instead sellers step up and what looks like a reaction high occurs, (b).

On continued light volume the stock drifts lower but to the great delight of those looking for a near-term bottom, the move lower does not eclipse the lows set at (a) and a new rally begins. This point, (c), plays an important role in investor sentiment because it appears as though the stock is making a series of higher lows. Speculators begin adding new long positions in anticipation of a much bigger rally—and for a short time they are rewarded.

Amid more optimistic comments from Wall Street analysts the stock rises beyond the level of (*b*) but not high enough to create a parallelogram with the lows. This is a defining point in time because it sets the wedge formation characterized by a narrowing price range. After several additional sessions the stock stops rising and a new short-term top becomes evident, (*d*).

At this point a new, negative fundamental development occurs and the stock begins to decline. Speculators rush to close long positions to avoid losses but buyers are few. The imbalance between motivated sellers and willing buyers leads to a watershed decline. This situation is made worse by a series of negative comments from Wall Street analysts in the days ahead. Weeks later the stock declines to a new low.

How Are Technical Targets Derived?

Technical targets for rising wedges are derived by subtracting the height of the pattern from the eventual breakout level, which is the lower trendline of the triangle. (See Figure 1.33.)

Figure 1.33 Rising wedge for QLogic.
Source: StockCharts.com.

Vital Signs

- Rising wedges can be either reversal or continuation patterns. When they occur in a downtrend, they are always continuation patterns.
- Although the news that is pushing the stock higher may be bullish, weak volume is an indication that professionals are not buying. Indeed, these investors are using strength to unwind existing long positions and/or establish new short positions.
- Rising wedge formations in downtrends are distributive in nature. The fact that price is rising but volume is declining is a good indication that the move higher is illegitimate.
- Downside breakouts often lead to two percent to three percent declines followed by an immediate test of the breakout level. If the stock closes above this level (now resistance) for any reason, the pattern becomes invalid.
- To swing-trade, place a limit order to sell short below the seemingly rising uptrend. To limit losses in case you're wrong, place an order to cover 5 percent or so above the breakout level.

Bedford completes about 30 trades per day based on these patterns, five days a week, for his hedge fund in Toronto. In the past five years, he says that double tops and double bottoms have worked the best, as reversal patterns suit his personality and outlook better than continuation patterns. If his success continues on track, in a few years he's looking forward to the biggest reversal pattern of them all—retirement to a beach in Florida and a new career as an artist.

Chapter 2

BERT DOHMEN

To anyone born in wartime Europe, trading volatile markets must seem like a walk in the park. Stock prices flying low and fast overhead have to pale in comparison to the constant threat of bombs, fire, hunger, and losing your mom or dad.

Bert Dohmen, a veteran swing trader and founder of Los Angeles-based investment research firm Dohmen Capital Group, grew up in Cologne, Germany, during the final stages of World War II. His father was a successful artist who specialized in designing stained glass windows for churches, as well as frescoes for public buildings. Dohmen recalls that his father didn't care for war and spontaneously declared Hitler "nuts" in a public place when it was announced that Germany had declared war on the United States. For this, he was almost arrested.

After being drafted, his father managed to stay away from the fighting at the front by creating oil paintings of his officers and their wives. Most artists don't make good soldiers. Bert recalls that his father's superiors ultimately did him a favor and discharged him for bad hearing.

The Dohmen family had their home destroyed three times during air raids by Allied bombers—first by the English with low-altitude bombing runs during the night, then by the Americans with high-altitude bombing runs during the day. "We'd run down to the basement and peek outside—it was exciting and frightening at the same time," he says. "You'd see the searchlights crisscross the skies at night, lock on a bomber, and shoot it down. Many times the German fighters were shot down as well. Then we'd scurry out the next day to look at the wreckage."

During the last year of the war, Bert recalls food getting more and more scarce. The stores were virtually empty. But his father would create small paintings at home and then ride his bicycle into the countryside to trade with farmers for eggs and milk. In the final weeks of the war, Bert says he could hear the cannons from the front for many hours each day as the Battle of the Bulge raged. One day in May 1945, suddenly it was quiet, and the rumors of a German surrender filtered into town. The people were first told to put a white flag outside their windows to show American troops that they were not hostile. Everyone put white towels or bed sheets out their windows on poles, brooms, or whatever they could find.

A few hours later, rumors had it that Nazi SS troops would arrive first and planned to torch with flamethrowers every house displaying a white flag. So in went the flags. After several hours of dead silence, with no one on the streets, U.S. troops rolled through, tank after tank, with German POWs in tow, holding their hands up. Rather than despair, Dohmen recalls a wonderful sense of jubilation and liberation. "People hated the Nazis—we loathed those arrogant clowns," he says.

After the war, Dohmen's father applied for visas to emigrate to the United States. To him it seemed that Europe would always be at war for some reason or other. Five years later, visas were granted and the family settled in the Midwest where an aunt, who had sponsored them, lived. Currency controls limited the amount of money they could take out of Germany, and they landed in the United States with $40 in their pockets. Dohmen said he and his family "loved it right off the bat—we were welcomed with open arms." His aunt told them to tell neighbors that they were from Switzerland, but he says he was honest and never encountered prejudice.

His father was offered work at two of the leading stained glass studios in the country. But he preferred to stay independent and start his own business. He was amazed that all you needed to start your own business was a letterhead and some ambition, without the many forms and permissions required in Europe. Peter Dohmen quickly got contracts designing stained glass windows for major churches in the Midwest, including ones at Notre Dame and Valparaiso universities.

With his mother in charge of administration of the business, Dohmen says business was always discussed at the dinner table—giving him practical lessons that he feels were better than the theoretical education received at school.

Not having inherited his father's artistic talents, Dohmen graduated from college with a degree in chemistry. He went on to study business in graduate school, but was bored with the outdated textbooks, many of which had been written decades earlier and seemed irrelevant. However, the stock market had gotten his attention. He opened a brokerage account at the same Wall Street firm where his parents had their account and started investing with $400. Bert says his first investment came on a recommendation from that firm to buy shares in a large copper mining firm, listed on the New York Stock Exchange. It was paying a 10 percent dividend, making it the highest yielding stock on the NYSE—for a good reason, he later found out. Its African mine was soon nationalized and the stock fell apart, giving him a distaste for brokerage recommendations that persists to this day.

Indeed, a growing distrust of fundamental analysis led him to learn the tools of technical analysis that characterized his next 30 years of success. He went to the library and read the sparse literature available on the subject and found it fit with his science background. At the time, Wall Street equated technical analysis with tarot-card reading; Malcolm Forbes, the magazine publisher, had called it "voodoo." Yet, today, every Wall Street firm has a large technical analysis department.

Dohmen said he felt he was wasting his time at business school, so he ditched it without getting a degree and took a job in the defense industry just as the war in Vietnam was heating up. He found the work stimulating. Learning which companies were expanding and doing well, he began investing in the strongest ones, using technical analysis for entry and exit points.

In time Bert was successful enough to quit his job and trade full time. He moved to Honolulu for better climate in 1976. In early 1977 he started an investment newsletter, called the *Wellington Letter*, to explain why he thought a new bear market was right around the corner. At the time, bullishness among mainstream analysts was peaking. A *Wall Street Journal* columnist detailed his prescient call several months later, bringing him into the national spotlight—and his new career as a newsletter publisher took off.

He added services over time, including letters covering commodities, mutual funds, and short-term trading. The latter, the daily *Smarte Trader*, provides market analysis and daily long and short stock picks for $3,500 per year. For that kind of money, readers expect Dohmen to catch swings in any environment with accuracy—and he has managed to catch most major market turns within a few days.

In 2001 Dohmen and his wife, Santy, moved to the mainland. Bert trades his own accounts every day until the market closes, then switches over to produce the advisory services for clients. He considers closing prices the most important of the day, since "everything else is just jumping around—running the stops on the upside and the downside, and creating a lot of noise."

Dohmen thinks the biggest mistakes of novice swing traders are trying too hard to bag big winners—and holding onto losing positions too long. "It's more important to exercise risk control than to hit home runs," he says. He advises traders to write down their stop losses and targets for each trade before initiating them, and then get out according to plan.

Now let's look at his favorite swing-trading setups or patterns, his methods of minimizing risk with thoughtful trade management, his strategies for controlling risk with stop losses, and his plans for exiting trades with profits.

Setups

Dohmen starts by determining the broad market trend, as he believes it is less risky to swing-trade with the supertrend than to trade against it. Like most other pros, he is always focused on conserving capital in the event that he's figured things wrong. If he wishes to short a stock and the major trend of the market is down, then he believes unexpected rallies will not last long. Likewise, if he wishes to go long a stock or sector and the major trend is up, he believes an unexpected decline is unlikely to last long. In other words, he says, "in a bear market it's less risky to be a short seller, while in a bull market it's less risky to be long."

It's more than just style: Dohmen believes that bull and bear markets are mirror images of each other, with opposite sets of rules. Techniques and indicators that work in a bull market will not work in a successive bear market. "The world is very simple—don't try to make things too complicated. In a bear market, you want to forget everything that was hot or worked well in the bull market," he says.

After settling on the market's major trend, Dohmen studies the charts and fundamentals of the 11 major industrial sectors and 3 major capitalization groups, and determines which are in the strongest bull and bear trends. Only then does he begin to focus on stocks. After all, he notes, even in a major overall bear market there are always certain sectors, styles, and capitalization groups that are humming along as if all is well in the world. In the 2000–2002 bear market, for instance, small-cap stocks, value stocks, homebuilders, restaurants, and defense contractors were all in powerful bull markets most of the time while the broad market averages dominated by large-cap growth stocks—the S&P 500 Index and the Nasdaq 100, specifically—plunged. But even those groups were not safe havens after May 2002. That's when technical indicators gave Dohmen sell signals that preserved nice profits.

How do you determine if a market, sector, or capitalization group is in a bull market? Again, keep it simple. The Dow Jones or Standard & Poor's sector indexes are making new highs, and a majority of stocks in the sector are making new highs. These indexes can be viewed online at any of the leading stock charts providers, such as Prophet.net.[1] (See Figure 2.1.) Nasdaq provides two easy-to-read tables of the major sectors and exchange-traded funds at its web site.[2] (See Figure 2.2.) Decision-point.com provides pages of the charts of all stocks that underlie the major and minor market indexes ranked by price-performance momentum. (See Figure 2.3.)

Dohmen loves to buy stocks making new highs, particularly if they are all-time highs with no overhead resistance from a high 3, 5, or 10 years back. If you buy new highs, he points out, you don't need to worry about moving averages, stochastics, or other indicators. "The key to trading is to keep it simple," he says. "If you are looking for strength, buy the strongest stocks in the strongest sectors. If you are looking for stocks to short, sell the weakest stocks in the weakest sectors." It's the law of the jungle. The strongest predators in the wild, let's say lions on the African savanna, always stalk the lamest members of an antelope herd for their next meal, not the fastest. In the generally down-trending market of 2000–2002, telecommunications

---

[1]Visit StockCharts.com, Decisionpoint.com, Prophet.net.
[2]Visit Nasdaq.com for a "heat map" or table that shows which exchange-traded funds tracking the leading indexes are doing well or poorly over a variety of time periods.

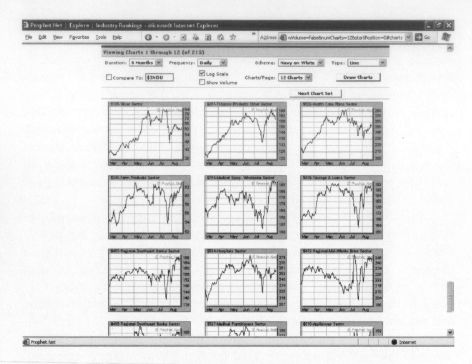

Figure 2.1   Prophet.net. In the Industry Ranks section of its Explore area, the free web site Prophet.net provides a performance-ranked view of the charts of 215 industries. Dohmen prefers to confine his swing-trading long candidates to top-performing sectors.
Source: © Prophet Financial Systems (www.prophet.net).

carriers and telecom equipment providers were the weakest members of the technology herd that proved easy prey for short-sellers. Likewise, utilities that depended on energy trading and high levels of debt to generate profits were the easiest prey for short-sellers in the wake of Enron's collapse. Short-sellers who tried to make money by shorting the stocks of home builders or restaurants, hoping for a reversal of their strength, faced a path of much greater resistance. Buy strength and sell weakness, and you've got more than half the swing-trading game mastered.

Some swing traders love to buy and sell stocks that move erratically, or up and down over time like a sine wave moving sideways. But Dohmen prefers stocks that trade in a smooth pattern either up or down

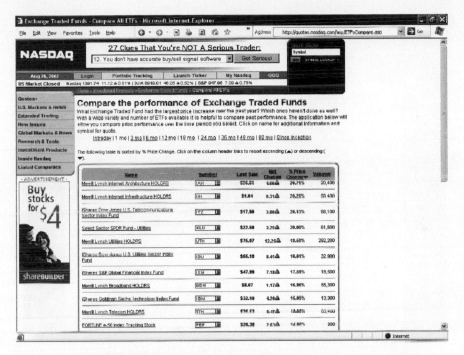

Figure 2.2 Nasdaq.com. Exchange-traded funds are special securities that track the performance of major market indexes, sector indexes, capitalization groups indexes, investment style indexes, and international indexes. Because most trade on the Nasdaq or American Stock Exchange, Nasdaq.com provides powerful screening tools to help investors track them in the Exchange Traded Funds section of its Investment Products area. Choose different time period links at the top of the page to re-sort the list to find potential candidates for longer or shorter trades.
Source: Nasdaq.com.

because he ideally wants to hold a position for several weeks or longer. If you use a trading software program like Metastock, you can draw trend channels or regressions based on standard deviations, and choose the ones with the narrowest channels. But you can also simply eyeball a chart to determine the ones that move progressively higher or lower with little interruption for weeks or months at a time. (See Figure 2.4.)

Once Dohmen finds the stocks consistently making new highs in sectors making new highs, he will just buy shares at the market on a break-

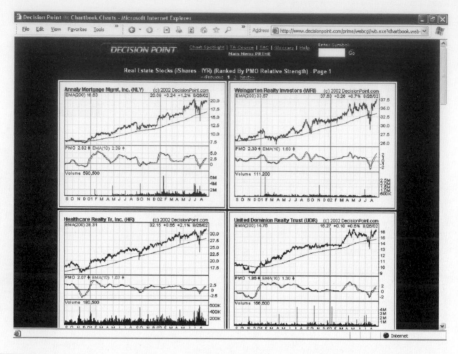

Figure 2.3   Decision Point. Decisionpoint.com provides quick access to charts of all stocks underlying every major and minor market index ranked by performance over the past 6 months or 24 months. Dohmen prefers to focus on stocks in strong industries that are breaking out to new highs for swing-trading long candidates.
Source: Courtesy of Decisionpoint.com.

out to new highs without waiting for a decline. Many traders, like Terry Bedford in Chapter 1, like to wait for a little pullback—but Dohmen believes that people who try to save a couple of bucks usually end up missing the best moves. "I see so many people concentrate on nickels and dimes," he says. "They see a breakout in price and volume and wait for a pullback—but that's a big mistake. Put a market order in and you're good to go." He likes to buy a stock the first day it breaks out to a new high, either with a market order or on a buy stop—which is a limit order that turns into a market order if a stock rises to a certain price. If you miss the first day of a powerful breakout, however, he admits that there's usually a little pullback on the second or third day when latecomers can enter a position. (See Figure 2.5.)

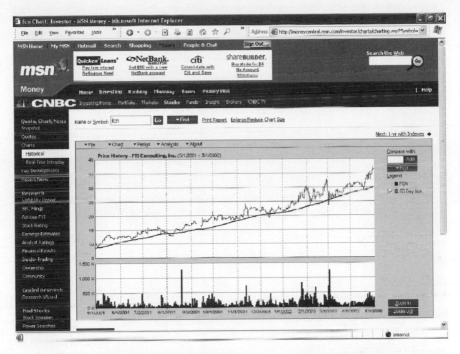

Figure 2.4 FTI Consulting. Shares of bankruptcy and litigation specialist FTI Consulting moved up in a steady pattern from May 2001 to May 2002 as its list of potential clients swelled amid bear-market blues. This is the type of pattern that Dohmen prefers to trade: nice and predictable.
Source: CNBC on MSN Money.

Of course, as with all other rules, there is an important caveat. Dohmen notes emphatically that he would not buy pullbacks in stocks whose sectors are in bear or sideways trends. For instance, in 2001, after the bull trend in home-building stocks was well-defined, he regularly recommended buying pullbacks of home builders' shares to support to prepare for their next breakouts. In generally down-trending sectors, however, pullbacks in stocks making nascent positive moves usually result in a bigger decline, as investors in the graphics processor manufacturer NVIDIA discovered in the first half of 2002. (See Figure 2.6.)

To repeat, Dohmen keeps his swing trading of longs simple by focusing on upside breakouts to one-year highs in the strongest stocks in the strongest groups. In these situations, there is no overhead supply of

Figure 2.5   W Holding Company. Shares of Puerto Rican bank holding company W
Holding were rising in a steady uptrend from September 17, 2001 to mid-June, 2002
when they broke through a four-year-old high at 14.25. Buying the breakout on the first
day resulted in a move that persisted to 19 two months later, though there was a short
pullback in early July to accommodate latecomers. Breakouts through multiyear highs in
predictably trending stocks are a favorite setup for Dohmen.
Source: CNBC on MSN Money.

shares—no buy-and-hold investors waiting patiently for a chance to sell
and get flat after weeks or months or years. Dohmen pounces on the first
day of the breakout, putting in his order in the last half hour of the day's
trade to ensure that the breakout is for real. However, before diving in
with his money, he looks back three to five years to see whether the stock
is within 15 percent of a high set in the past. If the new breakout is that
close to the old high, then he waits for it to clear that hurdle before purchasing. If the new one-year high is, let's say, 20 percent to 50 percent or
more below a three- to five-year high, then he'll buy the breakout on the
expectation that a great deal of supply from longtime holders won't come

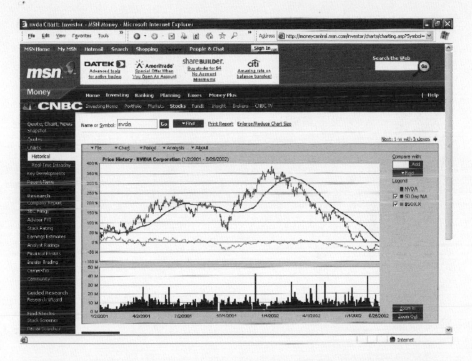

Figure 2.6 NVIDIA Corporation. Graphics semiconductor maker NVIDIA bucked the bearishness of the technology and chip groups during 2001, but its grace period ended in January 2002. Then every time it looked like the stock was ready to resume its uptrend, sellers piled on. Swing traders trying to repeat their 2001 successes with this stock by buying pullbacks in its few up moves in 2002 failed repeatedly. In this chart, the top line is NVIDIA; the bottom, the Philadelphia Semiconductor Index. Dohmen avoids buying breakouts or breakdowns in stocks that are bucking the big trend of their sector as they have no cavalry to fall back on for strength during periods of weakness.
Source: CNBC on MSN Money.

into the market until he's safely made and exited his trade. Let's take a look at four examples: Figures 2.7, 2.8, 2.9, and 2.10.

Selling

You haven't made a successful swing trade until you've sold or covered the stock, so now let's turn to look at the ways that Dohmen exits positions.

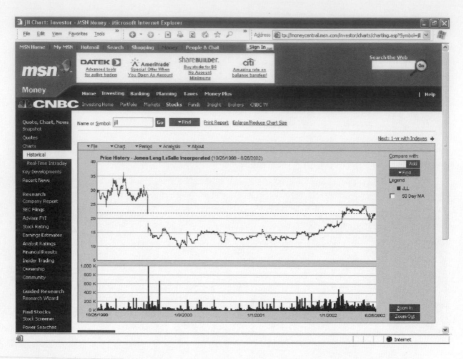

Figure 2.7   Jones Lang LaSalle Incorporated. Shares of Chicago-based real-estate services provider Jones Lang LaSalle broke out to a 52-week high at the end of June 2002 on strong volume, but that left the stock within 10 percent of its three-year high. This is the sort of upside breakout that Dohmen would not trade, expecting supply to hit the market for JLL shares after just a very short advance. Indeed, supply did return soon at that level, knocking the stock back below its presumed breakout level.
Source: CNBC on MSN Money.

A successful trader determines the conditions under which a stock will be sold or covered as part of the purchase or short decision. Dohmen, in fact, writes down his target sell price and initial protective stop in his trading journal alongside his purchase price. The first stop is perhaps the most important, as well as the easiest to place. Since he primarily buys breakouts of strong stocks in strong sectors, he sets the first stop a fraction below the low of the day prior to the breakout. That makes sense, right? If the stock declines to that level soon after your purchase, the breakout is invalidated and your whole reason for being in the game is out the window. (See Figure 2.11.)

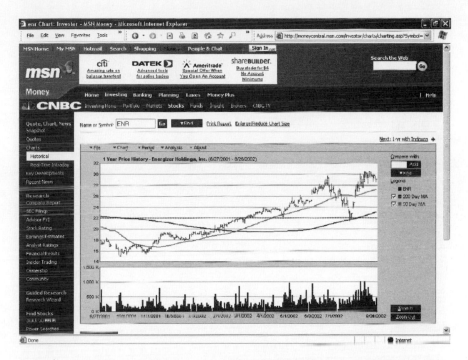

Figure 2.8 Energizer Holdings, Inc. Energizer Holdings, a maker of batteries, was the sort of uncomplicated consumer products company with regular earnings streams whose shares found strong demand in early 2002. This is the sort of stock that Dohmen likes to swing-trade on high-volume breakouts. Swing traders were successful trading it from the long side, on high-volume breakouts, as occurred in late January 2002 at $20.25 and again in late May at $28. On the first breakout, Dohmen would have bought at $20 with a stop under the recent low, around $18.50.
Source: CNBC on MSN Money.

After a stock has broken out and entered the expected trend, Dohmen places a mental stop 10 percent to 12 percent below each day's close, or just below the rising trendline or major simple moving average (21-day or 50-day). Some traders aren't willing to give up that much, and set their protective stops at 8 percent. Few successful swing traders are willing to hold a stock through a decline of larger than 20 percent.

Dohmen uses Fibonacci numbers to determine how far a retracement, or decline, from a new high can go. Or conversely, how far a re-

Figure 2.9 Blue Rhino Corporation. Another powerful earnings and "new product" story in 2001–2002, Blue Rhino Corporation sells propane in reusable containers to gas-grille owners through home-improvement stores and filling stations. After a decline in the second half of 2000, shares consolidated starting in January 2001 in an evenly paced "saucer bottom," then broke out in early 2002 around $6.50 over the 2001 high. That breakout signaled an important long-term trend change and provided an excellent entry point on the long side for swing traders. Volatility continued to be subdued after that breakout, a good sign that the new trend was strong, and two months later new breakouts at $8 and $10 proved to be more solid entry points for the sort of long-side swing trade Dohmen favors. (In July, a return to the stock's 2000 high in the high $14s provoked an outpouring of supply, briefly yielding an ideal setup for a short sale.)
Source: CNBC on MSN Money.

bound from a reaction low can rise. Fibonacci numbers, named for the Italian mathematician who first documented their pervasive existence in nature, are, for traders' purposes, 38 percent and 61 percent changes from a significant high or low on any chart, whether intraday, daily, weekly, or monthly. For example, if a stock moves quickly to $12 after a long consolidation around $10, its first Fibonacci retracement would

Figure 2.10 P.F. Chang's China Bistro, Inc. Restaurants go through regular periods of favor and disfavor on Wall Street. New dining concepts almost always hit investors' sweet tooth during the bull phases, and one of these in 2001–2002 was P.F. Chang's China Bistro—an upscale Chinese restaurant chain that offers large portions and consistent flavors and typically has long lines in its lively metropolitan locations.. In September 2001 shares were repelled after approaching their 2000 high, but in December 2001 the stock broke out to a new multiyear high and prior resistance level to provide a setup that perfectly fit the Dohmen model. A trailing 10 percent to 12 percent stop, or trendline stop, would not have been violated until the shares were up more than 90 percent in mid-2002.

Source: CNBC on MSN Money.

be to $11.24 (subtract 38 percent from the $2 move, or $.76) and its second Fibonacci retracement would be to $10.78 (subtract 61 percent from the $2 move, or $1.22). Most advanced charting software, as well as online sites such as StockCharts.com, does the math for you and shows the "Fib levels," as they're known, graphically. (See Figure 2.12.)

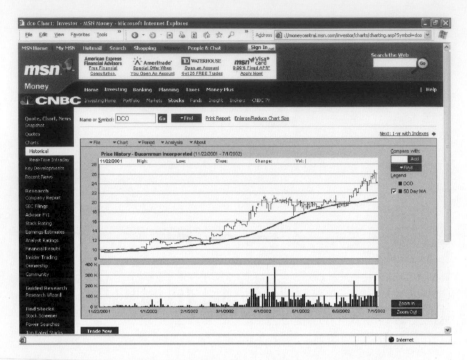

Figure 2.11 Ducommun Incorporated. Shares of small-cap aerospace defense contractor Ducommun traced out an almost perfect scenario from late 2001 through mid-2002, regularly rising sharply on higher and higher volume, then consolidating on low volume before another move. Swing traders who missed the first move in January 2002 got further chances in March, April, and July. Protective stops on the initial trades were easily defined as a fraction beneath the low of the day of the breakout: at $19.50, for instance, on June 10.
Source: CNBC on MSN Money.

Dohmen uses Fibonacci retracements as mileposts for *repurchase* or the initial purchase of a stock if he believes it is in an uptrend. In other words, if he has been long a stock that he likes from a breakout at $10 and sells after it stalls at $14, he will look to repurchase it when it has retraced 38 percent or 61 percent of the $4 move, or at around $12.48 or $11.66. Of course, there is nothing instantaneously magical about those exact levels; he would require some other confirming signal as well, such as a "hammer" formation on a candlestick chart or a strong reversal of the down move there on strong volume. (See Figure 2.13.)

Figure 2.12 Microsoft Corporation. To determine how far software maker Microsoft might rebound toward its January 2002 high from its July 2002 reaction low, traders who study Fibonacci retracements would expect a move at least to $52.35, a 38.2 percent retracement, and if that level was exceeded, then they would expect a move to at least $59.25, a 61.8 percent retracement. The levels can be easily drawn at the website StockCharts.com by creating a chart, then using the Annotate feature and choosing the Fibonacci tool from the top row of buttons.
Source: StockCharts.com.

Dohmen also watches for a break in a stock's trendline support as a signal to exit. "A trendline violation has to be honored," he says. The drawing of trendlines is an art, not a science. He looks for trends that are at least two months long and connects the lows of the days on the chart, not the closes. When a stock falls below the trendline connecting its two-month lows, that's a yellow light. Then he looks for other reasons why a stock may fall. The more distance between the two points in the trend-line, the more valid the signal.

A good example of the latter came in the winter and spring of 2002 with the terrific surge in defense contractor Lockheed Martin. The stock performed well immediately after the September 11 terrorist attacks, cresting on October 29, 2001 at $52.98 before going into a three-month consolidation. During that consolidation, a smart swing trader using Dohmen's methods would have put the stock on his radar screen awaiting a breakout above that high. The breakout finally came on February 4, 2002, when the stock surged to a high of $54.10

Figure 2.13 iShares. To determine where to buy iShares of the S&P 600 Index during its consolidation from lows in November 2001 to a reaction high in January 2002, traders who study the Fibs would have expected a retracement of at least 38.2 percent to around $111.00—a spot that turned out to be a very good re-entry point for the next move up.
Source: StockCharts.com.

on strong volume. The trader would have bought the stock around $53–$54 that day, and then immediately drawn the long-term trendline to determine the likely path of future trading if the uptrend continued. The first low would be touched on September 10, 2001 at $37.90, the day before the terrorist attacks. The next low was around $44 in mid-November, then $47 in late January. Drawing the line forward creates a psychological floor for the stock's future consolidations. As it turned out, the trendline would not have been violated until July 11, when shares slipped to $62. (See Figure 2.14.) A sale at that point would have brought the swing trader a profit of $18 per share. An investor who had not paid attention to the trend break would have lost all of his profit in the next two weeks, as the stock went on to fall right back to $52.30 by July 23 before rebounding. "This is why long-term investing makes no sense," says Dohmen. "Why let your profits turn into losses, when there's a clear signal to sell that lets you lock in a gain?"

When exactly do you pay attention to the breakout? Dohmen prefers to wait for end of day action before making his decision to place a stop loss order, as there is so much noise during the middle of the trading ses-

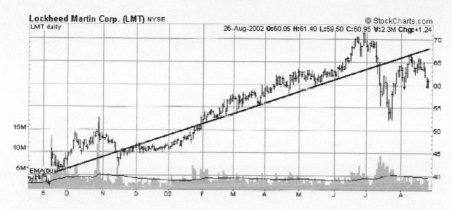

Figure 2.14 Lockheed Martin Corporation. A trendline connecting the lows in Lockheed Martin from September 2001 to February, March, April, May, and June 2002 lows was not violated until July 2002, leaving plenty of room for profit before a breakout would have suggested a sale initiated after February.
Source: StockCharts.com.

sion. If a stock penetrates its trendline in the last 20 minutes of trading, he will get out of it near the close. Otherwise, if it's close, he will wait until the open the next day.

Risk Control

Dohmen always scales into his swing-trade moves, putting in his largest chunk of money at the first breakout. If the trade works out and the stock continues to move in the expected direction, then he'll use pullbacks from the trend to add to the position in amounts that are always incrementally smaller than the initial purchase. This is a key element of risk control that distinguishes successful traders from unsuccessful traders. (See Table 2.1.) He avoids building an "inverted pyramid" in a position in which incrementally larger amounts of money are added to a position as it succeeds, so that at the end you have much more money invested at the top than at the bottom. The reason is obvious: In the latter case, a small decline near the top can wipe out all of your profits. (See Table 2.2.)

Table 2.1   Risk-Control Pyramid

Stock at	Buy Shares	Buy $	Total $
$10.00	1,000	$10,000	**$10,000**
$12.00	500	$6,000	**$16,000**
$14.00	250	$3,500	**$19,500**
Sell at	**Sell Shares**	**Sell $**	**Profit/Loss**
$16.00	1,750	$28,000	$8,500
Or, yikes!			
$12.00	1,750	$21,000	**$1,500**

When building a risk-control pyramid, more money is added to a position as shares move in the expected direction, but new amounts are always smaller than the initial amount. A sale upon reaching the target leaves the trader with a bigger gain than if he had not added to the position. A sale upon pullback to the middle of the trade range leaves the trader with a profit.

Dohmen likes to keep his money invested in a diversified basket of 10 to 20 positions in three or four sectors at any given time in a strong-trending market environment—though he is not at all opposed to holding cash if the environment turns uncertain. (He also goes fully to cash before heading out on vacation.) There's no magic number; it's all about what the trader believes he or she can manage. The real key to determining how many swing-trading positions to carry at any given time, he says, is that no more than five percent of your capital should be invested in any one position. He might start with two percent or three percent of his capital in a position, then build his pyramid until five percent of his capital is in a single position. That means if you're trading a portfolio worth $100,000, start each position out at around $2,500 and build to $5,000 if all goes well. That may not sound like much, but it should keep you out of trouble. "I have found that when I have violated this rule it's always a big mistake—the stocks you feel strongest about are the ones that come back to bite you," he says. "No one can know the future, no matter how well you are trading. The key to success is having your money diversified over a group of stocks and not overloading in a single position."

Table 2.2   Risky Inverted Pyramid

Stock at	Buy Shares	Buy $	Total $
$10.00	1,000	$10,000	**$10,000**
$12.00	1,500	$18,000	**$28,000**
$14.00	1,750	$24,500	**$52,500**
Sell at	**Sell Shares**	**Sell $**	**Profit/Loss**
$16.00	4,250	$68,000	$15,500
Yikes!			
$12.00	4,250	$51,000	($1,500)

In an inverted pyramid, a trader adds incrementally more money to a position as it moves in the expected direction. A sale upon reaching the target leaves the trader with a bigger gain than if he had either not added to the position or if he had pyramided his position with progressively smaller purchases. However, a sale upon pullback to the middle of the range leaves the trader with a loss.

To Dohmen, trading is a job like any other. He is at his desk working from an hour before the markets open in New York to a couple of hours after the close. That doesn't mean he's entering orders all day, every day. He's reading and analyzing the news, and monitoring the action in his stocks. When the market and his stocks are trending predictably, he trades more. When the markets are erratic and choppy—which is most of the time—he prefers to hold back and tread lightly.

The best way to know whether the market has entered an erratic phase? The perception will vary for each individual, but as a rule of thumb it might be when each day's action fails to follow through on the previous day's action, or you start to record a lot of losses in your trades, or none of your usual indicators seem to be working, or all of the above. Let's say you witness an upside breakout in a stock and all your indicators are flashing buy, and volume increases into the breakout. Bingo, an ideal trade, you're in. But then the stock reverses, falls back through its breakout point and volume then increases to a level higher than the breakout. That's a good indication that something is amiss, that dark forces have manipulated the breakout to trap bulls, and that it might be a good time to quit playing that stock for the day.

Timing

Dohmen sees the market and stocks through the prism of a variety of time frames: daily (short term), weekly (intermediate term), and monthly (long term). Sectors and stocks can thus be in an intermediate downturn amid a long-term up-move, and it's important to distinguish between the two to find the best entry points for swing trades.

To help determine the short- and intermediate-term trends, Dohmen uses a slow stochastic of his own invention that he declines to share with anyone, including this author. However, he says it's slower than what most charting programs call a "slow" stochastic, so let say it's set at 15–7. The exact setting doesn't really matter; what's important is that you test a variety of settings on a variety of stocks over many days and conditions, and determine if it works at signaling the change in the velocity of demand for shares. What Dohmen is looking for from the slow stochastic, as with most other oscillating indicators, are four clues to future price action:

1. A decline from "overbought" conditions at the 80 line (for shorts) or an advance from "oversold" conditions at the 20 line (for longs).
2. A cross of the signal line (usually red) over the indicator line (usually black).
3. A divergence from price action.
4. A pattern of higher highs or higher lows.

The first condition is the least reliable, as the problem with all oscillators is that they, quite obviously, always oscillate. They will always regularly move back and forth from oversold to overbought conditions regardless of whether any information is truly imparted. The second condition simply tells the chart reader when the "rollover" from overbought to oversold or from oversold to overbought has been completed.

It's the latter two conditions that really matter, and the third is the easiest to witness and act upon. Take the example of the iShare tracking the S&P Smallcap 600 Value Index (IJS) in April and May 2002. This was one of the best performing major indexes during the bear market until it ran into head winds after 18 months of strength, rising about 42 percent from July 2000 to April 2002, versus a 22 percent drop in the S&P 500 Index and a 60 percent drop in the Nasdaq Composite. By mid-April 2002, however, mainstream business newspapers and magazines had caught on and were calling readers' attention to the bull market in small cap value stocks. That normally means the jig is up for early buyers of the trend, but most await some sort of signal before dumping.

That's where observation of a top-formation process combined with the 15–7 stochastic helps a swing trader gain focus. As you can see in Figure 2.15, the S&P 600 Value Index made three stabs at getting through $99.50 from mid-April to mid-May. Daily volume increases over the average of the prior period on every failed attempt, and the 15–7 stochastic made a series of lower lows—first peaking at 95, then 86, then 75. The lower stochastic values show that there was increasingly less price acceleration toward each high, which is typically a deadly accurate sell signal. The index then went on to slip quietly under its 50-day moving average without much protest, whereupon it then plunged through its 200-day moving average as well en route to a ret-test of its post-September 11 lows. "It really is as simple as 1-2-3," Dohmen says. "At a third peak in price that's unconfirmed by the stochastic, you've got to sell."

Figure 2.15 iShares. The chart of the S&P Smallcap 600/Barra Value index tracking stock traced out a triple top pattern in May 2002 in which each successive peak was weaker than the last as shown in the sinking tops of the 15–7 slow stochastic. This is a type of pattern that Dohmen loves to swing-trade from the short side.
Source: StockCharts.com.

Another example of a topping formation that was made clear by proper use of a slow stochastic came in early 2002 with shares of the once-hot graphics semiconductor maker NVIDIA. The stock was one of the few stars of 2001 and it hit another in a seemingly endless set of peaks on December 17 at $68.95. After a brief consolidation, 10 days later the stock hit $69.69, fell back, then surged again to $72 on January 3, 2002—making unalert traders think that the new year would be just as colorful as the last. However, observers of the 15–7 stochastic would have noticed that something was amiss. The third peak—remember Dohmen's focus on 1-2-3—generated a stochastic level that was lower than the prior peak, and the prior peak generated a stochastic level that was lower than the peak before that. (See Figure 2.16.) To be exact, the stochastics peaked at 95, 88, and then 72. That was a nearly certain sign of waning momentum for the stock—just as a ball thrown into the air loses velocity near its apogee just as it is about to reverse. Swing-trade holders of the stock from much lower levels would have been smart to take that signal as an exit, for shares went on to plummet by more than 85 percent over the next eight months, finally hitting $8.50 in mid-August.

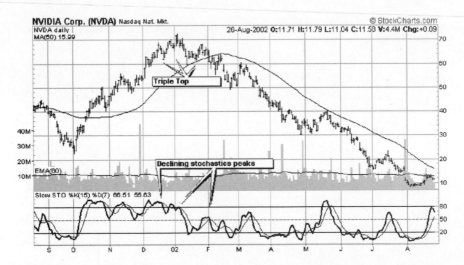

Figure 2.16   NVIDIA. The chart of the graphics chip maker NVIDIA traced out a triple top pattern from December 2001 to January 2002 as its 15–7 stochastic was sinking. It's hard to tell from the chart alone whether the stock is losing velocity, but the slow stochastic provides a powerful clue that its momentum is waning—an exit signal for swing traders like Dohmen.
Source: StockCharts.com.

"Always sell on the third peak when the stochastic is sinking, and you will virtually never regret it," says Dohmen.

Dohmen also uses the MACD, which acts similarly to the stochastic. The same rules apply as described for the stochastic. He also draws trend lines on the MACD, which work well to confirm a buy or sell signal.

Following these patterns may not generate the same level of excitement as the chases after fallen Allied jets that Dohmen experienced in his youth, but they are undoubtedly a lot more profitable.

Chapter 3

GEORGE FONTANILLS

George Fontanills works at a desk that looks as if it is floating on the Atlantic Ocean. From his vantage point in a condominium high above Miami Beach, he can see nothing but crystal-blue water, and as he clears his mind to prepare for trading he watches cruise ships slip past with a purposeful languor.

Born in Havana to first-generation Cubans whose own parents had emigrated from Spain, he took a tough road to his current perch as one of the nation's leading swing traders.

Fontanills and his family fled Cuba just after the Communist revolution in 1961 (when he was one year old) and landed on another planet: Syracuse, New York. His parents, an architect and a nurse, barely had $20 between them when they came to the United States, but they were sponsored by family members and worked hard. After a decade of cold winters and success, they packed up and moved to Miami, where Fontanills learned Spanish and went to high school, specializing in math, karate, and bodybuilding.

He earned a scholarship to the University of Florida at Gainesville, but soon after starting was diagnosed with Hodgkins disease and spent months going through rounds of chemotherapy and radiation. That brush with death led him to step up his ambitions, and he decided to head to New York University to study accounting and finance at the heart of the capitalist world so at odds with his native country. He went to work after graduation at accounting firms Delloite Haskins & Sells and Arthur Andersen, first as an auditor then as a computer systems consultant, but he

115

came to feel that it didn't fit his personality. A manager recommended that he apply to the Harvard Business School, and he won admittance to a class that would launch the careers also of former Microsoft Corporation chief financial officer Greg Maffei and Starwood Hotels & Resorts chief executive Barry Sternlicht. He recalls that the competititon made him learn to think quickly. "They throw a lot of data at you and teach you to make decisions quickly about what's useful and what's not—which turns out to be very good training for trading," he says.

After graduating with an M.B.A. in 1986, Fontanills fled New York again for Miami, where he joined his father in a family real estate development business. They bought and rehabbed apartment buildings, then graduated to luxury condominiums. Two years later, though, interest rates began to explode higher and the business fell apart—leading indirectly to his new career. On a slow day, one of his co-workers suggested that they start trading stocks. "I had no idea what that would entail, even after Harvard, but I was game," he recalls.

One thing he did learn in Cambridge was that if you don't know what you're doing, find people who do. So he and his partner hired three guys who called themselves professional traders. That turned out to be a lie, and in a month, they lost a good portion of their stake. Undeterred, with real estate still in a funk, Fontanills and his partner set up a little trading floor in their real-estate office and started trading options on the S&P 100 Index, or OEX. He started with options both for the leverage that they offered, and also because he quickly recognized that the most you can lose is the premium value of the option. With his background in computers from his days at Andersen, he began to write programs on the TradeStation platform to systemize trading of both those index options and commodities. "I truly studied at the school of hard knocks," he says. "But I had no choice. The only other business I knew was real estate, and the market for homes and condos at that time was just terrible."

Fontanills left his partner after three years and began to trade both for himself and build a trading-seminar business. He now has two lines of work: an educational workshop and a website business called Optionetics.com, and two hedge funds that are closed to new investors. He calls them two of the largest options trading funds in the world (though that's hard to verify), with assets leveraged up to notional positions of $1 to $2 billion. He said he wouldn't mind growing them larger, but already has a hard time because he has maxed out on many of the markets he trades.

To work off tension during the trading day, Fontanills likes to lift weights at the gym in his office. And then after hours, he is likely to roar out of town in his Lamborghini Diablo. Now let's see what sort of setups and trades make his trading desk zoom.

Stock Selection

Fontanills prefers the term "momentum trading" to swing trading to describe what he does, but it doesn't really matter. He's looking for jumpy, or high-beta, stocks with a big catalyst for medium-term movement in either direction, up or down. He tries to find big stocks that are in the news and the subject of a lot of institutional interest and then tag along for the ride. He religiously watches the news on cable financial channel CNBC, as he believes that stocks that are being talked about in public often have the greatest potential for big swings as pros and the public form divergent opinions that can send a stock flying.

Fontanills keeps his trading simple, with what he calls a "five-minute success formula." Basically, it comes down to finding stocks with the greatest short-term momentum that will turn into long-term momentum. Specifically, he's looking for shares that have moved at least 30 percent on high volume in a single day from the previous close as a result of high-impact news, such as an accounting irregularity, an investigation by federal regulators, or an extreme earnings surprise or disappointment. Much of the art is in determining whether a news catalyst is long lasting or will be a one-day wonder.

Consider this set of six rules to find these stocks. The stocks are

1. Up or down 30 percent in a single day on at least 300,000 shares traded or
2. Up or down 20 percent in a single day on volume of at least one million shares or
3. Up or down $5 in a single day on volume of at least one million shares and
4. Still trading at more than $7 and
5. Have options and
6. Have a long-term news catalyst. (Accounting fraud is better than quarterly earnings as a catalyst, for instance, because its effects tend to last through months of recriminations, while earnings can improve in a successive quarter.)

Looking for stocks like these used to be tedious, but stock-screening engines on the Web today make the task easy. The best is the Screener feature at MSN Money, where the URL is http://moneycentral.msn. com/investor/finder/customstocks.asp. If you're visiting for the first time, you will be asked to download a small bit of software. It's free, downloads quickly, and only works on Windows machines (sorry about that, Mac users).

Detailed instructions on using Screener are found in my book, *Online Investing: Second Edition* and in the Help section of the web site. But essentially you will want to create a screen that ultimately looks like Figure 3.1. To do so, follow these steps:

1. Click in the first blank under the title Field Name, and a fly-out menu will appear. Choose Stock Price History by clicking with your mouse, and another fly-out menu will appear. On this one, choose % Price Change Today. (See Figure 3.2.)

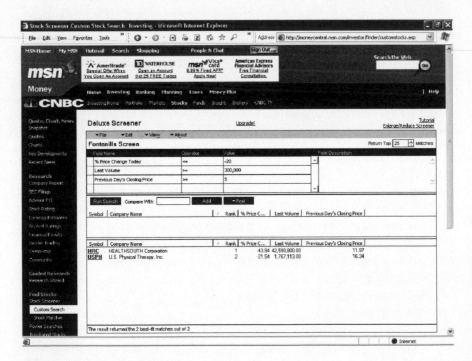

Figure 3.1 Deluxe Screener.
Source: CNBC on MSN Money.

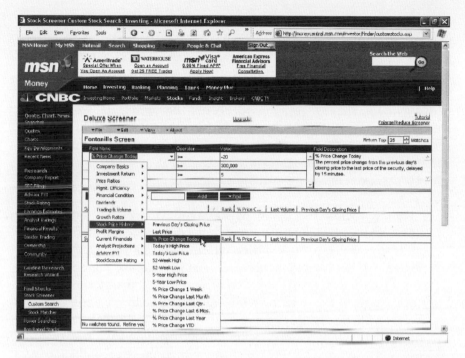

Figure 3.2   Price change today.
Source: CNBC on MSN Money.

2. Click in the first blank under the title Operator and choose </=.
3. Click in the first blank under the title Value and *type* in the number –20, including a hyphen to make the negative sign.
4. Click in the second blank under Field Name, and another fly-out menu will appear. Choose Trading and Volume with your mouse, and another fly-out menu will appear. On this one, choose Last Volume.
5. Click in the second blank under Operator and choose >/=.
6. Click in the second blank under Value and *type* in the number 300,000.
7. Click in the third blank under Field Name and choose Stock Price History again, but this time choose Last Price.
8. Click in the third blank under Operator and choose >/=.
9. Click in the third blank under Value and type in the number 7.

The list of stocks generated will be appropriate for further study for an intermediate-term trade. But first, you now need to figure out why they are up or down by 20 percent to 30 percent or more.

A move of that enormity signals that there has been an extreme imbalance of information about the company and its prospects between
bulls and bears. One group of investors has been very disappointed, and
another group rewarded. One side had correct beliefs about the future,
and the other had radically false beliefs. If the move is to the down side,
bulls figure that they've been misled, become disgusted, and are ready to
walk away. Fear becomes overwhelming, as they question all of their assumptions. As stocks enter a period of parabolic decline on increasing
volume, Fontanills often senses that institutional investors are jumping
out of the stock at intensifying volume.

> I like the stock to sink below its 50-day moving average on this
> move. You are looking for signs of fear, of desperation, of giving
> up. If you watch a stock during one of these moves with five-
> minute tick bars during the day, you can just feel the regret; you
> can sense how support levels crumble faster and faster as the
> stock sinks. You can keep following the stock lower until you
> feel the volume dry up, or decrease to the point that sellers are no
> longer the dominant force in the move, that they have become
> less aggressive and have reached an equilibrium or accommoda-
> tion with buyers.

Essentially, the 30 percent down move on a gap tells the bulls that
someone has information that they don't have, and that they should now
fear more skeletons in the company's closet. (If the move is to the upside,
the dominant motif from 1995 to early 2000, that magnitude of change
incites extreme feelings of greed, as sidelined investors pile on in an effort not to miss the move.)

What happens next is typically that the disappointed investors either
give up and the stock continues to move in the same direction as the initial explosion, or the disappointed investors regroup and try to persuade
the other side, plus previously disinterested parties, that the initial explosion was unwarranted and presents a reversal opportunity.

It's a simple matter to prove that this works. From March 2000
through the end of August 2002, according to research performed for me
by Logical Informations Machines of Chicago, 564 stocks sank by more
than 30 percent in a single day on at least 300,000 shares traded and
ended at a price greater than $7. (See Table 3.1.) A day later, the price of
the median stock was unchanged from its final price on the plunge day,

Table 3.1   30% One-Day Plungers: What Comes Next?

	Change After			
	1 Day	**1 Month**	**6 Months**	**12 Months**
Median	0.0%	–4.0%	23.3%	–51.5%
No. Up	287	260	154	103
No. Down	277	311	336	334
Pct. Down	49%	54%	69%	76%

Data: Logical Information Machines
Dates: March 2000 through August 2002

but a month later the median stock was down 4 percent. Six months later the median stock was down 23 percent and 12 months later the median stock was down 51 percent. Of the 437 stocks that had already completed 12 months of trading from their plunge date to August 30, 2002, and were still trading, 76 percent fell in price. This undoubtedly understates the effect, as many companies went out of business and were delisted before they could be counted.

During the 2000–2002 bear market, Fontanills played these 30 percent movers exclusively from the perspective of a intermediate-term short seller by buying out-of-the money put options that expired 3 to 12 months in the future. Then, he says, "We wait for the stock to do what it's destined to do, which is fall apart."

A good example: Tyco International, which came under unrelenting scrutiny over both its accounting and the practices of its executives and directors in 2002. The jolt in the company's shares was a big surprise to most market players, as shares hit an all-time high around $63 in early 2001, and revisited that level in December 2001. At the time, it was one of the 20 most widely held stocks on the New York Stock Exchange. Its acquisition strategy became a favorite of growth-stock managers, who had few good themes to play. Shares were remarkably nonvolatile during this time, never moving more than 7 percent in a day from August 2002 through December 2001, and typically less than 3 percent.

In mid-January 2002, however, the first crack in Tyco's story appeared when it announced that it would split up into four companies to make its accounting easier for analysts and shareholders to understand. That news was greeted with mild angst by investors. But two weeks later, the company slid $8.35, or 20 percent, to $33.65 on a single day of massive volume: 170 million shares. The catalyst was an announcement that it had richly compensated one of its directors for arranging the acquisition of CIT Group, a company in which the director held stock. The firm disclosed it had paid the director a $10 million fee and contributed another $10 million to a charity he controls.

The news clearly shocked the company's partisans, many of whom were still smarting over the conflicts of interest that emerged in the wake of the implosion of similarly acquisitive one-time growth favorite, the Houston-based energy merchant Enron Corporation. Fontanills' strategy is generally to wait a day or two for a mild rebound, then buy cheap out-of-the-money put options 3 to 12 months out to wait for disappointed investors to bail out as they are bombarded with negative vibes in the media. He likes shares of companies that regularly move at least $2 per day and about which there is a lot of uncertainty, pulling the stock in both directions. Wild oscillations reflexively create even more uncertainty, and persuade more longs to panic.

> CNBC is one of the best catalyst creators. We pay attention to what they're pounding on, like Tyco when the stock was falling apart. At times like that, it's Tyco, Tyco, Tyco eight times a day! If you go to any trading floor, they're listening to the same thing as me. That's a signal that it's one to start playing, it makes a great trade—because ultimately people who aren't sophisticated in trading will start to take the other side, and you can take their money.

The strategy certainly worked in this case. (See Figure 3.3.) Tyco shares rebounded modestly over the next three trading days, but Fontanills and others believed that an Enronlike set of disclosures was about to begin. Playing the stock from the short side, not as a candidate for reversal, was clearly the right path, as a week later it went on to have −16 percent and −23 percent days back to back as it fell to $23.10. For the next couple of months, the stock slowly worked its way back to the low $30s, but traders who came to believe that the −20 percent high-volume day signaled a change not just in price trend, but in opinion trend about the stock, did not need to wait long to be rewarded. In late

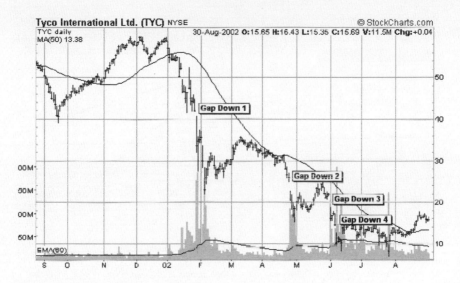

Figure 3.3 Tyco International Ltd.
Source: StockCharts.com

April further revelations resulted in three days of −19 percent, −4 percent, −14 percent as the stock sank further to $17. The cycle of reconciliation between bulls and bears then began anew, as the stock worked its way back to the mid-$20s before another disclosure sent shares reeling down 27 percent on June 3 to $16.05, followed by two more back-to-back days of −16 percent and −31 percent on June 6 and June 7, to $10. Once again, the cycle of reconciliation between bull and bear points of view recommenced, and shares drifted languidly back to $17 by late August 2002.

To study the effect of −20 percent moves in any stock that captures your interest, you must learn to export price data to a spreadsheet program like Microsoft Excel. It's easily done from charts on MSN Money. Start with a one-year chart by clicking Period on the chart's top menu bar and choosing 1 Year from the fly-out menu that appears. Then click File on the top menu bar and choose Export Data. (See Figure 3.4.) If you have Excel on your computer, the application will open and the daily high, low, close, and volume data will automatically appear on a new sheet. Next, prepare the sheet for your calculation of daily percent change. Eliminate all blank rows where market holidays appear. Either

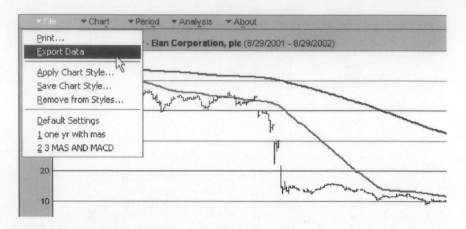

Figure 3.4   To export daily price data to Excel on your computer, visit the Chart section of the Stocks area of MSN Money, choose a 1-, 3-, or 5-year time period, then click File on the top menu bar. From the fly-out menu that appears, choose Export. The software then automatically opens a new spreadsheet and populates it with daily price data. If you have a 3-year weekly or 5- to 20-year monthly chart on your screen, the software will export weekly or monthly data to the spreadsheet.
Source: MSN.com.

delete these rows manually, or use Excel's AutoFilter tool on one of the columns, for instance, Column E, and choose Blanks from the list. (See Figure 3.5.) When only blank rows appear, delete them all and then un-filter the column by clicking All in the AutoFilter, revealing all the data again. Next, go to the bottom of the first open column and insert a for-mula that calculates daily percent change. (See Figure 3.6.).Then copy that formula up to the top, and change the format to percentage. (See Figure 3.7.) To spot the –20 percent rows more easily, choose Format/Conditional Formatting on the spreadsheets' top menu row and tell the software to turn all rows with less than –20 percent red. (See Fig-ure 3.8.) That's it. Now eyeball the list to see what's happened in that stock after 20 percent and 30 percent declines, or manipulate the data further to learn more.

Two more –30 percent collapses that Fontanills played in 2002 came in the shares of semiconductor designer Genesis Microchip and Irish drug maker Elan. In each case, the first watershed decline was the first of many en route to massive, multimonth plunges—particularly after the stocks had crossed below their 50-day moving averages.

Figure 3.5 Before you can calculate daily percent changes, you must eliminate all the blank rows that are the result of market holidays. To do this quickly, highlight the Date/High/Low/Close/Volume row of the spreadsheet, which is always Row 5, then choose Data on Excel's top menu bar. On the first fly-out menu that appears, choose Filter, and on the second choose AutoFilter. That will make each of the columns filterable. Next, choose any of the filter buttons—in this case, Volume was chosen—and drag the slider that appears to the bottom to find the term Blanks. When you click on Blanks, only blank rows will appear on the spreadsheet. Delete all of these rows (highlight them, then choose Edit and then Delete from the top menu bar). Next, return to the top of the filtered column (in this case, Volume), click the down-arrow button, and this time choose the term All. Now all the rows with data will reappear.
Source: CSI, Inc.

125

| Arial | | 9 | **B** *I* U | ☰ ☰ ☰ 📊 | $ % , | +.0 .00 |

AVERAGE ▾ ✗ ✓ *fx* =(D253-D254)/D254

	A	B	C	D	E	F	G
1	Historical stock prices provided by CSI, Inc. Historical mutual fund and industry pri						
2							
3	Tyco International Ltd. (TYC)						
4	Daily prices (8/29/2001 to 8/29/2002)						
5	DATE ▾	HIGH ▾	LOW ▾	CLOSE ▾	VOLUME ▾		
6	8/29/2002	15.85	15.31	15.65	15092200		
7	8/28/2002	16.78	15	15.91	22179800		
8	8/27/2002	17.34	16.46	16.98	18909200		
9	8/26/2002	16.89	16.29	16.49	18301100		
10	8/23/2002	16.88	15.86	16.31	19794900		
11	8/22/2002	17.75	16.52	16.72	29240200		
12	8/21/2002	16.75	15.62	16.72	32317400		
13	8/20/2002	15.5	14.4	15.35	22368400		
14	8/19/2002	15.04	13.34	14.5	29963300		
15	8/16/2002	13.85	12.9	13.3	12654400		
16	8/15/2002	13.45	12.49	13.26	20374200		
17	8/14/2002	12.91	12.03	12.9	11624000		
18	8/13/2002	12.91	12.31	12.42	13986100		
244	9/19/2001	46	42.42	43.75	19566600		
245	9/18/2001	46.5	44.25	44.75	13390200		
246	9/17/2001	46.58	44.9	45.1	16931700		
247	9/10/2001	48.1	46.29	47.71	10998700		
248	9/7/2001	48.8	46.51	46.58	16963200		
249	9/6/2001	49.8	48.3	48.38	10764100		
250	9/5/2001	50.48	48.51	50	20831900		
251	9/4/2001	52.2	50.4	50.48	9949300		
252	8/31/2001	52.63	51.55	51.95	5638200		
253	8/30/2001	53.15	51.65	51.85	7278000	=(D253-D254)/D254	
254	8/29/2001	53.05	52.3	52.35	5377600		
255							

Figure 3.6 To calculate the daily percent change for each day in the year, go to the next to last row in Column F and create the following formula using the appropriate cell numbers instead of the words used here: (Day 2-Day 1)/Day 1, and hit Enter. In this case, it's (D253-D254)/D254. Next, copy that formula all the way up the row by clicking in the lower right corner of the formula cell, and dragging it all the way to the top of the column, to F6. Then add a label for the top of the column by typing in % Chg.

Source: CSI, Inc.

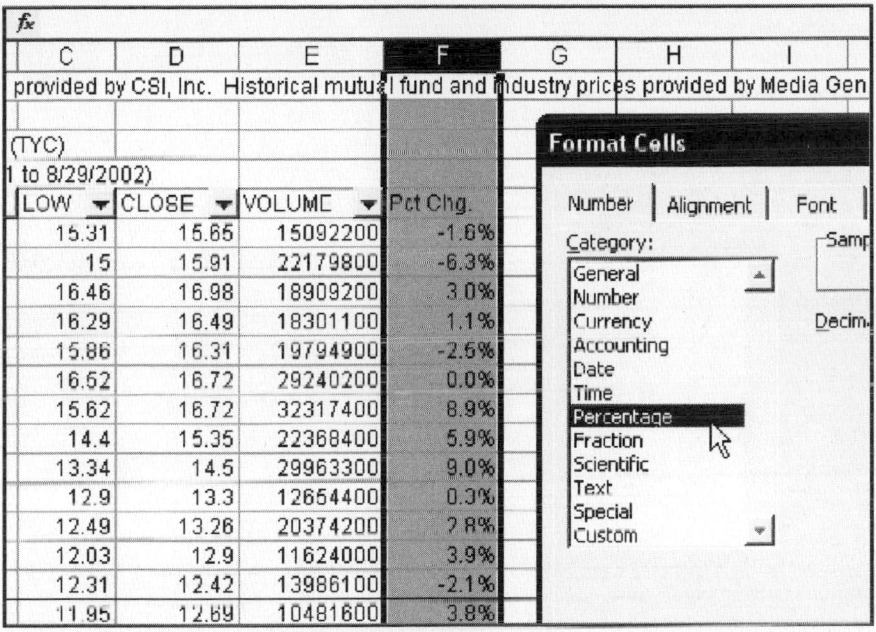

C	D	E	F	G	H	I
provided by CSI, Inc. Historical mutual fund and industry prices provided by Media Gen						

fx

(TYC)

1 to 8/29/2002)

LOW ▼	CLOSE ▼	VOLUME ▼	Pct Chg.
15.31	15.65	15092200	-1.6%
15	15.91	22179800	-6.3%
16.46	16.98	18909200	3.0%
16.29	16.49	18301100	1.1%
15.86	16.31	19794900	-2.5%
16.52	16.72	29240200	0.0%
15.62	16.72	32317400	8.9%
14.4	15.35	22368400	5.9%
13.34	14.5	29963300	9.0%
12.9	13.3	12654400	0.3%
12.49	13.26	20374200	7.8%
12.03	12.9	11624000	3.9%
12.31	12.42	13986100	-2.1%
11.95	12.69	10481600	3.8%

Format Cells

Number | Alignment | Font |

Category:

General
Number
Currency
Accounting
Date
Time
Percentage
Fraction
Scientific
Text
Special
Custom

Samp

Decim.

Figure 3.7 To view the column properly, highlight it and change its formatting to percentage either by clicking the % button on the top Excel menu or by choosing Format from the top menu bar, then choosing Cells, then Number, then Percentage.
Source: CSI, Inc.

In the case of Genesis, Fontanills said he bought puts not long after the first gap down, when the stock plunged to $23.49 from $41.00 on February 28, 2002. "When you have bad news in a bear market, you must assume that there will be more," he says. The company, designer, and seller of integrated circuits for flat-panel computer monitors and digital televisions, had been one of the rare technology favorites of bulls in 2001, so it had plenty of supporters willing to rush to its defense—and shares ultimately traded back as high as $31 two weeks later. Buying ran out of steam and shares drifted back to the reaction low of $20 by the end of April before bulls regathered their forces and took shares back to $31 one more time in late May. But that double top proved the kiss of death, and shares went on to sink more than 20 percent in a day twice more over

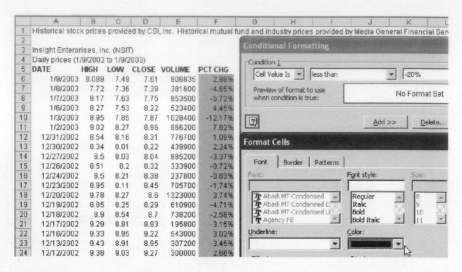

Figure 3.8   To see the useful information more easily, use the Conditional Formatting to turn the cells showing –20% red. Highlight the column again, then click Format on the top menu bar, then Conditional Formatting. Next, click the down arrows on the dialog box to make Condition 1 show that the Cell Value is "less than or equal to" –20%. Then click the Format button on the dialog box, click the down arrow on the Color button, and choose red. Click OK twice, and the cells with –20% or less will turn red. Now you can scan the sheet quickly for the most valuable data.
Source: CSI, Inc.

the next few months before sinking as low as $6.10 by mid-August. Buying far-month puts a week or two after the plunge proved to be the smart move and provides an ideal model for intermediate-term traders. (See Figure 3.9.)

The case of Elan, a Dublin-based developer of drugs and drug-delivery systems focused on pain management, autoimmune diseases, and Alzheimer's, shows again that intermediate-term traders did not have to be early to take advantage of the information imbalance. Shares collapsed the first time on January 17, 2002, when the company and two partners reported that it had suspended clinical trials of an Alzheimer's therapy after four patients in France had suffered nervous-system inflammation. (See Figure 3.10.) Fontanills said he did not buy

Figure 3.9 The painful saga of Genesis Microchip shares in 2002 starkly shows the value of buying puts, or shorting, stocks that gap down by more than 30 percent on high volume in a single day—particularly when the breakout occurs below the 50-day moving average. Following the script of many other major gappers in the 2000–2002 bear market, the first giant decline on February 28 (Gap 1) was followed by a sharp recovery as bulls rushed to its defense. But the information disequilibrium that favored bears the first time came into play again with a second big gap down on May 30 (Gap 2), and then again on June 14 (Gap 3). Buyers of six-month-out puts a few days after the first plunge would have had to wait patiently for the payoff, but it came ultimately in vivid color.
Source: StockCharts.com.

puts in part because it was not clear that the problem would be long lasting. A couple of weeks later, though, the stock gapped down again when the *Wall Street Journal* reported questionable accounting practices. The newpaper said the company had been shifting research and development costs off its books through joint ventures. The company protested. Fontanills said he didn't buy this gap down either, as it was not clear that the problem would be long lasting either, as the company protested its innocence.

With Elan now the subject of a high level of negative media buzz, the trader said he did finally buy puts on the next gap down, from $29

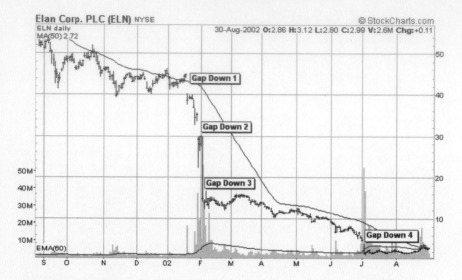

Figure 3.10   Shares of Irish drug maker Elan suffered four high-volume, high-percentage collapses from January through July 2002. The journey of this stock from the mid-$50s to around $3 is a classic tale of information imbalance, as bulls were repeatedly shocked and humiliated by a series of clinical trial failures, accounting troubles, regulatory probes, and sudden management exits. Intermediate-term traders who missed the first and second gap downs could still have taken advantage of the third. After that, the stock no longer fit the Fontanills model as the price was below $7.
Source: StockCharts.com.

to $14.85 on February 4. This one occurred when the company said it expected 2002 earnings to be slower than anticipated due to a slowdown in the introduction of new products and to its transformation from a drug-delivery company to a biotech drug developer. Even buying the puts this late in the information disequilibrium curve proved fruitful, as bulls quickly lost control of the stock from there. On February 7, the company announced that it was the subject of a U.S. Securities & Exchange Commission investigation, and on February 22 the *Washington Post* reported that Elan had halted trials of its Alzheimer's vaccine after more volunteers had become ill with brain inflammation. Showing how stubborn shareholders can be with the shares of an old bull-market favorite, the stock held fast in the $14 area for the next four and a half months until, in early July, the company announced that losses in its securities portfolio would lead to significant write-downs, and the chairman and chief executive stepped down. To be sure, it would have been best in retrospect to buy on the first gap down, but waiting to have a greater degree of certainty that problems would persist resulted in the potential at least for a successful multimonth short sell from $14 to around $3. Fontanills' January 2003 $10 puts on Elan, originally purchased in February 2002 at $.50, were worth $7.50 by late August 2002.

Trade Management

Of course, it's easy to see in retrospect that the stock would fall and fall and fall again. But in real time, an intermediate-term trader would have been sorely tempted to take profits after making just 50 percent or 100 percent on her puts, rather than more than 1,000 percent. Fontanills, indeed, encourages the taking of short-term profits. One of his rules is to sell half a position after doubling one's money—letting the rest ride until the momentum falters or reverses. Additionally, it is smart trade management to buy puts at least one month out after the initial gap, as time decay erodes the value of the option premium most dramatically in the 30 days prior to expiration.

Fontanills, who has written several books of his own about such sophisticated options strategies as "volatility crush," calendar spreads, and strangles, lastly proposes that relatively inexperienced medium-term traders not try to trade too many of these gappers at a time. "Get good at a few things—become a master of just a few stocks," he says. "Make thoughtful short-sells of no more than four or five of these sort of stocks at a time, then patiently wait for the information balance to shift in your expected direction."

Despite his success as an avid short seller and put buyer, Fontanills maintains a sunny disposition as he watches the tides of the Atlantic Ocean roll in to the Miami beach. His experience shows that a disciplined, methodical approach to intermediate-term sales of stocks trading down on high volume can put patient traders in command of the frequent information imbalances that arise in the shares of even the most well-followed companies. (See Table 3.2.)

Table 3.2   Big Bear-Market Down-Gappers

Stocks that sank at least 30% in a single day to at least $7 on volume of at least 300,000; March 2000 to August 2002

Date	Sym	% Chg 1 Day	% Chg 1 Mo.	% Chg 6 Mo.	% Chg 12 Mo.
3/1/2000	PRXL	35.29	11.03	17.65	96.32
3/1/2000	RFMI	−10.92	4.80	−40.61	−81.22
3/3/2000	FSCO	−6.04	−13.65	7.83	—
3/6/2000	CCCI	−6.17	−40.09	—	—
3/6/2000	FLIR	−3.75	−16.25	−35.63	−13.75
3/6/2000	TKSS	−6.17	−40.09	31.28	−85.02
3/6/2000	WSM	0.96	54.49	104.49	40.31
3/7/2000	NERX	−7.78	−52.79	−49.24	−81.73
3/7/2000	PG	−4.92	4.00	2.66	12.33
3/8/2000	CGN	−15.44	−29.41	−28.68	−50.06
3/9/2000	ULTR	13.33	−44.85	−77.58	−87.27
3/10/2000	PTRY	−3.08	11.54	53.85	20.00
3/13/2000	ITP	−8.33	0.00	5.42	−24.07
3/13/2000	ITP	−8.33	0.00	5.42	−24.07
3/13/2000	STRM	0.76	−27.79	−65.22	−89.79
3/16/2000	SDAY	−7.31	−46.12	−75.34	−87.21
3/17/2000	CAPA	7.47	−16.12	−55.96	−74.84
3/17/2000	SBSE	9.50	4.00	89.50	19.13
3/20/2000	GLGC	−3.09	−47.73	−48.19	−59.16
3/20/2000	MAXY	−14.08	−58.78	−58.40	−88.57
3/20/2000	MSTR	−16.64	−61.17	−68.88	−95.10
3/21/2000	CRXA	20.83	−20.64	46.21	−73.58
3/21/2000	EWB	11.75	−14.46	−5.12	−56.00
3/21/2000	MYGN	11.58	−35.56	63.80	−4.26
3/22/2000	MOV	−6.36	−13.29	42.20	29.48
3/22/2000	MOVA	−6.36	−13.29	42.20	29.48
3/24/2000	DDDC	22.22	−28.13	−69.79	−92.36
3/24/2000	POWI	−5.71	−31.92	−49.68	−39.53
3/27/2000	FNV	−21.08	−37.35	−67.47	−91.81
3/27/2000	TMBS	3.85	0.77	−30.77	−61.54
3/29/2000	HAUP	−18.29	−49.70	−69.51	−86.59
3/29/2000	LMLP	−15.46	−54.44	−82.89	−89.87
3/29/2000	MEDX	4.12	24.71	176.03	−27.06
3/29/2000	TZIX	−10.07	−36.57	−53.73	−63.81
3/29/2000	VLNC	9.93	−15.41	−5.48	−78.08
3/30/2000	CS	−1.67	−23.75	−1.67	−57.00
3/30/2000	ETS	−1.67	−23.75	−1.67	−57.00
3/30/2000	NEXL	−8.21	−32.84	−45.15	−91.60
3/30/2000	NQLI	13.79	−24.14	−59.05	−77.16
4/3/2000	EFNT	2.92	−40.24	−67.74	−77.74

Table 3.2   *(Continued)*

Date	Sym	% Chg 1 Day	% Chg 1 Mo.	% Chg 6 Mo.	% Chg 12 Mo.
4/3/2000	IMMR	8.29	−14.72	−64.81	−89.00
4/3/2000	LGTO	−12.26	−36.48	−42.45	59.75
4/3/2000	OPTV	0.53	−9.98	−60.70	−90.33
4/3/2000	PGEX	−20.43	−42.99	−84.76	—
4/3/2000	PMTC	−14.83	−24.13	1.74	−24.71
4/3/2000	SVNX	−3.70	−37.58	−46.45	−89.35
4/3/2000	SWCM	3.23	−4.04	92.80	—
4/4/2000	BVEW	0.00	−9.15	21.83	−66.20
4/4/2000	EXTN	−8.15	−41.20	−37.77	−82.30
4/4/2000	FSTP	−6.85	0.00	−34.93	−63.01
4/4/2000	ITIG	29.03	4.03	−88.91	−93.55
4/4/2000	ITIG	29.03	4.03	−88.91	−93.55
4/4/2000	PTSX	4.48	1.49	−37.31	−88.06
4/4/2000	REMC	59.88	61.99	−0.31	−69.67
4/4/2000	SYMX	−6.85	0.00	−34.93	—
4/4/2000	VDIM	4.48	1.49	−37.31	−88.06
4/5/2000	CAR	4.57	−21.57	—	—
4/6/2000	PRGN	−8.50	−34.69	−44.39	−41.37
4/6/2000	VIRS	2.14	−24.29	−9.64	−37.14
4/7/2000	MAPX	−2.30	−16.80	−17.56	−61.83
4/7/2000	MWY	6.72	−11.19	−19.40	−20.12
4/11/2000	ICCA	−20.32	—	−75.40	−86.18
4/11/2000	OPUS	−5.88	−36.03	−76.47	−97.76
4/11/2000	VPHM	−27.42	37.90	5.38	50.80
4/12/2000	BCSI	−15.32	−14.41	89.19	−90.83
4/12/2000	CFLO	−15.32	−14.41	89.19	−90.83
4/12/2000	CPWR	3.14	−12.05	−50.53	−24.36
4/12/2000	IQIQ	6.67	—	—	—
4/12/2000	ISYS	−3.27	−21.57	−30.07	−13.73
4/12/2000	LFMN	−1.28	−36.51	−72.16	−97.55
4/12/2000	IQIQ	6.67	—	—	—
4/12/2000	ISYS	−3.27	−21.57	−30.07	−13.73
4/12/2000	LFMN	−1.28	−36.51	−72.16	−97.55
4/12/2000	ONDS	−7.83	55.35	—	—
4/12/2000	RIMM	−7.10	−18.31	98.36	−38.21
4/12/2000	VLNK	6.67	2.86	−40.48	−79.28
4/13/2000	CYBR	5.75	8.73	−41.27	−71.43
4/13/2000	DTHK	0.67	28.00	129.33	−46.13
4/13/2000	ENPT	−17.48	−20.39	−59.22	−91.00
4/13/2000	FVCX	−21.92	−8.46	−66.92	−90.77
4/13/2000	LTNX	−25.68	−14.19	−59.46	−55.68
4/13/2000	MVSN	2.45	27.52	62.54	29.39
4/13/2000	SSPX	−25.68	−14.19	−59.46	−55.68

(Continued)

Table 3.2 *(Continued)*

Date	Sym	% Chg 1 Day	% Chg 1 Mo.	% Chg 6 Mo.	% Chg 12 Mo.
4/13/2000	WEBM	−29.50	−10.82	−15.02	−70.83
4/14/2000	BALT	35.24	32.38	16.75	−82.64
4/14/2000	CRDS	3.61	23.80	−88.16	−90.25
4/14/2000	DICE	−5.77	51.92	−1.92	−74.36
4/14/2000	DIGL	36.29	90.73	107.72	−27.14
4/14/2000	DLK	−18.48	32.48	−21.02	−80.64
4/14/2000	ELX	0.00	18.74	211.09	11.11
4/14/2000	EPNY	2.89	45.39	41.97	−68.52
4/14/2000	EWBX	−5.77	51.92	−1.92	−74.36
4/14/2000	FCEL	5.49	16.85	391.94	208.81
4/14/2000	FCL	5.49	16.85	—	—
4/14/2000	HEAR	−4.69	−15.63	−59.38	−94.13
4/14/2000	IIJI	49.62	92.05	7.01	−65.21
4/14/2000	INFA	−5.98	11.62	111.28	−3.51
4/14/2000	INTF	5.18	−9.76	—	—
4/14/2000	INTW	−11.86	−32.05	−86.86	−98.92
4/14/2000	LFMN	−10.47	−4.49	−68.38	−96.31
4/14/2000	LFMN	−10.47	−4.49	−68.38	−96.31
4/14/2000	LMLP	−20.48	45.71	−43.33	−60.76
4/14/2000	MOGN	−15.05	25.75	40.13	−41.89
4/14/2000	MYTN	25.65	55.74	−38.94	—
4/14/2000	NAVI	16.60	16.19	−62.55	−94.49
4/14/2000	NETP	53.66	87.20	−54.57	−90.24
4/14/2000	NTRX	0.00	49.61	—	—
4/14/2000	NXWX	0.00	49.61	−61.24	−88.22
4/14/2000	PKSI	6.14	35.45	−80.23	−88.80
4/14/2000	POCI	3.04	53.90	−12.61	−72.59
4/14/2000	RBAK	8.56	13.46	116.29	−68.50
4/14/2000	RRRR	25.96	20.00	−71.91	−90.40
4/14/2000	SFO	−27.56	—	—	—
4/14/2000	SIVB	−5.56	72.92	125.69	33.56
4/14/2000	SLTC	10.80	43.00	15.20	−85.15
4/14/2000	SOFO	−27.56	−16.87	−72.29	−91.47
4/14/2000	SVNX	−17.91	−22.79	−36.39	−80.46
4/14/2000	SWBD	−20.94	−30.77	−55.13	−79.42
4/14/2000	TLXS	17.25	−19.27	−86.24	−96.74
4/14/2000	UTSI	1.66	21.16	−43.57	−40.15
4/14/2000	VCNT	4.17	50.00	−35.00	−89.47
4/14/2000	VIAD	36.89	21.92	−66.85	−96.58
4/14/2000	VICL	−24.84	4.58	5.88	−27.84
4/14/2000	WAVX	24.47	28.98	−3.04	−70.20
4/14/2000	XLA	−8.82	11.76	−55.33	−88.47
4/14/2000	XLNK	−18.48	32.48	−21.02	—

Table 3.2 *(Continued)*

Date	Sym	% Chg 1 Day	% Chg 1 Mo.	% Chg 6 Mo.	% Chg 12 Mo.
4/17/2000	CALP	21.24	100.52	87.56	35.30
4/17/2000	CBST	78.99	79.35	130.43	54.26
4/17/2000	FDHG	59.70	−19.40	−79.10	−92.60
4/17/2000	MAJR	59.70	−19.40	−79.10	−92.60
4/17/2000	WFT	7.56	17.36	−2.57	38.34
4/19/2000	INSW	−5.81	2.33	−27.91	−59.07
4/19/2000	OMKT	−11.11	1.23	−69.14	87.16
4/19/2000	SGNT	0.43	38.53	−61.04	−74.37
4/24/2000	DIGX	2.07	−20.44	7.06	−75.86
4/24/2000	MCTR	−7.76	−22.67	−87.73	−95.28
4/24/2000	PVSW	−3.45	−31.03	−56.90	−75.86
4/25/2000	OSTE	−12.88	6.82	−22.73	41.82
4/25/2000	RGIS	2.89	8.67	39.31	67.77
4/26/2000	MRBA	0.34	−34.23	69.13	−84.97
4/26/2000	TSAI	13.62	−12.68	12.68	−39.83
4/27/2000	DFS	0.00	−2.74	52.74	−7.62
4/28/2000	MAI	0.00	−18.87	0.00	22.87
4/28/2000	RADS	8.05	−24.83	8.05	−10.87
5/3/2000	CUBE	−4.87	−13.18	−3.44	−24.95
5/3/2000	HCR	−7.50	0.00	119.17	231.33
5/3/2000	NOVL	4.71	−16.76	−16.76	53.88
5/3/2000	PCOP	−1.34	−10.71	−0.22	−32.25
5/15/2000	PMS	5.92	1.18	—	—
5/15/2000	YND	5.92	1.18	17.73	—
5/16/2000	CCE	2.40	10.80	25.20	16.10
5/16/2000	NTWK	−6.74	34.27	47.75	−78.65
5/22/2000	PTIX	−18.58	−21.31	31.69	16.20
5/22/2000	RT	−4.64	9.27	−14.57	38.81
5/24/2000	ELK	0.00	25.61	−23.18	9.31
5/24/2000	MTIC	−10.16	8.59	−0.39	−73.00
5/24/2000	RVSN	5.51	76.47	6.99	−54.12
5/26/2000	CLST	0.00	4.49	−23.08	−14.67
5/26/2000	PGNX	0.00	50.00	171.25	101.60
6/1/2000	UTSI	2.42	46.83	−17.82	13.11
6/6/2000	EFII	7.31	−1.31	−41.51	8.24
6/8/2000	GPSI	8.67	−16.47	158.96	—
6/12/2000	BPUR	3.89	36.58	65.37	56.58
6/12/2000	CTXS	12.08	−4.21	27.81	31.64
6/12/2000	HLIT	−1.98	−33.39	−69.35	−70.37
6/12/2000	MSTR	9.95	−16.53	−59.55	−90.65
6/13/2000	INDYY	−42.37	−8.47	—	—
6/13/2000	INTZ	4.26	31.91	−25.53	−63.23
6/14/2000	INDYY	−2.57	52.21	—	—

(Continued)

Table 3.2 *(Continued)*

Date	Sym	% Chg 1 Day	% Chg 1 Mo.	% Chg 6 Mo.	% Chg 12 Mo.
6/14/2000	INYY	−2.57	52.21	—	—
6/14/2000	NHAN	20.93	11.05	5.81	—
6/14/2000	VNWK	−14.48	−65.52	−90.60	−80.69
6/15/2000	NBTY	3.98	2.65	−36.73	72.46
6/15/2000	TCNO	0.41	18.67	−66.81	−38.59
6/16/2000	UB	6.90	−7.21	6.90	64.92
6/19/2000	CRDS	−11.90	−35.71	−78.69	−82.10
6/20/2000	ZOOX	14.42	−6.51	−83.49	−78.57
6/22/2000	PCOM	−3.13	25.00	−68.75	−89.33
6/26/2000	OCR	−2.00	−10.67	112.00	117.60
6/27/2000	HLIT	0.80	9.38	−74.40	−63.02
6/27/2000	SYB	2.32	5.63	—	—
6/29/2000	SCMM	12.94	−9.21	−38.46	−80.61
6/29/2000	UIS	1.69	−36.44	−0.85	−0.27
6/30/2000	HOLL	29.03	22.58	−50.00	−22.71
7/3/2000	ORCT	0.00	−58.25	−89.23	−90.41
7/5/2000	BMC	−1.17	−12.61	2.35	6.74
7/5/2000	BMCS	−1.18	−12.61	2.34	—
7/5/2000	CA	4.46	−8.49	−20.38	15.16
7/5/2000	ENTU	4.10	−25.43	−60.41	−86.38
7/6/2000	CLB	−3.30	4.62	20.79	0.06
7/6/2000	CPRKV	8.20	−56.25	—	—
7/6/2000	MDSI	18.61	14.29	−46.32	−67.79
7/7/2000	BRIO	3.32	−22.51	−17.34	−31.51
7/10/2000	TENF	−4.27	−22.26	−83.54	−96.49
7/11/2000	LMLP	7.24	−59.79	−58.58	−56.76
7/11/2000	PCLE	2.73	−6.12	−10.88	−44.27
7/11/2000	SCIL	−39.66	−54.60	−67.24	−83.17
7/12/2000	CNMD	−0.75	−21.51	7.92	73.52
7/13/2000	BBOX	9.39	−4.36	5.25	8.44
7/13/2000	JWL	−2.30	22.89	−21.38	22.25
7/13/2000	JWL	−2.30	22.89	−21.38	22.25
7/13/2000	TFS	3.16	−20.86	−34.64	−42.20
7/14/2000	XTND	5.37	−2.12	−62.67	−87.42
7/17/2000	MCTR	3.04	−45.11	−65.87	−92.29
7/20/2000	CBC	0.00	−6.90	−0.57	168.69
7/20/2000	CLKB	0.00	−6.90	−0.57	168.69
7/21/2000	A	4.21	27.37	38.03	−39.16
7/21/2000	CMTO	1.26	−22.33	−57.86	−93.96
7/21/2000	DCTM	−12.59	2.01	51.96	−54.93
7/21/2000	NXPS	1.35	−20.63	−81.17	−96.27
7/21/2000	VNTR	1.34	−20.63	−81.17	−96.27
7/25/2000	MEDQ	8.31	10.30	6.31	64.57

Table 3.2 *(Continued)*

Date	Sym	% Chg 1 Day	% Chg 1 Mo.	% Chg 6 Mo.	% Chg 12 Mo.
7/26/2000	LSI	3.82	14.50	−30.38	−41.53
7/26/2000	NIS	−1.59	25.92	51.85	—
7/26/2000	QRSI	−9.84	31.88	−36.08	14.68
7/26/2000	RMDY	6.70	5.03	10.34	48.78
7/27/2000	NUHC	53.79	77.88	−10.00	−29.84
7/27/2000	NVDM	8.60	5.95	−29.14	−0.51
7/27/2000	OCCM	−5.87	−3.52	−85.63	−98.45
7/28/2000	CELL	7.41	24.69	−3.70	−36.79
7/28/2000	CLRN	−4.85	6.10	−64.49	−83.87
7/28/2000	EGOV	−3.50	−13.23	−47.86	−61.90
7/31/2000	CEPH	1.86	24.80	45.11	58.51
7/31/2000	MDEA	−0.57	66.09	−70.62	−89.15
7/31/2000	NSTA	6.25	25.33	—	—
7/31/2000	WEBX	20.06	165.27	−12.57	9.75
8/1/2000	PROX	−7.59	52.68	9.38	−63.71
8/1/2000	TWP	3.36	−15.44	−21.10	−48.13
8/3/2000	F	−0.43	−14.53	−4.24	−14.70
8/3/2000	SFN	1.98	1.49	−6.06	−32.20
8/9/2000	LLY	1.67	−7.55	7.67	2.99
8/16/2000	MCTR	−10.51	3.50	−51.36	−87.30
8/18/2000	NTSL	2.42	6.45	−12.90	58.71
8/22/2000	ZD	1.82	−7.27	—	—
8/24/2000	BOL	−2.61	5.05	41.60	1.71
8/24/2000	CYBV	−0.77	−10.77	−46.15	−72.06
8/24/2000	NXTV	1.20	36.68	−78.93	−94.01
8/29/2000	GLIA	−12.88	−38.65	−73.01	−60.74
9/1/2000	VIAN	0.00	−28.24	−62.98	−85.34
9/12/2000	NTCR	−6.25	−37.50	—	—
9/12/2000	PRIA	2.17	37.44	−28.99	
9/20/2000	EDG	−60.94	−86.72	−94.75	−97.00
9/22/2000	ZOMX	−17.67	−30.08	−49.62	−48.87
9/25/2000	CLPA	−5.70	−16.11	−45.97	−62.31
9/25/2000	OTEC	−15.92	−3.98	−11.44	−39.10
9/26/2000	GES	1.90	−31.65	−39.75	−39.14
9/27/2000	LHSP	17.95	−35.26	—	—
9/27/2000	MSV	7.81	−30.21	−70.50	−66.25
9/27/2000	NEWH	−3.61	11.34	28.87	1.53
9/27/2000	PCLN	10.47	−47.67	−79.94	−68.56
9/27/2000	PRLX	5.83	−2.08	−35.63	−40.67
9/28/2000	CSGS	−3.13	67.01	42.59	36.95
9/29/2000	EXAP	−21.38	−31.03	−66.90	−97.13
10/2/2000	TFR	−2.48	−9.09	−74.88	−74.48
10/3/2000	DSET	−1.07	−6.95	−78.61	−94.91

(Continued)

Table 3.2 *(Continued)*

Date	Sym	% Chg 1 Day	% Chg 1 Mo.	% Chg 6 Mo.	% Chg 12 Mo.
10/4/2000	THOR	0.00	1.56	−41.67	50.00
10/5/2000	HLIT	−8.70	37.68	−68.60	−33.37
10/5/2000	PRDS	13.07	50.75	−86.93	−91.24
10/6/2000	CCRD	−5.56	−8.33	−20.83	−2.33
10/6/2000	HYSL	6.25	36.46	28.13	20.42
10/6/2000	RAZF	8.13	24.38	−91.88	−95.80
10/6/2000	SDRC	1.17	−8.77	32.16	—
10/6/2000	VECO	12.86	−2.50	−49.21	−57.68
10/11/2000	LU	1.18	2.94	−65.74	−68.56
10/11/2000	PHSY	−30.68	−10.76	78.49	−11.14
10/12/2000	BCRX	−6.52	30.43	−15.13	−52.70
10/12/2000	PHSY	2.87	28.74	158.39	28.37
10/13/2000	DCLK	−2.51	19.10	−3.44	−34.55
10/16/2000	NSS	−12.62	−26.21	33.50	−42.23
10/17/2000	EFII	5.76	26.18	119.06	53.88
10/17/2000	MRVL	−11.39	−20.48	−72.78	−60.73
10/17/2000	PCCC	−10.36	5.06	−65.61	−61.83
10/17/2000	VSEA	−3.30	11.85	65.38	17.06
10/18/2000	CMTN	−5.08	1.59	−70.74	−86.18
10/18/2000	CTLM	10.61	2.65	12.12	−78.33
10/18/2000	EFNT	33.11	40.13	—	—
10/18/2000	GSPN	3.35	−32.77	−72.64	−86.15
10/18/2000	MIKE	−3.15	45.11	66.31	137.63
10/18/2000	MIK	−3.15	45.11	66.31	137.63
10/18/2000	RFMD	19.74	55.70	69.33	40.35
10/18/2000	RNWK	27.73	23.53	−39.43	−60.74
10/18/2000	TERN	−2.20	−6.60	−82.44	−57.18
10/18/2000	TMWD	4.91	31.23	−92.53	−84.00
10/18/2000	TSTN	8.36	−53.13	−70.72	−87.53
10/18/2000	VRTA	4.13	−21.30	−55.06	−64.35
10/18/2000	XIRC	0.48	17.22	—	—
10/19/2000	NDN	−1.12	9.27	102.92	133.93
10/19/2000	NTRO	−0.85	−30.40	−77.05	−85.91
10/19/2000	RSYS	7.59	24.61	−11.46	−43.12
10/20/2000	CC	−5.88	−4.98	−1.47	−2.62
10/24/2000	NSM	−5.93	−7.99	9.48	15.05
10/24/2000	NUHC	−9.92	−32.06	−46.38	−54.14
10/25/2000	CCRT	1.72	−42.89	−64.41	−77.38
10/25/2000	CITC	2.90	30.43	190.20	—
10/25/2000	CTLM	35.02	8.21	15.94	−81.26
10/25/2000	THDO	−9.68	−29.03	−47.10	−48.65
10/26/2000	BRNC	−4.72	−29.92	−38.27	−47.58
10/26/2000	CLRS	−3.95	−5.08	−41.51	−68.99

Table 3.2 *(Continued)*

Date	Sym	% Chg 1 Day	% Chg 1 Mo.	% Chg 6 Mo.	% Chg 12 Mo.
10/26/2000	VRTA	0.00	39.03	−21.43	−34.39
10/27/2000	BRKT	2.94	−14.71	−50.82	−73.49
10/27/2000	MDRX	9.86	36.62	−48.73	−60.56
10/31/2000	EW	−3.26	19.53	61.12	89.02
11/2/2000	HABK	1.30	−32.47	−23.38	−72.36
11/2/2000	PSIXP	−17.19	−53.13	—	—
11/3/2000	MEAD	1.83	−18.90	−46.24	−52.29
11/3/2000	MLT	5.68	−18.18	−19.18	—
11/3/2000	NSIL	−3.03	−54.92	−54.06	−63.52
11/3/2000	TWP	2.81	−6.38	16.20	−42.90
11/3/2000	ZL	5.68	−18.18	−19.18	−23.45
11/6/2000	LNUX	−2.16	−54.32	−71.91	−91.60
11/6/2000	TSTN	10.24	−30.72	−28.87	−70.31
11/8/2000	NERX	−3.67	30.67	−29.60	−64.27
11/9/2000	BBY	2.73	−30.41	64.83	88.38
11/9/2000	BIGT	−17.99	0.00	−2.73	−94.24
11/9/2000	ICGE	−4.47	−45.81	−72.11	−90.17
11/9/2000	NENG	21.84	−46.60	−90.99	−92.16
11/9/2000	SCII	−4.73	−85.50	—	—
11/10/2000	JNIC	−8.29	−10.16	−81.03	−87.81
11/10/2000	JNIC	−8.29	10.16	−81.03	−87.81
11/17/2000	OVTI	−26.70	−7.39	−61.27	−66.09
11/20/2000	PLMD	17.48	19.17	20.78	−12.74
11/21/2000	BKI	6.91	22.87	−2.47	−15.32
11/21/2000	PUMA	9.70	−54.48	−50.09	−57.37
11/22/2000	BCSI	0.00	−31.74	−76.67	−94.50
11/22/2000	CFLO	0.00	−31.74	−76.67	−94.50
11/28/2000	MANH	19.49	38.31	11.51	−5.29
11/29/2000	TUTS	−33.33	−22.81	76.14	−87.46
11/30/2000	CATZ	17.65	20.59	−35.29	−59.47
11/30/2000	GTW	0.63	−5.32	−11.89	−50.53
11/30/2000	OAKT	−3.09	−28.35	−16.04	−4.00
11/30/2000	TUTS	1.32	15.79	−66.74	−81.75
12/1/2000	NVTL	0.00	28.57	−67.79	−92.52
12/4/2000	UTHR	−6.62	−31.71	−24.57	−49.77
12/5/2000	NAV	−11.57	25.07	27.25	72.78
12/5/2000	NMSS	2.82	−7.04	−19.89	−43.55
12/6/2000	ENWV	−24.07	−12.96	−46.67	−65.04
12/8/2000	CAMP	27.33	−13.66	−56.67	−45.54
12/8/2000	PCCC	19.75	5.73	50.93	80.69
12/11/2000	JNIC	−0.90	−30.76	−57.53	−70.91
12/11/2000	JNIC	−0.90	−30.76	−57.53	−70.91
12/12/2000	MAXM	−21.64	−56.72	−53.37	−58.03

(Continued)

Table 3.2   *(Continued)*

Date	Sym	% Chg 1 Day	% Chg 1 Mo.	% Chg 6 Mo.	% Chg 12 Mo.
12/12/2000	PEGS	−0.85	29.91	57.95	86.26
12/13/2000	RAZF	−17.86	21.43	−64.00	−85.71
12/14/2000	QLTI	2.90	2.67	−31.30	−18.79
12/14/2000	UDI	−2.56	14.87	—	—
12/15/2000	CUBE	−18.09	11.70	—	—
12/19/2000	DLTR	8.26	26.61	22.81	34.26
12/19/2000	GMCR	−19.92	30.86	68.44	70.31
12/19/2000	MERX	−3.55	48.22	27.59	52.53
12/19/2000	PKE	34.94	80.72	7.90	22.94
12/19/2000	TTMI	−2.50	31.25	−22.70	15.40
12/20/2000	EXTR	9.24	38.96	−19.00	−58.43
12/20/2000	FDRY	7.21	45.19	21.08	−40.85
12/20/2000	OPNT	−12.22	65.91	45.82	10.55
12/21/2000	BCSI	23.28	−29.85	−80.66	−87.82
12/21/2000	CFLO	23.28	−29.85	−80.66	−87.82
12/21/2000	CNXT	8.04	22.77	−44.07	−5.50
12/21/2000	GNSC	46.43	36.31	15.71	−62.10
12/21/2000	INFS	9.78	51.56	18.83	62.20
12/21/2000	PALM	15.12	−2.20	−82.36	−86.46
12/22/2000	CRO	0.00	15.71	−8.57	−34.06
12/28/2000	BCSI	−18.99	−8.31	−80.77	−87.47
12/28/2000	CFLO	−18.99	−8.31	−80.77	−87.47
12/28/2000	DSET	−15.44	72.06	−66.12	−86.35
12/28/2000	NICE	14.64	42.50	−27.60	−5.43
12/28/2000	VASC	−7.81	18.75	6.25	−65.38
1/2/2001	TMWD	−67.50	−46.88	−62.70	−43.50
1/2/2001	WGRD	−4.96	−23.22	−54.13	−69.18
1/4/2001	WGRD	7.18	24.16	−32.63	−44.88
1/5/2001	CVTX	−9.15	−11.99	41.20	26.51
1/8/2001	HSP	4.45	0.27	11.41	7.23
1/9/2001	DITC	2.22	47.11	−1.30	−11.11
1/10/2001	CLTK	4.80	−6.83	−26.14	−25.61
1/11/2001	BCGI	−4.41	−48.90	−10.29	−53.12
1/12/2001	CLSR	0.00	7.81	14.44	33.00
1/12/2001	SIPX	0.00	1.92	−22.31	−7.69
1/17/2001	MACR	1.44	1.86	−42.10	−34.02
1/18/2001	VIGN	−2.40	−19.20	−6.56	−40.99
1/19/2001	CPTH	0.69	−66.67	−91.22	−65.33
1/19/2001	LENS	−5.74	−4.78	−55.75	−39.90
1/19/2001	LENS	−5.74	−4.78	−55.75	−39.90
1/19/2001	SAGI	−0.58	−24.57	4.51	248.39
1/22/2001	TKTX	−7.84	−29.19	16.76	77.47
1/25/2001	LINK	11.54	−20.51	−53.13	−58.97

Table 3.2 *(Continued)*

Date	Sym	% Chg 1 Day	% Chg 1 Mo.	% Chg 6 Mo.	% Chg 12 Mo.
1/25/2001	MCOM	1.09	57.38	—	—
1/25/2001	SNDK	5.42	−23.29	−30.15	−49.01
1/26/2001	OTGS	−2.39	−16.27	−49.47	−7.75
1/26/2001	SAWS	7.86	−35.00	—	—
1/31/2001	CCRT	0.00	3.65	30.22	−36.23
2/1/2001	NDC	−3.38	−2.58	34.00	32.09
2/2/2001	CMNT	−3.51	−30.53	−48.80	16.72
2/2/2001	PDII	−2.86	−3.74	0.82	−69.51
2/7/2001	BCGI	2.17	−7.25	37.86	−13.86
2/8/2001	TMX	−1.26	4.41	10.59	12.09
2/12/2001	ELX	4.72	−45.82	−41.55	6.72
2/13/2001	PLT	0.83	−20.17	−30.63	−33.03
2/14/2001	CWTR	−4.69	−1.25	34.00	−29.60
2/14/2001	ITXC	5.17	−27.59	−50.34	−12.55
2/14/2001	ITXC	5.17	−27.59	−50.34	−12.55
2/16/2001	EMS	0.00	−38.02	−20.20	
2/16/2001	NT	0.00	−15.60	−65.35	72.20
2/23/2001	SMDI	4.36	−20.36	−13.77	−54.15
2/27/2001	FRNT	−3.60	−27.51	−21.58	33.20
2/28/2001	ELNT	0.63	35.96	106.94	54.55
3/1/2001	TVLY	−0.83	−1.25	59.47	72.47
3/2/2001	INTI	2.50	−20.00	−24.00	32.53
3/7/2001	CTS	2.52	−24.12	−29.28	−36.70
3/8/2001	CREE	−6.88	−25.94	10.00	7.43
3/12/2001	GILTF	4.04	−22.08	—	−72.09
3/12/2001	XXIA	28.33	33.24	—	−40.53
3/13/2001	HAKI	1.15	−24.27	—	−15.60
3/15/2001	RMBS	−34.41	−18.93	—	−66.46
3/15/2001	TTEC	−0.34	12.61	—	37.38
3/16/2001	CSC	0.92	1.16	—	59.79
3/16/2001	NUAN	10.97	44.52	—	−26.40
3/16/2001	RMBS	20.57	16.52	—	−48.86
3/16/2001	SPWX	0.00	63.42	—	20.34
3/19/2001	NOVT	3.30	5.44	−63.66	−50.30
3/21/2001	LTRE	8.54	32.03	31.58	62.87
3/22/2001	BDAL	6.63	31.57	20.67	−2.65
3/23/2001	IMNX	5.38	26.19	51.31	167.61
3/23/2001	PLMD	42.65	83.24	−15.59	49.41
3/26/2001	VYYO	−1.30	−26.03	−69.25	−48.88
3/28/2001	HAND	−8.05	32.41	−87.59	−57.15
3/28/2001	PALM	−0.78	−8.34	−81.89	−50.51
3/28/2001	XTND	0.59	−8.54	−77.28	−44.90
3/29/2001	SFNT	−3.41	18.79	−52.00	25.50

(Continued)

Table 3.2 *(Continued)*

Date	Sym	% Chg 1 Day	% Chg 1 Mo.	% Chg 6 Mo.	% Chg 12 Mo.
3/30/2001	PTA	−12.98	−78.37	−71.98	−44.54
4/2/2001	NOVN	0.00	24.97	−8.29	7.29
4/3/2001	BVSN	−1.05	136.80	−67.33	−51.49
4/3/2001	PPRO	−18.33	−10.40	−88.53	−82.40
4/3/2001	SIRI	−8.68	67.14	−49.75	−33.22
4/3/2001	SO	−0.91	1.22	15.61	21.04
4/3/2001	ZOLL	2.87	34.71	108.34	121.53
4/6/2001	EIX	8.12	12.12	93.09	109.70
4/6/2001	PCG	−4.17	25.00	147.92	215.97
4/10/2001	MDCC	−8.52	−4.24	−10.95	−28.81
4/10/2001	SRM	−3.08	12.31	86.92	—
4/16/2001	NCS	−14.86	2.09	3.21	94.78
4/25/2001	CHMD	−6.58	0.63	−61.01	−15.33
4/25/2001	PPRO	−25.93	−61.73	−86.91	−86.67
4/26/2001	FCGI	−4.50	−14.48	44.77	12.17
4/27/2001	SCMM	0.75	0.28	−19.96	16.11
4/30/2001	DG	−4.48	12.24	−14.91	−4.55
5/15/2001	CVS	1.85	−8.56	−53.42	−34.35
5/15/2001	RRRR	−5.50	−56.88	−39.45	−72.48
5/24/2001	PPRO	−7.19	−31.74	−58.08	−87.66
5/25/2001	DITC	0.00	−32.53	−42.74	−69.17
6/14/2001	MUSE	5.15	−12.59	−38.49	−74.48
6/15/2001	IRF	−0.51	−5.22	−4.97	16.21
6/15/2001	IRF	−0.51	−5.22	−4.97	16.21
6/19/2001	TWP	−2.38	29.89	8.11	54.05
6/20/2001	SYNP	18.38	−19.15	−11.15	−61.28
6/22/2001	EDEN	0.11	2.96	−47.21	−71.56
6/22/2001	MANU	−10.20	−28.15	−23.35	−78.11
6/22/2001	SYMC	4.63	18.07	69.43	56.66
7/2/2001	SMDI	10.05	−24.93	−43.38	−81.83
7/3/2001	IMNY	0.00	−31.60	12.47	−63.58
7/3/2001	ISSX	0.00	−24.57	14.80	−58.02
7/3/2001	ISSX	0.00	−24.57	14.80	−58.02
7/3/2001	MLTX	0.00	−39.66	−36.13	−54.74
7/10/2001	FTUS	10.10	−0.25	−1.45	−28.80
7/10/2001	GETY	−2.42	−6.47	36.20	16.86
7/10/2001	TNOX	−0.77	−8.73	10.63	−36.97
7/11/2001	CMVT	1.50	1.66	−10.25	−63.20
7/12/2001	BFR	2.74	13.03	−61.51	−87.58
7/16/2001	TWAV	−5.83	36.00	26.08	−37.50
7/17/2001	VTIV	−1.73	−6.50	−78.49	−81.61
7/18/2001	CTLM	−6.34	−39.27	−43.50	−64.59
7/20/2001	INFA	−3.50	−9.38	56.75	−8.25

Table 3.2 *(Continued)*

Date	Sym	% Chg 1 Day	% Chg 1 Mo.	% Chg 6 Mo.	% Chg 12 Mo.
7/20/2001	SFA	5.70	−6.14	17.11	−42.98
7/24/2001	CVAS	2.24	5.67	−5.01	−78.63
7/24/2001	TTP	0.42	−12.55	−33.47	−85.69
7/30/2001	CNO	−11.60	−16.13	−80.88	−92.15
7/31/2001	MRCY	4.08	−14.06	14.88	−38.45
8/1/2001	VTS	5.10	−6.77	−1.74	−18.71
8/2/2001	OO	19.49	23.75	56.21	20.94
8/3/2001	NOVN	1.48	16.81	−9.80	−41.99
8/6/2001	ETS	−0.51	−33.09	−64.15	92.07
8/6/2001	PLMD	−10.46	−38.55	−7.42	20.87
8/16/2001	CIEN	−4.28	—	−55.50	−78.64
9/4/2001	NOVT	−6.79	−31.34	−34.63	—
9/5/2001	TCP	−7.61	−42.63	−1.09	—
9/19/2001	LSS	−3.19	34.05	70.60	—
9/19/2001	NTLO	−16.77	3.28	−48.97	—
9/20/2001	IVX	5.59	11.17	0.61	—
9/20/2001	IVX	5.59	11.17	0.61	—
9/21/2001	CENX	4.15	38.86	77.46	—
9/25/2001	TWTC	−11.83	22.77	−30.25	—
9/26/2001	OCCF	−5.41	−32.97	−46.49	—
9/26/2001	WIN	−10.23	−13.70	30.94	—
9/27/2001	MRVL	11.50	86.17	234.65	—
10/8/2001	OCCF	0.00	−0.83	−17.36	—
10/11/2001	MBRS	−6.48	−25.11	48.77	—
10/12/2001	CTRA	7.80	5.53	−58.16	—
10/12/2001	PVN	1.12	−73.68	−42.83	—
10/15/2001	UTHR	0.10	−6.67	31.97	—
10/25/2001	HLIT	−4.74	35.64	14.74	—
10/30/2001	RHB	1.60	6.20	6.60	—
11/2/2001	CIMA	1.12	−5.70	−39.49	—
11/2/2001	NOVN	2.30	0.99	32.83	—
11/8/2001	BKS	−1.96	25.20	29.70	—
11/13/2001	PDII	−6.32	8.99	−0.33	—
11/13/2001	WPI	−2.31	8.16	−14.23	—
11/26/2001	MIKE	−2.51	—	—	—
11/28/2001	STRC	0.82	15.52	−2.26	—
11/30/2001	EOT	42.22	63.11	−40.56	—
12/7/2001	CWTR	8.98	7.85	2.54	—
12/7/2001	HAL	16.67	−8.08	47.33	—
12/13/2001	MACR	−15.73	15.73	−11.36	—
12/14/2001	PCYC	−2.88	−2.98	−55.27	—
12/14/2001	TTWO	31.27	83.93	89.25	—
12/20/2001	NOVT	−4.74	28.09	−39.20	—

(Continued)

Table 3.2   *(Continued)*

Date	Sym	% Chg 1 Day	% Chg 1 Mo.	% Chg 6 Mo.	% Chg 12 Mo.
1/2/2002	FMC	3.39	6.59	−11.67	—
1/3/2002	PRGN	1.51	−14.99	−95.69	—
1/9/2002	BREL	10.51	−32.02	22.33	—
1/14/2002	SLNK	3.35	−11.71	−4.92	—
1/17/2002	CBST	4.11	−3.94	−44.01	—
1/22/2002	CYBX	−2.96	12.63	−19.72	—
1/22/2002	EOT	−20.90	−35.82	−71.93	—
1/28/2002	WWCA	−21.72	−17.88	−71.72	—
2/1/2002	DYII	−20.34	28.48	78.74	—
2/4/2002	ELN	−5.79	−2.76	−86.33	—
2/6/2002	CRN	21.08	6.43	−1.71	—
2/6/2002	OVER	26.40	91.35	15.79	—
2/20/2002	PRX	3.35	30.06	71.12	—
2/25/2002	LUME	1.56	7.26	−35.20	—
2/28/2002	GNSS	8.56	10.69	−64.96	—
3/1/2002	PKI	2.92	18.10	—	—
3/7/2002	CURE	−7.07	10.61	—	—
3/7/2002	SEPR	−0.66	−20.82	—	—
3/26/2002	MROI	2.09	10.27	—	—
4/1/2002	DRIV	−3.94	−34.51	—	—
4/1/2002	SRP	−11.53	−24.81	—	—
4/1/2002	SRC	−6.59	−5.69	—	—
4/2/2002	GMST	6.55	−1.22	—	—
4/2/2002	LMNX	−2.59	−12.81	—	—
4/2/2002	PSFT	−1.59	−11.37	—	—
4/17/2002	MOGN	−5.12	−19.44	—	—
4/17/2002	MXT	−9.43	3.70	—	—
4/22/2002	MNS	−8.60	−7.85	—	—
4/24/2002	PRSE	−0.15	1.51	—	—
4/25/2002	CYTC	3.18	1.91	—	—
4/25/2002	DIGE	3.26	1.97	—	—
4/26/2002	VRSN	−18.40	1.92	—	—
4/30/2002	ICOS	−0.35	−11.61	—	—
5/1/2002	OVER	−3.59	−12.01	—	—
5/2/2002	TSO	16.97	−2.76	—	—
5/7/2002	MANU	32.82	−38.64	—	—
5/7/2002	MINI	3.29	12.08	—	—
5/10/2002	NTEC	4.76	−14.97	—	—
5/17/2002	MIMS	26.11	14.98	—	—
5/21/2002	CLHB	0.30	33.07	—	—
6/7/2002	RFMD	3.06	−9.39	—	—
6/7/2002	TYC	12.87	32.77	—	—
6/10/2002	PDX	2.10	8.89	—	—

Table 3.2 *(Continued)*

Date	Sym	% Chg 1 Day	% Chg 1 Mo.	% Chg 6 Mo.	% Chg 12 Mo.
6/11/2002	SKIL	0.41	−20.29	—	—
6/18/2002	GTIV	4.46	6.14	—	—
6/18/2002	MGAM	10.16	−1.91	—	—
6/21/2002	DOX	−16.86	−12.56	—	—
6/24/2002	MSCC	−4.53	−27.17	—	—
6/26/2002	RMG	−15.21	−4.61	—	—
7/1/2002	CATT	3.32	12.31	—	—
7/1/2002	DIAN	−3.69	6.39	—	—
7/1/2002	TRPS	−4.45	−33.53	—	—
7/3/2002	QGENF	0.00	−5.14	—	—
7/5/2002	JDAS	3.33	−20.00	—	—
7/5/2002	JDAS	3.33	−20.00	—	—
7/10/2002	BRKL	3.44	4.43	—	—
7/11/2002	ICN	5.38	14.84	—	—
7/17/2002	BUCA	1.40	−29.37	—	—
7/17/2002	COF	9.28	6.63	—	—
7/18/2002	ITRI	2.90	−1.96	—	—
7/18/2002	NSIT	17.44	−15.49	—	—
7/19/2002	CNX	−3.54	8.24	—	—
7/19/2002	GAS	2.15	26.46	—	—
7/19/2002	SFCC	14.56	24.85	—	—
7/23/2002	CDCY	−14.19	33.78	—	—
7/23/2002	FLS	18.21	25.02	—	—
7/23/2002	REI	−31.65	44.18	—	—
7/25/2002	DRD	4.11	1.10	—	—
7/26/2002	XEL	−25.03	33.77	—	—
7/30/2002	CSGS	10.19	—	—	—
7/30/2002	EMBX	−5.83	—	—	—
7/30/2002	SEE	−34.03	—	—	—
7/31/2002	HOTT	3.41	—	—	—
7/31/2002	NVDA	−9.58	—	—	—
8/6/2002	MSM	14.65	—	—	—
8/7/2002	CCRN	−14.16	—	—	—
8/7/2002	TMPW	4.29	—	—	—
8/8/2002	BBY	8.75	—	—	—
8/8/2002	ULTE	2.78	—	—	—
8/9/2002	FLX	−8.64	—	—	—
8/9/2002	MNTG	5.88	—	—	—
8/19/2002	OSIP	13.74	—	—	—
8/28/2002	CFI	6.94	—	—	—

Data: Logical Information Machines

Chapter 4

JON MARKMAN

For the better part of mid-2000 through 2002, my e-mail inbox resembled a cavalcade of sorrow and regret: Physicians, engineers, teachers, and ad salesmen bared their souls to admit repeated and unexpected failure as investors—buying tech stocks near highs in 1999 or 2000 and holding on as the market blasted them to bits.

I found these confessions intensely curious because they explode most assumptions about the link between speculation and emotionalism. These were not foolish people; they were logical, tenacious, high achievers who planned their long-term trades carefully. How could they fail so abjectly at the task of investing, which seems on the surface to reward the rational?

The answer is that the market does indeed reward reason, but in ever-changing ways both hidden and extremely complex. Like the locked-down rules of convention or science found in law and physics texts, the rules of stock investing begin from a steady and sensible base. But the rules can also mutate quickly, paradoxically, and capriciously. Nimble, experienced traders who observe and act upon these rule changes with ease extract huge sums of money from the market in short order. Investors who instead play strictly by a fixed set of rules—however useful and immutable they might once have seemed—are often their chastened counterparts, the losers of that money.

My quest to define a few sets of rules for market behavior led me to create the stock screens and mechanical portfolio-building techniques that have gone under the rubric SuperModels in the column that I have written at MSN Money since 1997. Many have worked very well, yet I've been frustrated by those ever-changing cycles which, with increasing speed, turn once-useful insights into useless trivia.

Recognizing the limits of my ability to capture the nature of *change* in the market, in 2000 I embarked on a new mission: to find a crack team of independent stock researchers that could define a dynamic group of rules that would bend fluidly with the market's extreme turbulence. Rather than codifying a fixed set of familiar precepts about the link between stock prices and earnings growth, I wanted to see if we could use the intensifying power of computers and software to find convention-shattering relationships buried below the surface of market movements. In short, I wanted to help create a new sort of stock-assessment system that embraced volatility, rather than ran from it, and that took a fresh approach to the standard one-size-fits-all market wisdoms.

The result of these efforts was StockScouter, a rating system that launched in June 2001 at MSN Money to help investors quickly assess a stock's potential for outperforming the broad market six months at a time—the ideal periodicity for a swing-trading candidate.

Working closely with Camelback Research Alliance, a research firm in Arizona at the cutting edge of financial engineering for institutional money managers, we identified statistically predictive traits that affect the performance of successful U.S. securities and developed a systematic way to help traders discover, research, hold, and sell them.

StockScouter, like similar systems that cost Wall Street pros hundreds of thousands of dollars per year, depends on advanced mathematics, an innovative mix of measurements and historical testing to attempt to forecast the short- and long-term outlook for all U.S. companies that have traded on the three major exchanges for at least the past six months. Through August 2002 that represented a universe of about 5,500 stocks.

In rating the outlook for stocks from strong to poor on a 10-point scale, StockScouter does not make subjective judgments. Instead, it compares the fundamental and technical qualities of individual companies and their stocks with benchmarks that have proved statistically predictive of stock performance in the past. It then assigns an expected six-month return to each stock based on this statistical profile and then balances that return against expected volatility. This ratio of expected return to expected volatility, or "risk," yields a stock's final overall rating. (See Figure 4.1.)

The balance of expected reward with expected risk is a key concept that sets StockScouter apart from other stock-rating systems, such as ones published by Value Line and Standard & Poor's. Stocks with expected high future returns would see their ratings reduced if the volatility of those returns is expected also to be high. Thus an ideal stock in the StockScouter system is expected to move briskly and directly to a higher price, rather than simply briskly.

StockScouter is not perfect; no predictive rating system could be. But its models have been tested to academic and professional standards using more than a decade of historical data—a period of time rich with variation. Also I believe that it has shown, in its first year of operation, that it helped individuals make more thoughtful investment choices by revealing the way successful professional money managers

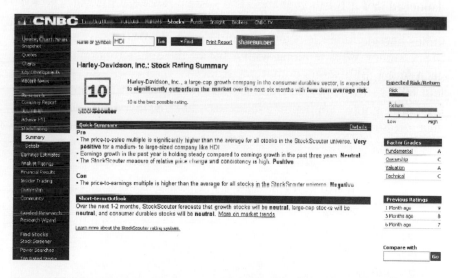

Figure 4.1 StockScouter rating. Approximately 5,500 stocks are rated 1–10 by the StockScouter system at MSN Money. Stocks rated 8–10 make the best swing-trading candidates on the long side; stocks rated 1–3 make the best swing-trading candidates on the short side. In early 2002, motorcycle maker Harley-Davidson was rated 10, which suggested zoomy prospects relative to all other stocks for the next one to six months.
Source: CNBC on MSN Money.

accumulate, sort, evaluate, and act upon financial information for intermediate-term trades.

How StockScouter Works

StockScouter rates each stock in its coverage universe from 10 to 1, with 10 being best. Ratings are scored on a bell curve. This means that there are fewer stocks with a rating of 10 than with a rating of 9 and fewer stocks with a rating of 9 than with a rating of 8; likewise, there are more stocks with a rating of 2 than with a rating of 1. (See Table 4.1.) Stocks thus bunch up in the middle, which is why stocks rated 4 to 7 are expected to perform more or less in line with the market. Ratings are recalculated and updated in the MSN Money database daily to reflect the most current technical, fundamental, ownership, and valuation data available.

The ratings derive from the Camelback research team's analysis of four key factors that either reflect a company's fundamental quality or investors' ardor for their shares. The system rates each factor's performance on a five-point scale from A to F, just as you'd see on a report card. These grades appear on StockScouter's Details pages on the MSN Money website along with a list of the subfactors that make up each factor. Subfactors do not get grades of their own; rather, the system tells you whether they add a positive, negative, or neutral bias to the factor grade. The factor grades are also displayed for quick reference on StockScouter's Summary page for each stock, and a pro/con

Table 4.1   The StockScouter Bell Curve

Rating	# of Stocks
10	178
9	361
8	660
7	826
6	805
5	843
4	820
3	666
2	351
1	176

Data: Sept. 1, 2002

list also summarizes the subfactors' findings. (See Figure 4.2.) Here are the four factors, and some of their key subfactors.

1. *Fundamentals.* This factor assesses a company's past earnings growth, its estimated future earnings growth, and its capacity to beat brokerage analysts' consensus estimates. To receive a high grade, a company generally must grow reasonably fast, beat analysts' growth estimates, and be expected by veteran analysts to grow earnings in the future. However, a powerful earnings surprise or big boost in estimates by an experienced analyst can also boost the grade of a stock with otherwise seemingly lackluster fundamentals.

2. *Ownership.* This factor assesses whether a stock is under accumulation by executives and board members. To receive a high grade, a stock generally must be under accumulation by high-ranking executives or board members in significant quantities.

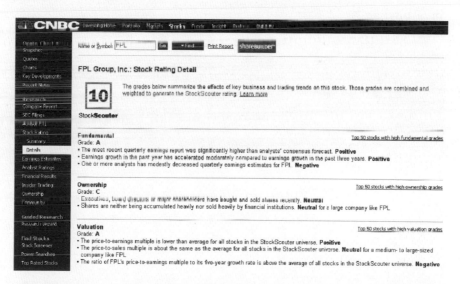

Figure 4.2 StockScouter summary page. Each security in the StockScouter universe at CNBC on MSN Money is rated from A–F in four key factors: fundamentals, ownership, valuation, and technical price action. In early September 2002, Florida-based energy merchant FPL Group earned an A for fundamentals, C for insider-trading trends, A for valuation, and C for price action. When averaged and combined with the stock's past volatility trends, it earned the highest rating, 10, for its potential to outperform the market with the least volatility.
Source: CNBC on MSN Money.

3. *Valuation.* This factor assesses whether a stock's price is high or low relative to its current level of sales, earnings, and expected earnings growth. It's counterintuitive, but our research shows that big companies' shares should be slightly more expensive than peers' to receive a high grade. Meanwhile, as you'd expect, small companies' shares must be much cheaper than peers' to receive a high grade.

4. *Technical.* This factor assesses whether a stock's price trend is positive or negative. To receive a high grade, a stock's price must either be rising over the past six months or must have risen on more days than it has declined over the past six months, or both. However, a stock with a very low price relative to its 10-week trend can receive a high grade if the system believes it has plunged to a level from which it is likely to rebound.

Traders who come to favor one of the four factors over the others can find the top-rated stocks for each factor on a separate page by clicking the appropriate Top 50 link on each summary page. (Figure 4.3.)

Top Rated Stocks

Top Rated by Ownership Grade   Return to Top Rated categories

Stock**Scouter**   Powered by Camelback   Quotes delayed 20 minutes

	Symbol	Name	Overall Rating	Ownership Grade	Last Price	Change
1	ALLE	Allegiant Bancorp, Inc.	10	A	16.15	+0.14
2	CNBKA	Century Bancorp, Inc.	10	A	28.27	+0.50
3	CNXS	CNS, Inc.	10	A	6.05	+0.05
4	EPN	ELPASO ENERGY PART	10	A	35.35	+0.41
5	IVX	IVAX Corporation	10	A	13.70	-0.14
6	KMP	Kinder Morgan Energy Partners, L.P.	10	A	32.56	-0.05
7	NYCB	New York Community Bancorp, Inc.	10	A	31.21	-0.54
8	POOL	SCP Pool Corporation	10	A	27.62	-0.22
9	CXW	Corrections Corporation of America	10	A	14.75	-0.21
10	ARLP	Alliance Resource Partners, L.P.	10	A	24.60	+0.21
11	BKMU	Bank Mutual Corporation	10	A	20.70	0.00
12	BRKL	Brookline Bancorp, Inc.	10	A	12.51	-0.04
13	COG	Cabot Oil & Gas Corporation	10	A	22.25	-0.38
14	CBAN	Colony Bankcorp, Inc.	10	A	16.10	unch
15	FCBP	First Community Bancorp	10	A	31.50	+0.25
16	HARB	Harbor Florida Bancshares, Inc.	10	A	22.51	-0.54

Figure 4.3 Top rated by grade. Intermediate-term traders who focus on highly rated stocks that have the highest grades in a particular factor can view 25 at a time on a single page at CNBC on MSN Money. In early September 2002, most of the high-rated stocks with strong grades for insider ownership were either small regional banks or gas drillers and distributors.
Source: CNBC on MSN Money.

Computing "Core" Ratings

StockScouter does not simply average subfactors to yield a factor grade. Instead, subfactors are added together in different weights that vary with a stock's size and sector. Likewise, factor grades are not simply added or averaged to yield a final overall rating. They are also weighted in a variety of ways according to a proprietary methodology developed by the statisticians and financial engineers at Camelback.

After all the factors and their constituent subfactors are measured and weighed, StockScouter awards each stock a "core" rating. The highest core rating would generally be straight A's; next would be three A's and a B, and so on. That core rating is then balanced against the standard deviation, or volatility, of the stock's price change over the past 12 months to yield the final overall rating. It's convenient to think of the overall rating as the ratio between expected return and expected risk. A stock with high expected return and high expected risk will generally receive a lower rating than a stock with modest expected return and very low expected risk.

A portfolio managed with guidance from the StockScouter system would attempt to stay invested in stocks rated 8 to 10 with high factor grades, and avoid, or short, stocks rated 1 to 3 with low factor grades. More specifically, the Camelback team has developed a variety of portfolio strategies that I share next. They are not strictly straightforward, but a little complexity is the price to pay for the system's potential power.

Let's look at several ways that intermediate-term traders can put the system to their advantage for one- to six-month plays.

Portfolio Management

Why one to six months? The problem with the future beyond half a year is that there's too damned much of it. It stretches in front of long-term investors like a black hole ready to suck in the best intentions with no remorse and little warning. The future is where big ideas go to die. The future is where big thinkers lose their naiveté and money.

And yet, skeptics of medium-term trading object that the prospect for the world economy over the next 10 years looks so clear. By 2013, there will be more people on Earth, and the disparity between rich and poor will widen. The less-developed world—particularly Brazil, India, and China—will have more smog, buzzing phones, and citizens with cholesterol problems. Fossil-fuel energy may become increasingly scarce, but alternative sources could take up the slack. Biotechnology will lead to new chemical compounds that will lengthen our ages and boost crop yields. And the third wave of Internet and wireless technology will connect us all in dizzying, perplexing new ways.

The usual method of translating these big thoughts into investment suggestions would lead us to pick a handful of companies today that are in the vanguard of these trends. Yet we would have learned nothing from the early 2000s bear market if we have not come to understand that over the long term, capital appreciation is less about the pure majesty of ideas than it is about people, things, psychology, and *value*. It is about nimble adaptation rather than heads-down determination. It is about flexibility, not certainty. It's about differentiating between good companies and good stocks. And it is about recognizing that between now and some idealized vision of 2010 and beyond, cleanup of the toxic telecom and Y2K bubbles could lead to one of the worst economic downturns since the 1930s.

In that vein, investors need to push aside their personas as dreamy futurists and focus on the pragmatic facts that they might have a son in college by 2010 and a daughter filling out applications. The future is anything but an abstraction in this context. Rather than a self-indulgent game, the goal is to find a way to piggyback on the expected long-term growth of world business and the mathematical miracle of compounding rates of return to solve real future financial needs—in this case, $300,000 to $500,000 in projected college education costs for the kids no matter what happens to the economy. You can't hide out in bonds and meet these goals.

I feel most strongly about a parent's ability to invest for the future one to six months at a time, rather than a decade at a time, by using a well-tested statistical-arbitrage system like StockScouter than by trying to gaze into a crystal ball and project the decision-making prowess of individual executives and the fundamental prospects of their rapidly obsolescent business lines.

The historical record offers tons of reasons to discount the pure long-term fundamentalists' chances for success, for their views of the value of decade-long investing are biased by experience in the past 20 years, when the Dow Jones Industrials rose 243 percent from August 1981 to August 1991, and 245 percent from August 1991 to August 2001. In contrast, from August 1951 to August 1961, the Dow rose just 26 percent in total, or about 2.3 percent per year; from August 1961 to August 1971, the Dow rose only 10 percent, or less than 1 percent per year.

It's fair to suggest that the "stretch" goal for traders using StockScouter heuristics is to attain the 28 percent annual returns recorded historically by StockScouter in the six-months-at-a-time mechanical, long-only system, though I'm sure anyone these days would settle for 12 percent. If you were to start with $100,000, your most ambitious effort would wrest $1.3 million from the market gods. Take away 50 percent overall because of stupid mistakes or because stocks fail to rise at all for multiyear periods, and with discipline one should still meet that goal. (Later in this chapter, I explain ways to use StockScouter to build moderate-risk, high-return *monthly* portfolios.)

Investing without such an historically tested methodology would be like asking a novice baker to take a pile of ingredients and produce an award-winning cake. The baker must know when too much sugar or yeast will ruin the cake; the investor must know when too much of a good thing like earnings growth or parabolic price advancement will ruin a stock's chances to move higher. It's all about understanding correct proportions, and the way certain ingredients interact positively or negatively with each other. And even after the cake is mixed, all that good work can be ruined if you leave it in the oven too long.

I'll start with a strategy, or recipe, developed by Camelback that has yielded a 13.25 percent return in a 50-stock test portfolio every six months on average since 1990, with a low 15.4 percent standard deviation. Here's the strategy:

1. Query the MSN Money Stock Screener database for stocks with StockScouter ratings of 8, 9, or 10.
2. Add criteria requiring StockScouter Fundamental, Valuation, Ownership, and Technical grades higher than or equal to C.
3. Add criteria requiring StockScouter Return expectation >/= High.
4. Eliminate stocks with average daily trading volume in the past three months less than 100,000 shares, or a closing price under $3.
5. Sort by StockScouter Rating as high as possible. (See Figure 4.4.)

To aspire to the benchmark six-month, you would have to buy the top 50 stocks and hold for half a year, then rebalance. Camelback has also tested several portfolios that hold just 10 stocks, as you'll see in a moment. But to winnow the list down to the 10 names on your own, start with the top 15 or 20 and reduce your exposure to a single industry as much as possible. In August 2001, for instance, I created a portfolio for readers of my column with the 10 top-rated stocks listed in

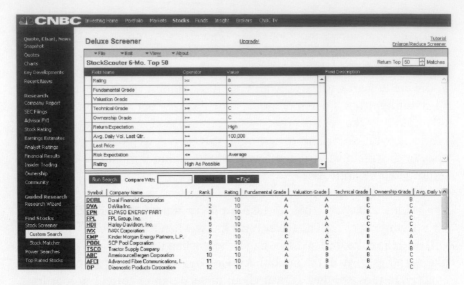

Figure 4.4   StockScouter six-month top rated. To find a list of 50 stocks that would either make suitable six-month holds as a group, or suitable candidates for further swing-trade research, build a screen in the Screener tool at MSN Money. In late September 2002, the top candidates were an eclectic mix of small regional banks, energy distributors, drug makers, retailers, and technology.
Source: CNBC on MSN Money.

Table 4.2, eliminating some regional banks to achieve some sector and market-capitalization diversity.

You can see that this portfolio was still overweighted in regional banks spread around the country: Washington Mutual, based in Seattle; North Fork Bancorp, based in New York; and BankAtlantic, based in Florida. The model and market loved those stocks in the summer of 2001 because when interest rates decline, these companies get to borrow cheap while continuing to lend dear to customers, especially their mortgage customers. This free pass to profits would eventually vanish, but the model clearly didn't think it would happen for at least six months.

Beyond them, the model favored an eclectic bunch. Barr Labs is a leading maker of generic and proprietary drugs; Packaging Corporation of America makes container board that is turned into corrugated boxes; St. Jude Medical is one of the world's largest manufacturers of artificial heart valves; UST is the world's largest maker of smokeless tobacco, as well as the owner of Northwest winery Chateau Ste. Michelle; SPX makes valves, motors, and other components used in the auto industry

Table 4.2 StockScouter 10—July 26, 2001

Company	Industry	Rating	July 26 01	Jan 25 02	Pct Chg
North Fork Bancorp	Banking	10	$31.80	$35.35	11.2%
Packaging Corp. of America	Packaging	10	$19.10	$18.10	−5.2%
Barr Laboratories	Health Care	10	$84.25	$77.25	−8.3%
Washington Mutual	Savings & Loans	10	$40.35	$35.14	−12.9%
St. Jude Medical	Health Care	10	$35.10	$39.50	12.5%
SPX Corp.	Industrial Products	10	$118.05	$141.92	20.2%
UST	Tobacco	10	$29.40	$34.45	17.2%
BankAtlantic Bancorp	Banking	10	$9.89	$10.98	11.0%
Energen	Public Utility	10	$26.25	$22.95	−12.6%
Fiserv	Business Software	10	$38.34	$43.29	12.9%
Average					**4.6%**
S&P 500 Index			1,204.00	1,138.00	−5.5%
Nasdaq Composite			2,025.00	1,951.00	−3.7%

and elsewhere; Fiserv provides transaction services to more than 10,000 financial institutions; and Energen is a driller and distributor of natural gas in Alabama.

The strategy was effective, as the group weathered the slide of summer 2001 well, then outperformed the market during the terrorist-induced turmoil of fall and persisted nicely into its sixth month. Not including costs, which would shave one percentage point off results, the group rose 4.6 percent over six months, versus a 5.5 percent slide in the S&P 500 and a 4 percent slide in the Nasdaq Composite.

What Makes for a Long-Term Winner?

Before we study ways to play StockScouter for monthly, rather than half-yearly, trades, let's take just one moment's time out to consider again how much harder it is to be a long-term investor. To find stocks that could potentially be held for the next 10 years, you need to leave the shores of science and sail into the realm of pure speculation.

A couple of years ago, I investigated the top stocks of each of the past five decades looking for reliable patterns. Here are the raw numbers, which came from researcher James O'Shaughnessy. (See Table 4.3.)

A study of each stock made it clear that each decade's superstock started the period either as a small private or public company—surely less

Table 4.3   Top Stocks of the Past Five Decades

Decade	Rank	Company	Price Gain
1950s	1	Polaroid	8,366%
	2	Avon	3,799%
1960s	1	Masco	10,177%
	2	Xerox	5,146%
1970s	1	Keystone Int.	2,393%
	2	ChemFirst	2,170%
1980s	1	Circuit City	8,265%
	2	Mark IV	6,998%
1990s	1	Dell Computer	89,820%
	2	CMGI	87,603%

Data Source: James O'Shaughnessy

than $10 billion in market capitalization, and usually less than $1 billion. Except for CMGI Inc. in the 1990s, all sold *things*, not services, to the public or to other businesses. Each addressed a very, very large market. Yet, few were able to sustain their brilliance through the next decade. CMGI, in fact, has lost 99.8 percent of its market value since peaking in early 2000.

It seems fair to say that if FBI profilers were looking for a common theme among these stocks, they might suggest looking for companies that somehow combine retail expertise with technology and communications. Superstock companies a profiler would not look for, based on past experience: banks or brokerages; consulting firms; services or media firms; heavy industrials; or any company focused on a single niche, such as apparel or temporary workers.

Practically speaking, experts believe that what long-term investors should look for in companies that could survive and thrive in the next 10 years are battle-tested management teams who have proven capacity to

- Transition regularly to new product cycles
- Gain market share in downturns
- Increase gross margins and free cash flow annually
- Build a healthy research and development program
- Maintain credibility with Wall Street via solid business forecasting

This is a tall order, and few companies meet all the criteria—or even half of them. The normal difficulty is exacerbated by the fact that prosperous, smart technology companies in the late 1990s suffered through two business bubbles: an unprecedented buying of PCs in advance of Y2K, and the telecom spending spree encouraged by the gobs of money shoveled at dot-coms and wanna be phone companies. You can blame individual investors for their investment losses in dot-com stocks, but you really can't blame executives at data-storage hardware maker EMC Corporation or Finnish wireless products manufacturer Nokia for building capacity and inventory to sell products into seemingly fantastic waves of demand. It's fair to say that tech companies that survive the 2000–2002 body slam will have successfully navigated one of the most severe tests of business skills in the past half-century.

Ride Market Tailwinds to Short-Term Scouter Profiits

Over the past few pages, I've explained how to use our new StockScouter rating system to choose relatively low-risk stocks to hold for six months at a time. But what about the short term?

For investors who prefer frequent turnover, StockScouter assesses three "market preferences" that tend to boost or hinder securities' performances over one- to three-month periods. Studies have shown that stocks with favorable market preferences tend to yield the strongest performances for as long as those preferences are in favor. Think of these as tailwinds, if they are in a stock's favor, or as headwinds, if they are not.

The market preferences are recalculated weekly and updated on Tuesdays on the Market Trends page at CNBC on MSN Money. (See Figure 4.5.) They are:

- *Sector.* StockScouter divides its universe of stocks into 12 industrial sectors, such as technology or health care, by their federal identification code. Generally, investors prefer a third or fewer of these sectors at any given time. When they do, Scouter calls them "in favor." The rest are either "out of favor" or in a no-man's land called "neutral." Academic and professional research indicates that as much as 50 percent of a stock's performance derives from the strength or weakness of its sector.
- *Market cap.* StockScouter divided its universe into four market-capitalization categories: The top 400 stocks by market cap are "large cap"; the next 1,000 are "mid cap"; the next 2,500 are "small cap"; and the rest, around 2,100 stocks in June 2001, are "micro cap." Generally, investors prefer only one or two groups at

Figure 4.5   StockScouter market trends. The Market Trends page in the Markets area of CNBC on MSN Money displays the stock sectors, capitalization, and investment style groups that StockScouter considers in favor, out of favor, or neutral at any given time. The determinations are made weekly.
Source: CNBC on MSN Money.

a time. Again, the groups investors prefer are considered "in favor." The rest are either "out of favor" or "neutral."

- *Style.* StockScouter divides its universe into two investment styles by price/sales ratio. High-priced stocks are categorized as part of the "growth" style of investing, while low-priced stocks are categorized in the "value" style. Generally, investors prefer one style or the other for periods lasting a year or more. Scouter rates each "in favor," "out of favor," or "neutral."

How to Use Market Preference Data

Camelback Research Alliance, the Arizona company that created the StockScouter system, says their studies show that the best stocks to own over one-month periods are rated 8, 9, or 10 and are a member of two, but preferably three, categories preferred by the market. In the short term, StockScouter would prefer a stock rated 8 or 9 with three "in favor" tailwinds over a stock rated 10 with just one "in favor" tailwind. When no sectors, market caps, or style are rated "in favor," the system prefers stocks with "neutral" tailwinds. At the very least, research suggests that it's best to avoid sectors, market caps, or styles with "out of favor" headwinds if you're aiming for a one-month hold. (Note: Stocks are sorted into sector, market cap, and style categories monthly to maintain stability, but market preferences are updated weekly to maintain freshness.)

Camelback has tested three 10-stock portfolios and one 50-stock portfolio managed according to these rules against data from the past 10 years of market history. In cases where a tiebreaker was required to choose between stocks with identical ratings and market preferences, Camelback recommends purchasing ones with the lowest expected risk. No stop losses were used.

Over the past decade, StockScouter's benchmark monthly rebalanced 50-stock portfolio advanced 39 percent per year, versus a 13.3 percent annual increase in the Wilshire 5000 Index. The average six-month return for StockScouter was 19 percent versus 5.4 percent for the Wilshire 5000. The standard deviation, or volatility, for the StockScouter system was slightly higher than the Wilshire 5000 at 22 percent per year versus 13 percent per year. (See Table 4.4.)

To determine whether a system takes on too much risk for each unit of return, academics and professionals calculate a Sharpe ratio of return minus the return of a risk-free investment (e.g., a 5 percent Treasury bond) divided by risk. (The measure is named for Stanford University professor William Sharpe, who shared in the Nobel Prize in economics in 1990 for his work on measuring risk and return on investments.) Any value over 1.0 is considered very good, and the higher the better. The Sharpe ratio for StockScouter's 50-stock monthly portfolio is 1.46 over the past 10 years; the ratio for the S&P 500 is 0.89.

Additionally, the StockScouter benchmark portfolio beat the S&P 500 in 82 percent of all months. While the StockScouter-based portfolio performed well when the market performed well, it really shined when the market performed poorly. In the 10 worst months for the Wilshire 5000 Index over the past 10 years, the StockScouter short-term portfolio registered monthly gains seven times.

The beauty of the monthly portfolio methodology is that sectors and capitalizations have come to move in and out of favor very rapidly in the past couple of years. Staying with mostly in-favor groups and avoiding out-of-favor groups should help rational investors sidestep potential trouble. As an example, in March 2000 the 50-stock monthly portfolio consisted of about half large-cap tech stocks, a quarter mid-cap energy stocks, and a quarter mid-cap utility stocks. After the late March tech-stock rout that year, however, tech stocks fell out of favor and never regained their tailwinds the rest of the year—even as many investors desperately hoped they would. In April 2000 the monthly portfolio was composed mostly of energy and utility

Table 4.4 StockScouter Monthly 50 (Historical Simulation through 2000)

	Scouter 50	S&P 500
Return 1990	20.27%	0.35%
Return 1991	109.78%	26.31%
Return 1992	82.70%	4.46%
Return 1993	39.65%	7.06%
Return 1994	13.29%	−1.54%
Return 1995	40.81%	34.11%
Return 1996	47.40%	20.26%
Return 1997	71.31%	31.01%
Return 1998	20.52%	26.67%
Return 1999	32.07%	19.53%
Return 2000	27.12%	−10.14%
Return 2001	9.26%	−13.04%
Return 2002 (thru August)	9.08%	−20.60%
Ann. Average (1990–2001)	*42.85%*	*9.57%*
Std. Deviation	*30.6%*	*16.3%*
Beta vs. S&P 500	*74.01%*	
Correlation vs. S&P 500	*57.07%*	
# Months with ret < −1%	32	47
# Months with ret < −2%	26	38
# Months with ret < −3%	18	25
# Months with ret < −4%	10	19
# Months with negative return	42	58
# Months with positive return	110	94
Real–Time Results, June '01 to Aug '02*		
June '01	2.976%	−2.359%
July '01	3.515%	−1.221%
August '01	−4.720%	−6.411%
September '01	−2.902%	−8.172%
October '01	1.156%	1.810%
November '01	0.659%	7.518%
December '01	6.637%	0.757%
January '02	3.085%	−1.557%
February '02	3.168%	−2.077%
March '02	5.578%	3.674%
April '02	3.999%	−6.142%
May '02	3.238%	−0.908%
June '02	−0.994%	−7.246%
July '02	−11.527%	−7.900%
August '02	3.300%	0.500%

*Portfolios published on MSN Money at start of each month
Source: Camelback Research Alliance.

stocks—and Scouter beat the badly slumping market, and especially the Nasdaq Composite. Likewise, the monthly benchmark portfolio rose in every month of 2001 except August and September largely on the basis of a heavy reliance on small-cap financial, energy, and home-building stocks. In 2002 the model suffered just two down months, versus six for the broad market largely due to its ability to focus on small-cap value stocks in the finance, home-building, and consumer nondurable sectors.

To build a monthly portfolio like this yourself, visit the Screener at MSN Money again and use these criteria. The first few are similar to the ones listed for the six-month portfolio.

* StockScouter Rating/Rating >/= 8
* StockScouter Rating/Fundamental Grade >/= C
* StockScouter Rating/Valuation Grade >/= C
* StockScouter Rating/Ownership Grade >/= C
* StockScouter Rating/Technical Grade >/= C
* StockScouter Rating/Return Expectation >/= Very High
* StockScouter Rating/Risk Expectation </= Average
* Stock Price History/Last Price >/= $5
* StockScouter Rating/Market Cap Market Preferences "Display Only"
* StockScouter Rating/Sector Market Preferences "Display Only"
* StockScouter Rating/Growth versus Value Market Preferences "Display Only"
* StockScouter Rating/Size "Display Only"
* StockScouter Rating/Sector "Display Only"
* StockScouter Rating/Style "Display Only"
* StockScouter Rating/Rating "High as possible"
* In the Return Top Matches box in the upper right, type the number 100.
* Press Run Search.

Now it gets a bit tricky. I don't think I said it was easy. You must export this list of 50 stocks to Excel for some manipulation and analysis. As explained in more detail in Chapter 3, click File on the Screener's top menu, then choose Export/Results to Excel. If you have Excel on your computer, the program will automatically open and the spreadsheet will be populated with the results of your screen.

To determine which stocks have the greatest number of tailwinds, we must now convert some text to numbers. Choose Edit on the top Excel menu, then click Replace on the fly-out menu that appears. (Alternatively, press Control-H on your keyboard). Now a Find/Replace dialog box is on top of your spreadsheet. In the *Find What* edit box, type the words "In-Favor" without the quotation marks but with the hyphen. In the *Replace With* edit box, type the number 3. Click Replace All. Next, press Control-H again and in the Find What edit box, type the words "Neutral" without the quotation marks; in the Replace With edit box, type the number 2. Click Replace All. Last, press Control-H again and in the Find What edit box, type the words "Out-of-Favor" without the quotation marks; in the Replace With edit box, type the number 1. Click Replace All. If your dialog box appears after any of the pressings of Replace All that says Excel cannot find any data to replace, it means there are no stocks on your list with that designation. (See Figure 4.6.)

Next, insert a new column in the spreadsheet to the left of the Growth vs. Value Market Preferences column. If you have created the formula exactly as described, insert the column to the right of column M by choosing Insert on the top Excel menu and clicking Columns. The new column is N. Now type the words "Preference Avg." without quotation marks in Cell N1. Then determine the average market preference of each stock in your list by clicking in N2 and creating the formula that averages K, L, and M as shown in Figure 4.7. To create the

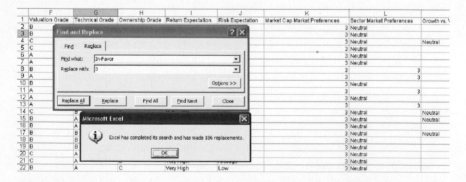

Figure 4.6 To create a monthly StockScouter portfolio, you must convert the market preference "tailwinds" to numbers, determine the average tailwind score for each stock, and then rank them by this figure. (Before snapping this screen shot, I cleaned up the spreadsheet by formatting the columns. First, highlight all columns by pressing the cell in the far upper-left corner of the spreadsheet, or pressing Control-A. Then choose Format on the top menu bar, and click Columns/Autofit Selection.)

K	L	M	N
Market Cap Market Preferences	Sector Market Preferences	Growth vs. Value Market Preferences	Preferences Avg.
3	2	3	=average(K2:M2)
3	2	3	
3	2	2	
3	2	3	

Figure 4.7   Create a formula averaging the market tailwinds to sort StockScouter stocks properly for the monthly 50 portfolio.

average, type *=average(K2:M2)* in Cell N2, including the equals sign, and press Enter. Now copy that formula all the way down Column N. To do this easily, first click in Cell N2. Next, hover your cursor, which starts out as a wide white cross, over the lower-right corner of Cell N2 until it turns into a narrow black cross. Now click the lower-right corner of N2 and drag it all the way down Row N. The formula that you created will replicate itself all the way down the column. Now sort highlight the whole sheet by pressing Control-A, and sort the spread sheet by Column N.

Voilà, you are now facing a list of stocks that is rank-ordered according to the StockScouter Monthly 50-portfolio criteria. The standard portfolio purchases the top-ranked 50, but you do not need to run a 50-stock portfolio with monthly rebalances to take advantage of the StockScouter system, however. Simply taking the top 10 of the top 50 works quite well also, though with more volatility. And there are two additional ways to narrow down the list to 10, as you will see in a moment.

Also you can simply consider these companies as an appropriate starting place for further research into swing-trading candidates by utilizing techniques found elsewhere in this book. For instance, if you fancy yourself an investor in small-cap stocks, filter the spreadsheet to show you only the small-cap names. Or if you prefer stocks favored by corporate insiders, then use the Screener to find high-rated stocks with Ownership grades of "A."

Alternative 10-Stock StockScouter Portfolios

Very often, simply taking the top 10 names in the 50-stock list will either leave you overly exposed to a single sector or, if micro-cap stocks are the only ones in favor, leave you overexposed to the risk of stocks that trade in low volume. That is why Camelback tested flavors of the monthly system that focus on diversifying the number of sectors in a 10-stock list, and another that focuses on requiring that each stock trade in relatively high volume.

The first, which Camelback calls Scouter 10 Sector-Constrained, or Scouter 10 SC, is exactly the same as the StockScouter 50 explained before, except that it prohibits the portfolio builder from taking more than two stocks from a single sector. For instance, if the first five are all financials, then take the first two, then skip to the sixth, and so on. The tested results of this strategy are impressive. (See Table 4.5, page 167.)

The second alternative approach, which Camelback calls Scouter 10 Volume-Constrained, or Scouter 10 VC, is the same as the StockScouter 50 explained in Table 4.5, except that it requires that each stock trade at least 100,000 shares on average in the past quarter. To check on the volume of the stocks in a 50-stock model, add the criteria Trading & Volume/Avg. Daily Volume Last Qtr. >/= 100,000 to your initial screen. Then proceed as before, taking the top 10 names. The tested results of this strategy are also impressive. (See Table 4.6, page 168.)

The Genesis of the StockScouter Metrics

At the start of all the other chapters in this book, I tell the stories of the men or women behind the ideas. I would be remiss if I didn't do the same for StockScouter's two lead inventors, Carr Bettis and Donn Vickrey. Each took widely divergent paths to their places of prominence in the world of quantitative investment research.

Vickrey, a principal at Camelback Research Alliance, is an accomplished race-car driver who grew up all over the country as his father, a widely published accounting professor, moved around to teach accounting at colleges in Texas, Arizona, and Florida. Donn's father did pioneering quantitative work in the early 1960s that proved to be a precursor to Donn's, including the first study into how the market reacted to dividend announcements. (Donn's father was also keenly interested in whether traders paid any attention to the information published in the quarterly reports to the Securities & Exchange Commission called 10-Qs. He proved that they did.)

Vickrey says he had no interest in stocks as he attended high school in Tucson, Arizona, in the mid-1970s. Business wasn't cool

Table 4.5 StockScouter Monthly 10 SC (Sector Constrained)

	Scouter 10 SC	S&P 500
Return 1990	–9.12%	–7.76%
Return 1991	89.08%	26.31%
Return 1992	111.79%	4.16%
Return 1993	80.19%	7.06%
Return 1994	24.28%	–1.54%
Return 1995	44.86%	34.11%
Return 1996	66.93%	20.26%
Return 1997	29.10%	31.01%
Return 1998	13.92%	26.67%
Return 1999	39.61%	19.53%
Return 2000	18.72%	–10.14%
Return 2001	35.37%	–13.04%
Annualized Mean Return	**39.08%**	**11.13%**
Annualized Sharpe ratio	1.61	0.45
Annualized standard deviation	20.99%	14.33%
Beta vs S&P 500	65.17%	
Correlation vs S&P 500	44.65%	100.00%
# Months with ret < –1%	32	41
# Months with ret < –2%	24	33
# Months with ret < –3%	15	22
# Months with ret < –4%	13	16
# Months with negative return	43	49
# Months with positive return	96	90
Sample Months*		
August '01	–4.19%	–6.41%
September '01	0.20%	–8.17%
October '01	0.96%	1.81%
November '01	1.25%	7.52%
December '01	11.19%	0.76%
January '02	4.03%	0.00%

*Historical simulation through 2000. Portfolios published on MSN Money starting August 2001.
Source: Camelback Research Alliance.

Table 4.6 StockScouter Monthly 10 VC (Volume Constrained)

	Scouter 10 VC	S&P 500
Return 1990	16.17%	6.28%
Return 1992	66.29%	4.46%
Return 1993	76.87%	7.06%
Return 1994	47.41%	−1.54%
Return 1995	71.18%	34.11%
Return 1996	56.40%	20.26%
Return 1997	71.45%	31.01%
Return 1998	46.16%	26.67%
Return 1999	58.47%	19.53%
Return 2000	35.38%	−10.14%
Return 2001	1.24%	−13.04%
Annualized Mean Return	**46.80%**	**11.54%**
Annualized Sharpe ratio	1.55	0.49
Annualized standard deviation	27.01%	14.29%
Beta vs S&P 500	88.4%	
Correlation vs S&P 500	94.0%	
# Months with ret < −1%	31	37
# Months with ret < −2%	26	30
# Months with ret < −3%	20	19
# Months with ret < −4%	16	13
# Months with negative return	41	43
# Months with positive return	82	80
Sample Months*		
August '01	−6.50%	−6.41%
September '01	1.25%	−8.17%
October '01	−0.06%	1.81%
November '01	−3.79%	7.52%
December '01	6.04%	0.76%
January '02	7.87%	0.00%

*Historical simulation through 2000. Portfolios published on MSN Money starting August 2001.
Source: Camelback Research Alliance.

at that time—it was the bane of all right-thinking flower children. He attended the University of Arizona and the University of Tulsa in Oklahoma when his father transferred there, trying majors in architecture and information management before settling on his father's specialty. Numbers had appealed to him all his life—particularly when it came to compiling statistics on baseball—though he never noticed it until his sophomore year. After graduating with a master's degree in accounting from Tulsa, he went on to earn a doctorate in the subject at Oklahoma State.

What really got Vickrey going were advances in the field of behavioral finance, which attempts to understand how human behavior influences financial activity. Behavioral finance specialists are constantly battling with the conventional wisdom at universities, which holds that markets are efficient discounters of all known information about a company and it shares. "Efficient market" theorists hold that current stock prices are based on rational expectations and the profit maximization aims of both companies and investors.

Rebel finance professors in the early 1980s began to smash that totem with research that showed things don't happen in real life as they do in theoreticians' heads—and that individuals' financial behavior reflects biases and decision heuristics that are suboptimal.

For instance, consider the "anchoring and adjustment" heuristic. Think of a trader or analyst who has a value in mind for a company's earnings. When new information comes along—let's say, in a quarterly earnings release—the trader tends to base his next estimate on an adjustment of the original estimate, rather than purely on the new information. That is, the original view is the anchor that tends to make an adjustment to a new estimate less accurate. (Several studies have shown that this is one of the key problems with brokerage analysts. They tend not to adjust adequately from their original anchor.)

Another related problem is what behavioralists call the "availability" heuristic. This describes situations in which investors base their judgments about the future on a memory that is the most conveniently available. If August was great for a trader last year, for example, he might come to the conclusion that "all Augusts are good for stocks."

Market efficiency adherents have ready replies for all of these behavior scenarios. They say that while individuals may not seek profit maximization individually, ultimately all odd human behaviors get arbitraged away in big, liquid markets—and in the end the market always reaches an efficient price. That is to say, despite all of our human inconsistencies, once we all form a market then we efficiently arrive at a price that reflects all known information about a company.

All of this humanistic interest notwithstanding, Vickrey's doctoral thesis focused on the dull but important topic of how the market reacts to cash-flow and accrual effects. He broke a large set of companies' earnings down to accruals and cash, and tried to learn whether there were different market reactions over time. It helped him formulate new ways to think about earnings quality. (Cash flow, for the record, was determined to be the highest quality while accruals led to fudging.) That early research ultimately led to a line of research at Camelback that was launched in mid-2002: Earnings Quality Analytics.

Vickrey taught accounting and financial statement analysis at the University of San Diego and was tenured in 1998. That's typically a sign that you have published in enough good academic journals and stayed on the good side of everyone with a say in the process, from fellow faculty to the dean. Throughout his pursuit for tenure, he had told his father he thought he could develop consulting work or trading strategies for financial institutions, but his dad told him not to bother—since no one would pay for anything but tax accounting research. But in the late 1990s he met Carr Bettis at an academic conference, and they decided to combine their work to develop unique trading models and sell them to financial institutions. Both kept their jobs as professors and cooked up their strategies on nights and weekends. In Vickrey's case, that meant taking precious time away from road-racing his Mazda RX7 and more importantly from his wife, Kim, and children, Natalie, Haley, and Cole. But it seemed like a good investment.

Bettis, who is co-founder and chief executive of Camelback, was born in Stockton, California, but moved clear across the world six weeks later when his father enrolled in a United Pentecostal Church seminary in Sydney, Australia. His father went on to become president of a bible college there, then moved the family west to Adelaide about the time that Carr reached elementary-school age. While his father and mother were organizing churches, Carr went to a private, all-boys Church of England school with his brother—and played a lot of cricket, Australian Rules football, and basketball when he wasn't running track or racing road bikes. He loved the semiarid climate close to the ocean and the slow pace of life. "It was truly a perfect life," he says, all traces of his Australian accent now gone. "I wouldn't have changed a thing."

Bettis was a prefect and "captain" at his schools, where math, physics, and chemistry were his favorite subjects. School counselors urged him to study nuclear or civil engineering at one of the Australian universities. But his parents moved to Guam to organize new churches there, and he and his brother, Leland, followed them. Bettis studied accounting and finance at the University of Guam, and after graduating took his CPA exam and got a job at the accounting and consulting firm of Touche Ross International (now Delloite & Touche). He had become fascinated with economic forecasting models and dove into work doing studies of rate changes for Guam's power company. After a while, the government asked Touche to volunteer a staffer to work on fiscal policy issues, and before he knew it at age 22 he had become head of a coordinating committee responsible for formulating new economic and tax policy for the U.S. protectorate. In the mid-1980s, personal computers were just becoming available and Carr built forecasting models in Lotus 1-2-3 for the government. His work caught the attention of the island's governor, and soon he was named tax commissioner, director of revenue, and territorial securities administrator, responsible for hundreds of territorial and federal employees.

It was fun, but Bettis decided he wanted a more formal set of intellectual tools, so he applied and received scholarships and fellowships to graduate business programs around the United States and chose Indiana University. He earned a doctorate in capital markets with specialties in economic methods and quantitative analysis and wrote his Ph.D. thesis on the profitability of insider trading. His dissertation committee was scared of the topic, as the conventional wisdom at the time was that you couldn't make money in the market mimicking insiders. But he believed that assumptions were wrong and that the techniques were crude, and ultimately he was proven right.

After four years in graduate school, he recalls, it's easy to become brainwashed into thinking that the best career path is to become a professor and publish papers the rest of your life. But Bettis felt that he wanted to straddle two worlds: publish to be sure, but also to sell his ideas commercially to financial institutions. He extended his research beyond that which he published in his thesis and then hired software developers on the side and together with them wrote code to turn his ideas into a product marketed for a long time by Thomson Financial called Signal—the first quantitative alpha forecasting model based on insider behavior. He went to Arizona State University because he wanted to return to a warm sunny place and believed that he would be able to do commercial work outside the classroom. He started his first company, Quantech Corporation, a year after arriving at the university in 1991. He went on to build a more sophisticated version of Signal, which was a popular insider factor among Thomson's institutional clients for a decade.

Bettis continued to meld academic and commercial work, developing increasingly complex analytical factors and founding Camelback Research Alliance in 1996 to sell them to Thomson, BARRA and Primark, owner of major quantitative units like IBES for earnings data and Disclosure for insider data. Camelback now creates and produces quantitative models, alpha-generating variables, and portfolio-performance and risk-management systems for institutional clients worldwide. In 2001 Bettis added a money management arm, called Pinnacle Investment Advisors, which is manager of three quantitative hedge funds. He and his wife have three daughters—Sydney, Reilly, and Carly—and most mornings, before dawn, you will find him riding his road bike or racing his mountain bike through the desert mountain trails outside Scottsdale.

Working together originally by phone and e-mail while still teaching, Vickrey and Carr built their first model for Primark (now a unit of Thomson Financial) based on their view that stocks could be rated based on changes in reported mutual fund holdings. They failed to secure enough data to make the work meaningful, but Primark liked their work and contracted with them to create new financial software and other models. The work started off at a slow simmer, but ultimately boiled higher and higher until both had to do the unthinkable: Give up their tenured faculty positions. Carr's wife Stephanie also left Andersen Consulting (now Accenture) taking with her other former Andersen IT professionals to join Camelback. The goal was to build a technology team that could support a production environment and models that were developed by Carr, Donn, or other financial engineers working with them.

Now it's important to keep in mind what made this pair unusual. The prevailing point of view in business schools around the country is that no one can have an edge in the market. Both of these guys were postulating that individuals can have an edge. Strangely enough, despite the fact that thousands of independent and institutional traders make millions of dollars in the market, this is still considered a radical point of view.

Bettis and Vickrey started their more complex work on finding lucrative creases in the financial markets' time–space warp by first examining the academic research on well-documented anomalies. These included:

- *The P/E effect*: Academic research has determined that stocks with low price/earnings ratios tend to outperform the market. Researchers essentially sort all stocks with positive P/Es into 10 buckets from high to low. Ones in the lower deciles tend to outperform ones in the higher deciles. The evidence isn't completely conclusive, but Vickrey and Carr consider it to be a robust anomaly that has stood the test of time.
- *Post-Earnings announcement drift*. The basic idea is that stock prices don't fully reflect all information known about any individual company's earnings—and don't fully adjust when the latest earnings information is released. The anomaly suggests that stocks, however, will drift in the direction of the earnings surprise. Carr and Vickrey believe that this anomaly does exist; it has been documented for 25 years and doesn't seem to go away. The best explanation is the anchoring heuristic, as noted before; traders seem to resist jettisoning their prior beliefs about earnings.
- *The Value Line effect*. Academics have spent years trying to explain how and why—and whether—Value Line's top-ranked stocks have outperformed the market. Adherents to conventional wisdom proposed that Value Line doesn't really outperform once you adjust for risk. But behavioral finance partisans shoot back that it outperforms even if you do control for risk.
- *Insider trading and ownership*. The academic community is virtually unanimous by now in agreeing that insiders at corporations do tend to make prescient purchases of their own stock during price troughs. Vickrey and Bettis have documented that the most powerful signal, however, comes when large trades are made in clusters at significant lows by high-ranking executives, such as chief executives and chief financial officers. Additionally, Vickrey and Bettis have documented that the *net change* in mutual fund holdings of a stock—not the absolute value of holdings—provides a significant positive or negative signal about future price action.

In all of these cases, and others, Bettis and Vickrey are seeking the "information coefficient" contained in a signal. That is, they try to determine the expected return to a stock once a set of conditions are met, and the variance, or standard deviation, of those returns. Ideally, they are seeking signals, also known as "factors," that augur high returns with low variance. Generally speaking, it's easier to find strong high-return, low variance signals with small-cap stocks than with large caps.

Most of the quantitative-research shops on Wall Street develop models that have many more variables than StockScouter and tend to be much more complex in the way that they are operationalized, or implemented. They are also obligated to fit into a single investment-style niche, such as value or growth or insider or health care, since that is the way their funds or research services are typically purchased a la carte by clients. Yet they face a danger of being so complex that they lose degrees of freedom—for example, they include so many variables that they explain the past perfectly but fail to predict the future. StockScouter, on the other hand, was meant to cover the waterfront, offering heuristics for every type of investor, with an economical list of variables that preserves the maximum degrees of freedom. And while it needed to be somewhat complex under the hood, on the surface it needed to be understandable to private investors who do not have the benefit of a graduate finance degree.

The majority of stock-rating strategies that preceded StockScouter, such as Value Line or Zacks Investment Research, were essentially price- or earnings-momentum strategies. Both strategies, which worked well during the 1990s, have not worked well in this decade due to two factors: Earnings growth has been harder to come by, and too many quantitative players crowded into the space, depleting the value of the anomaly. Indeed, it's a brutal fact of life in the quantitative investment field that if you develop a powerful strategy using historical data and then explain it to the world via a popular newsletter or publication, the phenomenon will disappear. As a result, most good quants clam up when asked to explain what they do.

Without giving away all the salient details, it suffices to say that Camelback's approach differs from that of other quant shops in that it tends to be more event driven. That is, Bettis and Vickrey tend to focus on specific informational events and determine what should be expected to happen a week or month or six months down the road. Additionally, they try to determine excess returns, or returns greater than the market, that will transpire when combinations of those information events occur—for instance, when insiders are buying at 52-week lows *and* earnings-estimate revisions are rising. Other shops tend to smooth out their variables. As an example, when it comes to insider data,

Camelback would count the most recent insider actions and project a return forward from the date of the transactions, while others would take a moving average of insider activity at a company and look for price trends in that continuum. Camelback's method assumes that the market reacts to the news itself and that investors have a relatively brief period of time in which to act on that information. They believe that approaches that constantly roll up 90 days' worth of information water down the signal. In other words, Camelback believes that prices are news driven and move in spurts, while others think that prices flow like a river.

In the end, however, what makes StockScouter unique at uncovering stocks that will help swing traders find multiweek ideas is that it picks up on a variety of anomalies and combinations of anomalies and offers a basket of stocks that should do well for different reasons. That is a very cool concept and should help the system generate more consistent returns over time than models that are highly dependent on the success of a single factor, like earnings momentum.

HiMARQ Analysis

An alternative approach to finding stocks that are likely to succeed as long or short positions in the coming weeks and months is to seek 5 to 10 stocks that have historically outperformed or underperformed in the coming month. In the online Appendix of my last book, *Online Investing: Second Edition*, I explain how to use Excel to determine the average return of a stock in any month. The Appendix was hard to find, however, so with permission from that book's publisher, Microsoft Press, I have reproduced those instructions here. Additionally in Tables 4.8 and 4.9 at the end of this chapter, you will find a list of the best- and worst-performing 50 stocks for each month.

I call my methodology for studying individual stocks' sensitivity to seasons and months HiMARQ, which is short for historical monthly average return quotient. Understanding the typical monthly or quarterly trading patterns of a stock or an index can be invaluable for swing traders. Strong historical patterns obviously do not provide a holy grail, since very often exogenous factors will trump the seasonal pattern. But all other things being equal, you're better off trading with the historical trend than against it.

I have found it profitable over the past two years to start with each month by studying a long list of best and worst HiMARQ stocks, then applying the swing-trading or StockScouter principles explained elsewhere in this book. Very often stocks that tend historically to record extremely strong or weak results in a month, currently show promising chart or trading patterns, and have high or low StockScouter scores, make terrific multimonth holds or shorts over subsequent months.

In Table 4.7, you can see the HiMARQ stocks that I proposed for readers of my column either in *Stock Traders's Almanac Newsletter* or MSN Money from December through August 2002, and their results from inception through August 30, 2002. Most of the successful holds were shorts, as would be expected for a bear market period. (In some cases, as noted, the transactions were initiated at the end of the third week of the prior month; in others the transactions were initiated on the last day of the prior month. The variation stemmed from my publishing schedule.)

I will now explain how to build a HiMARQ worksheet yourself and then provide tables containing the stocks with the best HiMARQ records for each month.

Creating Your Own HiMARQ Worksheet

To find any stock or index's HiMARQ number, you must have Microsoft Excel loaded on your personal computer. If you do, follow these instructions:

1. Enter its symbol on the home page of MSN MoneyCentral Investor, choose Charts from the drop-down list, and click Go.
2. On the chart control, click Period and choose All Dates from the drop-down menu. Then click Period a second time, choose Custom, and set Display Detail to Monthly.
3. Click File on the chart control, and choose Export Data. The monthly close for the stock is then automatically sent to an Excel spreadsheet.
4. Switch to Excel. On the spreadsheet, immediately delete rows 1–4 and columns B, C, and E (which are the stock's high, low, and volume for each month). Then type "% Chg" (without the quotation marks) as a label in Cell C1 for the new, blank column C. Next, highlight the column and change the format to Percentage. (With

Table 4.7 HiMARQ Monthly Picks, January to August 2002

JANUARY 2002 HiMARQ			Transactions 12/17/01
Company	Sym	8/30/02	Pct. Chg.
Long Positions (only)			
Providian Financial Corporation	PVN	$ 5.68	125.40%
Alabama National BanCorporation	ALAB	$42.25	25.80%
BankAtlantic Bancorp, Inc.	BBX	$10.25	21.30%
PennFed Financial Services, Inc.	PFSB	$26.25	20.90%
Hudson River Bancorp, Inc.	HRBT	$25.64	12.50%
Midwest Banc Holdings, Inc.	MBHI	$18.76	−3.70%
Brookline Bancorp, Inc.	BRKL	$12.51	−16.80%
Capital One Financial Corporation	COF	$35.67	−25.50%
MBNA Corporation	KRB	$20.20	−37.20%
		Longs	**13.63%**
		S&P 500	−17.04%

FEBRUARY 2002 HiMARQ			Transactions 1/29/02
Company	Sym	8/30/02	Pct. Chg.
Long Positions			
FirstFed Financial Corp.	FED	$28.25	10.60%
Meridian Gold Inc.	MDG	$19.15	59.92%
Genesco Inc.	GCO	$14.79	−38.34%
Nautica Enterprises, Inc.	NAUT	$11.94	−15.05%
Ross Stores, Inc.	ROST	$36.11	3.46%
Sylvan Learning Systems, Inc.	SLVN	$14.19	−44.87%
SunGard Data Systems, Inc.	SDS	$24.65	−11.27%
Ventana Medical Systems, Inc.	VMSI	$22.29	1.89%
Trigon Health Care	TGH	$101.70	40.20%
Short Positions			
AMERCO	UHAL	$9.75	44.37%
LeCroy Corporation	LCRY	$10.12	45.67%
Pittston Company	PZB	$24.10	−16.17%
Sapient Corporation	SAPE	$1.27	73.39%
Sykes Enterprises, Incorporated	SYKE	$6.46	23.72%
Casella Waste Systems, Inc.	CWST	$8.22	41.83%
Encompass Services Corporation	ESR	$0.22	89.75%
Headwaters Incorporated	HDWR	$13.40	−5.63%
		Longs	0.73%
		Shorts	37.1%
		Combined	**18.92%**
		S&P 500	−19.00%

(Continued)

Table 4.7   *(Continued)*

MARCH 2002 HiMARQ			Transactions 2/17/02
Company	Sym	8/30/02	Pct. Chg.
Long Positions			
Global Industries, Ltd.	GLBL	$ 4.88	−40.34%
Northwest Airlines Corporation	NWAC	$10.17	−32.83%
Dollar Thrifty Automotive Group, Inc.	DTG	$17.55	11.43%
Dollar General Corporation	DG	$14.98	2.46%
QUALCOMM Incorporated	QCOM	$27.71	−25.91%
Short Positions			
Vical Incorporated	VICL	$ 9.75	43.85%
Emisphere Technologies, Inc.	EMIS	$10.12	80.78%
Cell Therapeutics, Inc.	CTIC	$24.10	75.95%
Protein Design Labs, Inc.	PDLI	$ 1.27	50.19%
ImmunoGen, Inc.	IMGN	$ 6.46	74.26%
		Longs	−17.04%
		Shorts	65.0%
		Combined	**23.98%**
		S&P 500	−17.04%

APRIL 2002 HiMARQ			Transactions 3/28/02
Company	Sym	8/30/02	Pct. Chg.
Long Positions			
Cooper Cameron Corporation	CAM	$44.84	−12.26%
FTI Consulting, Inc.	FCN	$36.41	17.55%
JDA Software Group, Inc.	JDAS	$12.67	−60.25%
TriQuint Semiconductor, Inc.	TQNT	$ 5.30	−55.87%
Quest Diagnostics Incorporated	DGX	$56.04	−32.34%
Short Positions			
Acclaim Entertainment, Inc.	AKLM	$ 2.75	39.42%
CKE Restaurants, Inc.	CKR	$ 7.32	18.21%
Immunomedics, Inc.	IMMU	$ 5.75	69.67%
Transkaryotic Therapies, Inc.	TKTX	$34.63	19.53%
Euronet Worldwide Inc.	EEFT	$ 9.22	45.76%
		Longs	−28.63%
		Shorts	38.5%
		Combined	**4.94%**
		S&P 500	−20.00%

Table 4.7   *(Continued)*

MAY 2002 HiMARQ		Transactions 4/30/02	
Company	**Sym**	**8/30/02**	**Pct. Chg.**
Long Positions			
JLG Industries, Inc.	JLG	$ 9.18	−44.22%
Concord Camera Corp.	LENS	$ 4.70	−38.96%
Noven Pharmaceuticals, Inc.	NOVN	$12.92	−35.68%
Shoe Carnival, Inc.	SCVL	$19.00	−7.54%
Tropical Sportswear Int'l. Corporation	TSIC	$17.95	−34.96%
Short Positions			
Open Text Corporation	OTEX	$22.50	−4.74%
E*TRADE Group, Inc.	ET	$ 4.34	42.44%
First Consulting Group, Inc.	FCGI	$ 7.25	19.44%
Level 3 Communications, Inc.	LVLT	$ 5.18	−26.96%
Knight Trading Group, Inc.	NITE	$ 4.23	24.59%
		Longs	−32.27%
		Shorts	11.0%
		Combined	**−10.66%**
		S&P 500	−15.00%

JUNE 2002 HiMARQ		Transactions 5/17/02	
Company	**Sym**	**8/30/02**	**Pct. Chg.**
Long Positions			
Oracle Corporation	ORCL	$ 9.59	0.10%
Sinclair Broadcast Group, Inc.	SBGI	$12.63	−13.01%
Wild Oats Markets, Inc.	OATS	$11.24	−25.31%
Aftermarket Technology Corp.	ATAC	$15.51	−35.98%
Endocare, Inc.	ENDO	$11.06	−41.48%
Short Positions			
ABIOMED, Inc.	ABMD	$ 5.28	24.57%
Presstek, Inc.	PRST	$ 3.04	58.91%
PacifiCare Health Systems, Inc.	PHSY	$22.99	15.87%
Trendwest Resorts	TWRI	$23.68	3.42%
Midas, Inc.	MDS	$ 7.07	47.55%
		Longs	−23.14%
		Shorts	30.1%
		Combined	**3.46%**
		S&P 500	−16.80%

(Continued)

Table 4.7 *(Continued)*

JULY 2002 HiMARQ			Transactions 6/28/02
Company	**Sym**	**8/30/02**	**Pct. Chg.**
Long Positions			
Interpool, Inc.	IPX	$ 9.59	−22.88%
Wintrust Financial Corporation	WTFC	$12.63	−7.43%
New Century Financial Corporation	NCEN	$11.24	−12.09%
Dril–Quip, Inc.	DRQ	$15.51	−22.20%
Prosperity Bancshares, Inc.	PRSP	$11.06	4.61%
Short Positions			
Boyd Gaming Corporation	BYD	$ 5.28	−13.19%
CSG Systems International, Inc.	CSGS	$ 3.04	37.87%
BEA Systems, Inc.	BEAS	$22.99	35.75%
DoubleClick, Inc.	DCLK	$23.68	22.34%
		Longs	−12.00%
		Shorts	20.7%
		Combined	**4.35%**
		S&P 500	−7.40%

Source: Camelback Research Alliance.

the column highlighted, right-click with your mouse, choose Format Cells, and double-click on the word Percentage.)

5. Next go to the cell in column C that is one row above the last row in columns A and B. You need to make this column show the percentage change between the very earliest month listed for the stock and the following one. So if the last month in column B is Cell B181, the formula would be =(B180–B181)/B181). Hit the Enter key, and you should see a percentage figure. For instance, if B180 is 11 and B181 is 10, the figure in Cell C181 will be 10%.

6. Select and drag the formula all the way up the column to Cell C2, and you'll see the percentage changes for each month of the stock's public life.

7. Now it gets tricky. Click Cell B2 (or any lower row in column B), click Data on the Excel menu, and then choose PivotTable And PivotChart Report. You'll see the PivotTable And PivotChart Wizard now; click Next, and you'll see a flashing dotted line form around all the data in columns A, B, and C.

8. Click Next again on the PivotTable And PivotChart Wizard step 2 of 3, and then click Finish on step 3 of 3. You're now looking at the blank PivotTable form. You must next click on the label DATE in the PivotTable Wizard, hold it down with the left mouse button, and drag it to Column A in the area labeled Drop Row Fields Here. Then click on the label % Chg on the PivotTable form and drag it to the area labeled Drop Data Items Here.

9. Now double-click the button in Cell A3 labeled Count Of % Chg, and in the PivotTable Field dialog box that appears, click and highlight the word Average in the area labeled Summarize By. Then click the Number button, and in the dialog that follows, choose Percentage. Then click OK twice.

10. Last, click on any cell in column A, and then click Data on the top menu of Excel, choose Group And Outline from the submenu, and then choose Group from the menu that appears. In the dialog box that then appears, choose Months and Quarters and click OK.

11. That's all there is to it. You can experiment further on your own—for instance, you can choose to look at standard deviations of return instead of just the average return or seek out the maximum and minimum returns. More important, if you double-click on any of the Total return figures in column C, Excel will open another worksheet and display the monthly data behind that roll-up number.

HiMARQ analysis is most useful in the extremes. That is, if a stock has been up 6 times in the past 10 Marches and down 4 times, no useful information is imparted. But if a stock's been up 9 times in the past 10 Marches, and down just once, it's fair to bet that it'll be up the next March, all other things being equal. In Tables 4.8 and 4.9, stocks are sorted first by month, then by batting average (the percentage of times the stock has been up over our recorded history period), and then by average mean return in the period. To be included, stocks must have had at least four years of history in each month. Table 4.8 shows the best potential longs each month based on this analysis, while Table 4.9 shows the best potential shorts. (Data updated through 2003 is available at http://jonmark.com/himarq.htm.)

Even swing traders who do not trade systematically should be able to make use of StockScouter ratings or HiMARQ analysis to winnow down the list of possible choices of stocks to go long or short at any time.

Table 4.8 HiMARQ Longs—Best Long Candidates Historically by Month*

Month	Sym.	Name	Mean Chg.	Std. Dev.	Mos. Up	Mos. Dwn	Batting Avg.
January	MIMS	MIM CORP	58.2%	70.5%	4	0	1.000
January	GLGC	GENE LOGIC INC	48.7%	75.6%	4	0	1.000
January	PEGA	PEGASYSTEMS INC	40.3%	51.1%	5	0	1.000
January	CYMI	CYMER INC	33.2%	38.8%	5	0	1.000
January	PGNX	PROGENICS PHARMACEUTICALS INC	30.8%	19.4%	4	0	1.000
January	TSM	TAIWAN SEMICONDUCTOR MFG CO LTD	30.4%	8.3%	4	0	1.000
January	TRKN	TRIKON TECHNOLOGIES INC	30.2%	22.4%	5	0	1.000
January	LOGI	LOGITECH INTERNATIONAL SA	25.6%	28.8%	4	0	1.000
January	ASML	ASML HOLDING NV	25.4%	19.7%	6	0	1.000
January	ILXO	ILEX ONCOLOGY INC	24.9%	13.7%	4	0	1.000
January	ASCA	AMERISTAR CASINOS INC	24.7%	25.6%	8	0	1.000
January	ALXN	ALEXION PHARMACEUTICALS INC	23.1%	23.3%	5	0	1.000
January	IART	INTEGRA LIFESCIENCES HOLDINGS CORP	22.8%	12.2%	6	0	1.000
January	NUCO	NUCO2 INC	22.6%	18.2%	6	0	1.000
January	VSAT	VIASAT INC	21.0%	17.5%	5	0	1.000
January	USNA	USANA HEALTH SCIENCES INC	20.8%	21.1%	4	0	1.000
January	AVCT	AVOCENT CORP	20.7%	4.6%	4	0	1.000
January	SNAP	SYNAPTIC PHARMACEUTICAL CORP	19.0%	10.1%	6	0	1.000
January	NTEC	NEOSE TECHNOLOGIES INC	18.6%	20.0%	5	0	1.000
January	URI	UNITED RENTALS INC NEW	17.0%	9.4%	4	0	1.000
January	ANST	ANSOFT CORP	16.9%	8.2%	5	0	1.000
January	REMX	REMEDYTEMP INC	16.3%	6.9%	5	0	1.000
January	SEAC	SEACHANGE INTERNATIONAL INC	16.3%	11.2%	5	0	1.000
January	PEAK	PEAK INTERNATIONAL LTD	15.8%	11.5%	4	0	1.000

*Constraints: At start of historical month, split-adjusted price greater than $2. Also, minimum price in June 2002 greater than $5 and average daily volume greater than 25,000.

January	PT	PORTUGAL TELECOM SGPS SA	15.1%	6.8%	6	0	1.000
January	ATTC	AT&T CANADA INC NEW	14.9%	11.7%	4	0	1.000
January	MAXS	MAXWELL SHOE CO INC	12.6%	10.3%	7	0	1.000
January	PSEM	PERICOM SEMICONDUCTOR CORP	12.2%	13.7%	4	0	1.000
January	ADIC	ADVANCED DIGITAL INFORMATION CORP	11.7%	7.6%	5	0	1.000
January	AOL	AOL TIME WARNER INC	11.2%	3.8%	4	0	1.000
January	TI	TELECOM ITALIA SPA	10.2%	3.8%	6	0	1.000
January	UMPQ	UMPQUA HOLDINGS CORP	9.9%	6.0%	4	0	1.000
January	FTE	FRANCE TELECOM	9.9%	8.9%	4	0	1.000
January	PETD	PETROLEUM DEVELOPMENT CORP	9.0%	8.9%	5	0	1.000
January	WXH	WINSTON HOTELS INC	8.5%	7.8%	4	0	1.000
January	APU	AMERIGAS PARTNERS L P	8.5%	6.1%	6	0	1.000
January	MMA	MUNICIPAL MORTGAGE & EQUITY L L C	8.1%	6.3%	5	0	1.000
January	RWT	REDWOOD TRUST INC	8.0%	5.9%	6	0	1.000
January	EME	EMCOR GROUP INC	7.9%	7.3%	6	0	1.000
January	DOM	DOMINION RESOURCES BLACK WARRIOR TRUST	7.8%	5.0%	7	0	1.000
January	ADO	ADECCO SA	6.8%	4.0%	6	0	1.000
January	SHFL	SHUFFLE MASTER INC	6.3%	5.7%	8	0	1.000
January	CRUS	CIRRUS LOGIC INC	13.2%	12.5%	11	1	0.917
January	MCRI	MONARCH CASINO & RESORT INC	20.3%	16.6%	6	1	0.857
January	ALLE	ALLEGIANT BANCORP INC NEW	11.0%	8.2%	5	1	0.833
January	ADRX	ANDRX CORP ANDRX GROUP	20.8%	24.6%	4	1	0.800
January	TMPW	TMP WORLDWIDE INC	12.7%	17.7%	4	1	0.800
January	FBAY	FRISCO BAY INDUSTRIES LTD	18.7%	20.1%	3	1	0.750
January	NFI	NOVASTAR FINANCIAL INC	15.5%	19.1%	3	1	0.750
January	HEII	HEI INC	18.7%	19.3%	7	3	0.700

(Continued)

183

Table 4.8 (Continued)

Month	Sym.	Name	Mean Chg.	Std. Dev.	Mos. Up	Mos. Dwn	Batting Avg.
February	MEDC	MED DESIGN CORP	35.5%	28.6%	6	0	1.000
February	PHCC	PRIORITY HEALTHCARE CORP	22.6%	27.7%	4	0	1.000
February	KNDL	KENDLE INTERNATIONAL INC	19.9%	19.6%	4	0	1.000
February	KNSY	KENSEY NASH CORP	16.4%	17.2%	6	0	1.000
February	IFNY	INFINITY INC	16.3%	10.6%	6	0	1.000
February	PBR	PETROLEO BRASILEIRO	9.5%	9.0%	5	0	1.000
February	RLRN	RENAISSANCE LEARNING INC	9.1%	10.9%	4	0	1.000
February	PFB	PFF BANCORP INC	7.6%	4.6%	5	0	1.000
February	LBY	LIBBEY INC	7.4%	6.4%	8	0	1.000
February	JAKK	JAKKS PACIFIC INC	6.9%	7.2%	5	0	1.000
February	EME	EMCOR GROUP INC	6.6%	8.0%	6	0	1.000
February	SKP	SCPIE HOLDINGS INC	6.3%	8.4%	5	0	1.000
February	NAT	NORDIC AMERICAN TANKER SHIPPING LTD	5.1%	3.6%	4	0	1.000
February	GCS..B	GRAY COMMUNICATIONS SYSTEMS INC	4.4%	2.7%	5	0	1.000
February	ROV	RAYOVAC CORP	4.0%	3.9%	4	0	1.000
February	ARE	ALEXANDRIA REAL ESTATE EQUITIES INC	3.5%	1.5%	4	0	1.000
February	UU	UNITED UTILITIES PLC	1.7%	0.9%	4	0	1.000
February	MKL	MARKEL CORP NEW	6.2%	9.6%	14	1	0.933
February	SDS	SUNGARD DATA SYSTEMS INC	12.7%	8.2%	11	1	0.917
February	LUX	LUXOTTICA GROUP SPA	12.8%	14.8%	9	1	0.900
February	EP	EL PASO CORP	7.0%	5.5%	8	1	0.889
February	QUIX	QUIXOTE CORP	8.0%	9.0%	14	2	0.875
February	PHSY	PACIFICARE HEALTH SYSTEMS INC NEW	8.0%	14.0%	14	2	0.875

February	NC	NACCO INDUSTRIES INC	7.2%	10.5%	14	2	0.875
February	TFX	TELEFLEX INC	6.7%	7.0%	14	2	0.875
February	HNI	HON INDUSTRIES INC	6.2%	6.9%	14	2	0.875
February	CORS	CORUS BANKSHARES INC	5.4%	6.2%	14	2	0.875
February	TRW	TRW INC	5.2%	7.1%	14	2	0.875
February	REPB	REPUBLIC BANCSHARES INC	4.9%	9.0%	7	1	0.875
February	CINF	CINCINNATI FINANCIAL CORP	4.3%	4.3%	14	2	0.875
February	FVB	FIRST VIRGINIA BANKS INC	4.1%	6.8%	14	2	0.875
February	DJ	DOW JONES & CO INC	4.0%	6.6%	14	2	0.875
February	TNC	TENNANT CO	3.8%	4.7%	14	2	0.875
February	FTN	FIRST TENNESSEE NATIONAL CORP	3.4%	10.7%	14	2	0.875
February	PCLE	PINNACLE SYSTEMS INC CA	16.1%	16.5%	6	1	0.857
February	GDI	GARDNER DENVER INC	14.5%	22.5%	6	1	0.857
February	GDT	GUIDANT CORP	10.0%	11.7%	6	1	0.857
February	ADO	ADECCO SA	8.3%	7.7%	6	1	0.857
February	IVX	IVAX CORP	7.9%	9.2%	12	2	0.857
February	GG	GOLDCORP INC NEW	7.8%	11.0%	6	1	0.857
February	FED	FIRSTFED FINANCIAL CORP	8.6%	7.8%	13	3	0.813
February	KMI	KINDER MORGAN INC NEW	4.6%	6.3%	13	3	0.813
February	ZION	ZIONS BANCORPORATION	3.4%	5.8%	13	3	0.813
February	CFBX	COMMUNITY FIRST BANKSHARES INC	3.9%	4.7%	8	2	0.800
February	GCOM	GLOBECOMM SYSTEMS INC	22.6%	21.5%	3	1	0.750
February	GLH	GALLAHER GROUP PLC	9.2%	11.1%	3	1	0.750
February	ATR	APTARGROUP INC	6.6%	7.4%	6	2	0.750
February	TT	TRANSTECHNOLOGY CORP	3.9%	5.4%	12	4	0.750
February	FCN	FTI CONSULTING INC	6.5%	7.8%	3	2	0.600

(Continued)

Table 4.8 *(Continued)*

Month	Sym.	Name	Mean Chg.	Std. Dev.	Mos. Up	Mos. Dwn	Batting Avg.
March	HOTT	HOT TOPIC INC	32.6%	28.7%	5	0	1.000
March	DTG	DOLLAR THRIFTY AUTOMOTIVE GROUP INC	22.3%	15.4%	4	0	1.000
March	CWST	CASELLA WASTE SYSTEMS INC	19.8%	17.6%	4	0	1.000
March	GTRC	GUITAR CENTER INC	19.2%	9.6%	4	0	1.000
March	GRTS	GART SPORTS CO	14.9%	11.0%	4	0	1.000
March	OCLR	OCULAR SCIENCES INC	14.8%	15.1%	4	0	1.000
March	ACMR	A C MOORE ARTS & CRAFTS INC	14.4%	8.3%	4	0	1.000
March	TLM	TALISMAN ENERGY INC	14.3%	20.5%	4	0	1.000
March	BJ	BJ S WHOLESALE CLUB INC	14.1%	6.5%	4	0	1.000
March	BFAM	BRIGHT HORIZONS FAMILY SOLUTIONS INC	13.1%	12.6%	4	0	1.000
March	SYKE	SYKES ENTERPRISES INC	12.6%	9.0%	5	0	1.000
March	CBI	CHICAGO BRIDGE & IRON CO NV	12.4%	6.4%	4	0	1.000
March	MINI	MOBILE MINI INC	12.2%	5.2%	8	0	1.000
March	NWAC	NORTHWEST AIRLINES CORP NEW	10.7%	8.8%	7	0	1.000
March	BCM	CANADIAN IMPERIAL BANK OF COMMERCE	8.1%	5.8%	4	0	1.000
March	ASVI	A S V INC	7.8%	3.7%	6	0	1.000
March	WG	WILLBROS GROUP INC	6.9%	9.9%	5	0	1.000
March	HH	HOOPER HOLMES INC	6.9%	2.5%	4	0	1.000
March	SURW	SUREWEST COMMUNICATIONS	6.6%	7.7%	5	0	1.000
March	CNI	CANADIAN NATIONAL RAILWAY CO	6.5%	6.8%	5	0	1.000
March	MDS	MIDAS INC	6.0%	6.0%	4	0	1.000
March	NAT	NORDIC AMERICAN TANKER SHIPPING LTD	5.8%	5.0%	4	0	1.000
March	BCS	BARCLAYS PLC	4.1%	3.9%	4	0	1.000

March	CPO	CORN PRODUCTS INTERNATIONAL INC	3.0%	2.4%	4	0	1.000
March	LOW	LOWE S COS INC	8.8%	8.6%	11	1	0.917
March	UNH	UNITEDHEALTH GROUP INC	6.5%	9.4%	10	1	0.909
March	ANN	ANNTAYLOR STORES CORP	8.3%	9.6%	9	1	0.900
March	SMRT	STEIN MART INC	16.9%	23.5%	8	1	0.889
March	DG	DOLLAR GENERAL CORP	10.9%	9.7%	8	1	0.889
March	PZZA	PAPA JOHN S INTERNATIONAL INC	12.4%	14.3%	7	1	0.875
March	QCOM	QUALCOMM INC	10.9%	17.5%	7	1	0.875
March	CC	CIRCUIT CITY STORES CIRCUIT CITY GROUP	9.9%	16.9%	14	2	0.875
March	BKS	BARNES & NOBLE INC	9.4%	11.6%	7	1	0.875
March	GSB	GOLDEN STATE BANCORP INC	9.1%	10.4%	7	1	0.875
March	CVX	CHEVRONTEXACO CORP	5.2%	6.7%	14	2	0.875
March	MAS	MASCO CORP	4.6%	7.1%	14	2	0.875
March	OTTR	OTTER TAIL CORP	3.5%	4.6%	14	2	0.875
March	APC	ANADARKO PETROLEUM CORP	7.8%	10.3%	13	2	0.867
March	AKS	AK STEEL HOLDING CORP	8.1%	6.4%	6	1	0.857
March	ATU	ACTUANT CORP	6.0%	5.4%	12	2	0.857
March	TYC	TYCO INTERNATIONAL LTD BERMUDA	9.8%	15.4%	8	2	0.800
March	IBOC	INTERNATIONAL BANCSHARES CORP	3.1%	2.4%	4	1	0.800
March	HITK	HI TECH PHARMACAL CO INC	11.8%	14.2%	7	2	0.778
March	ISLE	ISLE OF CAPRI CASINOS INC	9.2%	15.4%	7	2	0.778
March	OFIX	ORTHOFIX INTERNATIONAL NV	6.5%	8.7%	7	2	0.778
March	LFUS	LITTELFUSE INC DE	5.3%	8.4%	7	2	0.778
March	JBX	JACK IN THE BOX INC DE	2.5%	6.2%	7	2	0.778
March	AME	AMETEK INC NEW	7.0%	5.3%	3	1	0.750
March	RAH	RALCORP HOLDINGS INC NEW	6.3%	10.0%	3	2	0.600

(Continued)

Table 4.8 (*Continued*)

Month	Sym.	Name	Mean Chg.	Std. Dev.	Mos. Up	Mos. Dwn	Batting Avg.
April	FCN	FTI CONSULTING INC	23.3%	4.1%	4	0	1.000
April	DGX	QUEST DIAGNOSTICS INC	23.2%	17.1%	5	0	1.000
April	GPI	GROUP 1 AUTOMOTIVE INC	22.3%	22.0%	4	0	1.000
April	RWY	RENT WAY INC	21.9%	15.7%	8	0	1.000
April	JILL	J JILL GROUP INC	19.4%	18.4%	6	0	1.000
April	ROCK	GIBRALTAR STEEL CORP	18.2%	8.0%	8	0	1.000
April	ALTR	ALTERA CORP	17.4%	13.8%	7	0	1.000
April	IM	INGRAM MICRO INC	15.4%	9.6%	5	0	1.000
April	STM	STMICROELECTRONICS NV	14.8%	10.6%	7	0	1.000
April	ASF	ADMINISTAFF INC	14.6%	14.6%	5	0	1.000
April	MGM	METRO GOLDWYN MAYER INC NEW	14.6%	4.6%	4	0	1.000
April	AVX	AVX CORP	14.2%	10.1%	6	0	1.000
April	RS	RELIANCE STEEL & ALUMINUM CO	14.2%	11.1%	7	0	1.000
April	WFSI	WFS FINANCIAL INC	13.8%	20.4%	6	0	1.000
April	BEIQ	BEI TECHNOLOGIES INC	13.6%	16.3%	4	0	1.000
April	MLNM	MILLENNIUM PHARMACEUTICALS INC	13.4%	8.2%	5	0	1.000
April	UMPQ	UMPQUA HOLDINGS CORP	12.6%	13.2%	4	0	1.000
April	HCM	HANOVER CAPITAL MORTGAGE HOLDINGS INC	12.6%	10.4%	4	0	1.000
April	CBKN	CAPITAL BANK CORP	12.5%	15.5%	4	0	1.000
April	STJ	ST JUDE MEDICAL INC	11.5%	7.5%	4	0	1.000
April	SWBT	SOUTHWEST BANCORPORATION OF TEXAS INC	11.5%	15.0%	5	0	1.000
April	CTV	COMMSCOPE INC	11.2%	5.2%	4	0	1.000
April	DLTR	DOLLAR TREE STORES INC	10.9%	5.3%	7	0	1.000

April	TLM	TALISMAN ENERGY INC	10.4%	9.8%	4	0	1.000
April	CAM	COOPER CAMERON CORP	9.6%	3.5%	6	0	1.000
April	SRI	STONERIDGE INC	9.1%	7.7%	4	0	1.000
April	PEGS	PEGASUS SOLUTIONS INC	8.7%	7.3%	4	0	1.000
April	CTS	CTS CORP	8.7%	5.4%	16	0	1.000
April	MBHI	MIDWEST BANC HOLDINGS INC	8.5%	5.2%	4	0	1.000
April	IEX	IDEX CORP	8.2%	5.0%	12	0	1.000
April	CPS	CHOICEPOINT INC	7.9%	8.2%	4	0	1.000
April	FAB	FIRSTFED AMERICA BANCORP INC	7.6%	3.3%	5	0	1.000
April	CNI	CANADIAN NATIONAL RAILWAY CO	7.3%	4.4%	5	0	1.000
April	HH	HOOPER HOLMES INC	7.2%	8.2%	5	0	1.000
April	ASTSF	ASE TEST LTD	5.7%	6.2%	5	0	1.000
April	HC	HANOVER COMPRESSOR CO	5.6%	4.6%	4	0	1.000
April	MTX	MINERALS TECHNOLOGIES INC	5.6%	3.0%	9	0	1.000
April	IBOC	INTERNATIONAL BANCSHARES CORP	5.6%	6.2%	5	0	1.000
April	APU	AMERIGAS PARTNERS L P	5.5%	5.5%	6	0	1.000
April	ICBC	INDEPENDENCE COMMUNITY BANK CORP	6.5%	4.6%	4	0	1.000
April	SUR	CNA SURETY CORP	5.9%	2.4%	4	0	1.000
April	FFIC	FLUSHING FINANCIAL CORP	5.4%	2.8%	6	0	1.000
April	BRK..B	BERKSHIRE HATHAWAY INC NEW	4.1%	1.5%	5	0	1.000
April	DOM	DOMINION RESOURCES BLACK WARRIOR TRUST	3.9%	1.8%	7	0	1.000
April	GSB	GOLDEN STATE BANCORP INC	10.7%	11.5%	7	1	0.875
April	PPS	POST PROPERTIES INC	3.8%	3.1%	7	1	0.875
April	BCGI	BOSTON COMMUNICATIONS GROUP INC	16.9%	14.1%	4	1	0.800
April	FRED	FRED S INC	4.4%	3.5%	8	2	0.800
April	SIB	STATEN ISLAND BANCORP INC	6.3%	5.0%	3	1	0.750
April	PETD	PETROLEUM DEVELOPMENT CORP	4.8%	5.7%	4	2	0.667

(Continued)

Table 4.8 (*Continued*)

Month	Sym.	Name	Mean Chg.	Std. Dev.	Mos. Up	Mos. Dwn	Batting Avg.
May	DAVE	FAMOUS DAVE S OF AMERICA INC	22.2%	19.8%	5	0	1.000
May	TSIC	TROPICAL SPORTSWEAR INTERNATIONAL CORP	20.6%	8.9%	4	0	1.000
May	KOSP	KOS PHARMACEUTICALS INC	14.7%	13.8%	5	0	1.000
May	HDWR	HEADWATERS INC	13.2%	14.3%	4	0	1.000
May	VIBC	VIB CORP	11.6%	7.3%	5	0	1.000
May	CBI	CHICAGO BRIDGE & IRON CO NV	11.0%	9.9%	5	0	1.000
May	STJ	ST JUDE MEDICAL INC	10.7%	8.9%	4	0	1.000
May	URI	UNITED RENTALS INC NEW	9.8%	11.4%	4	0	1.000
May	CERS	CERUS CORP	9.7%	8.2%	5	0	1.000
May	STRC	SRI SURGICAL EXPRESS INC	9.5%	4.9%	5	0	1.000
May	DRD	DUANE READE INC	9.3%	7.0%	4	0	1.000
May	PLB	AMERICAN ITALIAN PASTA CO	7.7%	6.4%	4	0	1.000
May	NWPX	NORTHWEST PIPE CO	7.3%	7.9%	6	0	1.000
May	MATW	MATTHEWS INTERNATIONAL CORP	7.1%	5.1%	7	0	1.000
May	WG	WILLBROS GROUP INC	6.5%	7.3%	5	0	1.000
May	TGI	TRIUMPH GROUP INC DE	6.5%	4.8%	5	0	1.000
May	LBAI	LAKELAND BANCORP INC	6.2%	2.5%	4	0	1.000
May	CECO	CAREER EDUCATION CORP	5.4%	2.7%	4	0	1.000
May	BKNW	BANK OF THE NORTHWEST	5.4%	4.5%	4	0	1.000
May	ANH	ANWORTH MORTGAGE ASSET CORP	4.9%	4.4%	4	0	1.000
May	RBA	RITCHIE BROS AUCTIONEERS INC	4.9%	4.7%	4	0	1.000
May	CEFT	CONCORD EFS INC	4.8%	5.4%	6	0	1.000
May	AFC	ALLAMERICA FINANCIAL CORP	4.4%	3.7%	6	0	1.000
May	MAT	MATTEL INC	7.2%	6.3%	14	1	0.933

May	FAST	FASTENAL CO	7.1%	7.9%	12	1	0.923
May	RDA	READER S DIGEST ASSOCIATION INC	4.6%	5.0%	11	1	0.917
May	XRAY	DENTSPLY INTERNATIONAL INC DE	4.4%	3.1%	10	1	0.909
May	REM	REMINGTON OIL & GAS CORP	9.6%	14.0%	9	1	0.900
May	NAUT	NAUTICA ENTERPRISES INC	9.3%	11.2%	9	1	0.900
May	FD	FEDERATED DEPARTMENT STORES INC NEW	6.6%	6.2%	9	1	0.900
May	YRK	YORK INTERNATIONAL CORP	5.8%	5.2%	9	1	0.900
May	BBOX	BLACK BOX CORP	13.1%	18.2%	8	1	0.889
May	SCVL	SHOE CARNIVAL INC	12.6%	15.4%	8	1	0.889
May	ARRO	ARROW INTERNATIONAL INC	7.5%	6.9%	8	1	0.889
May	TOM	TOMMY HILFIGER CORP	7.3%	10.9%	8	1	0.889
May	RCL	ROYAL CARIBBEAN CRUISES LTD	4.8%	5.1%	8	1	0.889
May	JLG	JLG INDUSTRIES INC	17.0%	13.3%	7	1	0.875
May	CEI	CRESCENT REAL ESTATE EQUITIES CO	4.1%	5.7%	7	1	0.875
May	AGM	FEDERAL AGRICULTURAL MORTGAGE CORP	14.3%	10.1%	5	1	0.833
May	AGN	ALLERGAN INC	6.9%	6.7%	10	2	0.833
May	EE	EL PASO ELECTRIC CO	5.6%	5.4%	5	1	0.833
May	NASI	NORTH AMERICAN SCIENTIFIC INC	18.3%	12.8%	4	1	0.800
May	HOEN	HOENIG GROUP INC	8.7%	10.5%	8	2	0.800
May	PNRA	PANERA BREAD CO	8.4%	13.5%	8	2	0.800
May	CUNO	CUNO INC	6.9%	8.0%	4	1	0.800
May	HAFC	HANMI FINANCIAL CORP	5.5%	5.4%	4	1	0.800
May	EPIQ	EPIQ SYSTEMS INC	8.8%	10.5%	3	1	0.750
May	SPI	SCOTTISH POWER PLC	5.9%	7.0%	3	1	0.750
May	PNP	PAN PACIFIC RETAIL PROPERTIES INC	4.2%	4.4%	3	1	0.750
May	CTWS	CONNECTICUT WATER SERVICE INC	3.2%	5.0%	11	5	0.688

(Continued)

Table 4.8 (Continued)

Month	Sym.	Name	Mean Chg.	Std. Dev.	Mos. Up	Mos. Dwn	Batting Avg.
June	RMBS	RAMBUS INC	50.5%	49.3%	5	0	1.000
June	BRCM	BROADCOM CORP	37.0%	21.8%	4	0	1.000
June	BCGI	BOSTON COMMUNICATIONS GROUP INC	30.9%	17.6%	5	0	1.000
June	ADRX	ANDRX CORP ANDRX GROUP	27.1%	24.4%	5	0	1.000
June	ICLR	ICON PLC	24.9%	34.5%	4	0	1.000
June	NAP	NATIONAL PROCESSING INC	24.9%	26.1%	5	0	1.000
June	SEBL	SIEBEL SYSTEMS INC	24.1%	14.8%	5	0	1.000
June	VSAT	VIASAT INC	22.7%	15.6%	5	0	1.000
June	NPSI	NORTH PITTSBURGH SYSTEMS INC	21.8%	16.6%	5	0	1.000
June	TMPW	TMP WORLDWIDE INC	20.6%	11.5%	5	0	1.000
June	OATS	WILD OATS MARKETS INC	19.3%	16.0%	5	0	1.000
June	ORCL	ORACLE CORP DE	18.2%	13.3%	7	0	1.000
June	VRSN	VERISIGN INC	18.0%	10.0%	4	0	1.000
June	SONO	SONOSITE INC	17.6%	18.8%	4	0	1.000
June	ATAC	AFTERMARKET TECHNOLOGY CORP	17.2%	14.0%	5	0	1.000
June	DRTE	DENDRITE INTERNATIONAL INC	17.2%	10.3%	6	0	1.000
June	CVD	COVANCE INC	16.6%	8.9%	5	0	1.000
June	KNDL	KENDLE INTERNATIONAL INC	16.4%	13.3%	4	0	1.000
June	SBGI	SINCLAIR BROADCAST GROUP INC	16.0%	9.8%	6	0	1.000
June	CHL	CHINA MOBILE HONG KONG LTD	15.2%	12.1%	4	0	1.000
June	WCNX	WASTE CONNECTIONS INC	14.4%	11.6%	4	0	1.000
June	FDCC	FACTUAL DATA CORP	13.7%	18.1%	4	0	1.000
June	AVCT	AVOCENT CORP	13.1%	15.9%	5	0	1.000
June	CEFT	CONCORD EFS INC	11.5%	9.2%	7	0	1.000

192

Month	Ticker	Company					
June	PLT	PLANTRONICS INC DE	11.4%	10.1%	8	0	1.000
June	WGOV	WOODWARD GOVERNOR CO	11.1%	6.1%	5	0	1.000
June	CSTR	COINSTAR INC	11.0%	8.7%	4	0	1.000
June	SHPGY	SHIRE PHARMACEUTICALS GROUP PLC	11.0%	6.2%	4	0	1.000
June	ISSX	INTERNET SECURITY SYSTEMS INC DE	10.9%	15.2%	4	0	1.000
June	DELL	DELL COMPUTER CORP	9.2%	4.3%	5	0	1.000
June	CTBK	CITY BANK WA	8.8%	7.8%	4	0	1.000
June	ANF	ABERCROMBIE & FITCH CO DE	8.2%	9.4%	5	0	1.000
June	STNR	STEINER LEISURE LTD	8.2%	11.2%	5	0	1.000
June	DGX	QUEST DIAGNOSTICS INC	8.1%	8.3%	5	0	1.000
June	FFIC	FLUSHING FINANCIAL CORP	7.3%	8.7%	6	0	1.000
June	JKHY	JACK HENRY & ASSOCIATES INC	7.0%	4.4%	6	0	1.000
June	COST	COSTCO WHOLESALE CORP DE	7.0%	5.2%	8	0	1.000
June	BJ	BJ S WHOLESALE CLUB INC	6.9%	4.6%	4	0	1.000
June	DA	GROUPE DANONE SA	6.7%	4.9%	5	0	1.000
June	PSMT	PRICESMART INC	5.4%	5.3%	4	0	1.000
June	CCU	CLEAR CHANNEL COMMUNICATIONS INC	5.0%	6.8%	9	0	1.000
June	FSCI	FISHER COMMUNICATIONS INC	5.8%	4.7%	5	0	1.000
June	OCFC	OCEANFIRST FINANCIAL CORP	5.6%	4.0%	5	0	1.000
June	CCBG	CAPITAL CITY BANK GROUP INC	5.3%	3.8%	5	0	1.000
June	ALLE	ALLEGIANT BANCORP INC NEW	5.0%	7.5%	6	0	1.000
June	ULTE	ULTIMATE ELECTRONICS INC	13.1%	10.7%	7	1	0.875
June	TGIC	TRIAD GUARANTY INC	12.7%	10.3%	7	1	0.875
June	FPIC	FPIC INSURANCE GROUP INC	11.7%	9.0%	4	1	0.800
June	ENDO	ENDOCARE INC	10.7%	10.6%	4	1	0.800
June	AMV	AMERIVEST PROPERTIES INC	5.5%	4.6%	4	1	0.800

(Continued)

Table 4.8 *(Continued)*

Month	Sym.	Name	Mean Chg.	Std. Dev.	Mos. Up	Mos. Dwn	Batting Avg.
July	FCGI	FIRST CONSULTING GROUP INC	20.0%	11.6%	4	0	1.000
July	CTSH	COGNIZANT TECHNOLOGY SOLUTIONS CORP	17.9%	15.3%	4	0	1.000
July	ICLR	ICON PLC	17.3%	7.4%	4	0	1.000
July	NCEN	NEW CENTURY FINANCIAL CORP	16.4%	12.8%	5	0	1.000
July	RGX	RADIOLOGIX INC	16.2%	11.0%	4	0	1.000
July	RACN	RACING CHAMPIONS ERTL CORP	12.1%	13.3%	4	0	1.000
July	SNBC	SUN BANCORP INC NJ	10.3%	12.0%	5	0	1.000
July	RAS	RAIT INVESTMENT TRUST	4.8%	6.1%	4	0	1.000
July	SOI	SOLUTIA INC	3.5%	2.4%	4	0	1.000
July	AXM	APEX MORTGAGE CAPITAL INC	3.4%	2.6%	4	0	1.000
July	HARB	HARBOR FLORIDA BANCSHARES INC	3.4%	2.2%	4	0	1.000
July	SYK	STRYKER CORP	9.5%	6.5%	13	1	0.929
July	SWY	SAFEWAY INC	6.4%	6.8%	11	1	0.917
July	HDI	HARLEY DAVIDSON INC	6.5%	5.9%	10	1	0.909
July	SWFT	SWIFT TRANSPORTATION CO INC	6.1%	6.4%	9	1	0.900
July	IPX	INTERPOOL INC	10.7%	7.0%	8	1	0.889
July	DORL	DORAL FINANCIAL CORP	6.5%	7.1%	8	1	0.889
July	MCHP	MICROCHIP TECHNOLOGY INC	11.7%	11.8%	7	1	0.875
July	PLT	PLANTRONICS INC DE	10.2%	7.8%	7	1	0.875
July	AEOS	AMERICAN EAGLE OUTFITTERS INC NEW	7.1%	12.3%	7	1	0.875
July	SSD	SIMPSON MANUFACTURING CO INC	5.9%	9.5%	7	1	0.875
July	GMCR	GREEN MOUNTAIN COFFEE INC	3.9%	14.8%	7	1	0.875
July	BHI	BAKER HUGHES INC	4.0%	10.1%	13	2	0.867

July	NET	NETWORKS ASSOCIATES INC	8.3%	12.6%	6	1	0.857
July	BSY	BRITISH SKY BROADCASTING GROUP PLC	7.1%	10.2%	6	1	0.857
July	GDT	GUIDANT CORP	5.8%	8.5%	6	1	0.857
July	APU	AMERIGAS PARTNERS L P	4.7%	3.1%	6	1	0.857
July	IART	INTEGRA LIFESCIENCES HOLDINGS CORP	15.0%	19.0%	5	1	0.833
July	GNWR	GENESEE & WYOMING INC	10.2%	11.7%	5	1	0.833
July	NICE	NICE SYSTEMS LTD	9.4%	11.4%	5	1	0.833
July	NWPX	NORTHWEST PIPE CO	4.7%	6.6%	5	1	0.833
July	PY	PECHINEY SA	3.6%	4.7%	5	1	0.833
July	PCZ	PETRO CANADA	2.5%	6.9%	5	1	0.833
July	AMGN	AMGEN INC	7.8%	10.3%	9	2	0.818
July	CBSH	COMMERCE BANCSHARES INC	3.7%	4.8%	13	3	0.813
July	BKH	BLACK HILLS CORP NEW	3.6%	5.8%	13	3	0.813
July	CNI	CANADIAN NATIONAL RAILWAY CO	3.1%	7.8%	4	1	0.800
July	MTG	MGIC INVESTMENT CORP	7.5%	8.8%	8	2	0.800
July	CFCP	COASTAL FINANCIAL CORP DE	3.8%	11.5%	7	2	0.778
July	SBIT	SUMMIT BANCSHARES INC TX	3.9%	7.3%	7	2	0.778
July	CXP	CENTEX CONSTRUCTION PRODUCTS INC	11.5%	16.7%	6	2	0.750
July	BEAV	BE AEROSPACE INC	9.7%	21.0%	9	3	0.750
July	CWST	CASELLA WASTE SYSTEMS INC	5.1%	4.6%	3	1	0.750
July	MCBC	MACATAWA BANK CORP	4.9%	3.6%	3	1	0.750
July	WPC	W P CAREY & CO L L C	4.8%	5.3%	3	1	0.750
July	DOM	DOMINION RESOURCES BLACK WARRIOR TRUST	4.3%	5.4%	6	2	0.750
July	FDEF	FIRST DEFIANCE FINANCIAL CORP	4.1%	4.7%	6	2	0.750
July	CHS	CHICO S FAS INC	7.6%	23.9%	5	2	0.714

(Continued)

Table 4.8 *(Continued)*

Month	Sym.	Name	Mean Chg.	Std. Dev.	Mos. Up	Mos. Dwn	Batting Avg.
August	SMTC	SEMTECH CORP	29.3%	18.6%	6	0	1.000
August	TRMS	TRIMERIS INC	25.7%	10.2%	4	0	1.000
August	KNSY	KENSEY NASH CORP	23.0%	21.9%	6	0	1.000
August	NTAP	NETWORK APPLIANCE INC	14.1%	9.8%	5	0	1.000
August	TIER	TIER TECHNOLOGIES INC	12.4%	13.6%	4	0	1.000
August	KRON	KRONOS INC	7.1%	3.8%	10	0	1.000
August	IRETS	INVESTORS REAL ESTATE TRUST	4.1%	1.5%	4	0	1.000
August	GYMB	GYMBOREE CORP	8.5%	16.6%	8	1	0.889
August	CAKE	CHEESECAKE FACTORY INC	6.1%	9.9%	8	1	0.889
August	SCSC	SCANSOURCE INC	12.6%	16.4%	7	1	0.875
August	WIND	WIND RIVER SYSTEMS INC	6.9%	12.0%	7	1	0.875
August	NFX	NEWFIELD EXPLORATION CO DE	5.8%	12.8%	7	1	0.875
August	GDI	GARDNER DENVER INC	3.9%	10.1%	7	1	0.875
August	RMD	RESMED INC	8.8%	11.6%	6	1	0.857
August	LTUS	GARDEN FRESH RESTAURANT CORP	3.8%	8.2%	6	1	0.857
August	ALXN	ALEXION PHARMACEUTICALS INC	17.9%	28.6%	5	1	0.833
August	IDPH	IDEC PHARMACEUTICALS CORP	17.6%	21.0%	5	1	0.833
August	LXK	LEXMARK INTERNATIONAL INC	14.3%	13.0%	5	1	0.833
August	KDE	4 KIDS ENTERTAINMENT INC	12.1%	27.0%	5	1	0.833
August	CLTK	CELERITEK INC	8.9%	15.1%	5	1	0.833
August	MCRS	MICROS SYSTEMS INC	7.2%	14.9%	10	2	0.833
August	ADRX	ANDRX CORP ANDRX GROUP	5.8%	9.6%	5	1	0.833

August	PRGX	PRG SCHULTZ INTERNATIONAL INC	5.6%	14.6%	5	1	0.833
August	IMN	IMATION CORP	2.7%	5.7%	5	1	0.833
August	AACB	ALLIANCE ATLANTIS COMMUNICATIONS INC	1.5%	13.5%	5	1	0.833
August	ANS	AIRNET SYSTEMS INC	0.9%	6.6%	5	1	0.833
August	INFS	INFOCUS CORP	7.6%	15.0%	9	2	0.818
August	HAE	HAEMONETICS CORP	4.8%	5.6%	9	2	0.818
August	VHI	VALHI INC	11.0%	18.8%	13	3	0.813
August	HRB	H & R BLOCK INC	4.1%	6.1%	13	3	0.813
August	UWN	NEVADA GOLD & CASINOS INC	15.0%	8.6%	4	1	0.800
August	DAKT	DAKTRONICS INC	14.4%	21.0%	4	1	0.800
August	GILD	GILEAD SCIENCES INC	10.2%	18.8%	8	2	0.800
August	ZOLL	ZOLL MEDICAL CORP	9.9%	20.8%	8	2	0.800
August	PEAK	PEAK INTERNATIONAL LTD	9.8%	13.0%	4	1	0.800
August	XLNX	XILINX INC	3.5%	11.4%	8	2	0.800
August	BSG	BISYS GROUP INC	8.0%	7.2%	8	2	0.800
August	ADIC	ADVANCED DIGITAL INFORMATION CORP	6.2%	15.4%	4	1	0.800
August	LKFN	LAKELAND FINANCIAL CORP	5.5%	10.2%	4	1	0.800
August	RAH	RALCORP HOLDINGS INC NEW	4.9%	7.1%	4	1	0.800
August	IFC	IRWIN FINANCIAL CORP	3.8%	12.5%	8	2	0.800
August	KMP	KINDER MORGAN ENERGY PARTNERS L P	3.6%	5.2%	8	2	0.800
August	GRKA	GREKA ENERGY CORP	27.0%	34.6%	7	2	0.778
August	CGX	CONSOLIDATED GRAPHICS INC TX	13.0%	15.1%	6	2	0.750
August	HTBK	HERITAGE COMMERCE CORP	9.5%	11.5%	3	1	0.750
August	PXD	PIONEER NATURAL RESOURCES CO	3.9%	11.8%	8	3	0.727

(Continued)

197

Table 4.8 *(Continued)*

Month	Sym.	Name	Mean Chg.	Std. Dev.	Mos. Up	Mos. Dwn	Batting Avg.
September	SCHS	SCHOOL SPECIALTY INC	22.3%	16.8%	4	0	1.000
September	CRN	CORNELL COS INC	14.7%	18.5%	5	0	1.000
September	CBK	CHRISTOPHER & BANKS CORP	13.5%	7.3%	4	0	1.000
September	SRZ	SUNRISE ASSISTED LIVING INC	12.1%	10.3%	6	0	1.000
September	IMH	IMPAC MORTGAGE HOLDINGS INC	9.0%	5.8%	6	0	1.000
September	NVS	NOVARTIS LTD	6.0%	3.3%	5	0	1.000
September	RA	RECKSON ASSOCIATES REALTY CORP	5.0%	3.5%	7	0	1.000
September	MVBI	MISSISSIPPI VALLEY BANCSHARES INC	2.9%	3.3%	9	0	1.000
September	GVA	GRANITE CONSTRUCTION INC	6.9%	7.2%	11	1	0.917
September	AMHC	AMERICAN HEALTHWAYS INC	15.5%	12.6%	10	1	0.909
September	FHCC	FIRST HEALTH GROUP CORP	8.8%	12.7%	10	1	0.909
September	STE	STERIS CORP	12.9%	13.6%	9	1	0.900
September	SCHL	SCHOLASTIC CORP	11.1%	8.5%	9	1	0.900
September	ROP	ROPER INDUSTRIES INC	8.5%	11.4%	9	1	0.900
September	VICL	VICAL INC	14.2%	17.1%	8	1	0.889
September	PDCO	PATTERSON DENTAL CO	10.7%	9.9%	8	1	0.889
September	MHC	MANUFACTURED HOME COMMUNITIES INC	6.1%	7.1%	8	1	0.889
September	CIMA	CIMA LABS INC	19.8%	19.6%	7	1	0.875
September	MHR	MAGNUM HUNTER RESOURCES INC	13.6%	8.4%	7	1	0.875
September	ATVI	ACTIVISION INC	12.4%	17.8%	7	1	0.875
September	PHLY	PHILADELPHIA CONSOLIDATED HOLDING CORP	11.4%	17.0%	7	1	0.875

September	MRR	MID ATLANTIC REALTY TRUST	5.1%	5.1%	7	1	0.875
September	CGI	COMMERCE GROUP INC	4.5%	5.1%	7	1	0.875
September	SMT	SUMMIT PROPERTIES INC	3.8%	5.3%	7	1	0.875
September	MKL	MARKEL CORP NEW	5.6%	5.4%	13	2	0.867
September	DSTM	DATASTREAM SYSTEMS INC	20.1%	36.2%	6	1	0.857
September	PSUN	PACIFIC SUNWEAR OF CALIFORNIA INC	18.2%	19.1%	6	1	0.857
September	ABC	AMERISOURCEBERGEN CORP	14.5%	12.6%	6	1	0.857
September	HNCS	HNC SOFTWARE INC	14.0%	19.4%	6	1	0.857
September	GDT	GUIDANT CORP	10.6%	11.5%	6	1	0.857
September	DRI	DARDEN RESTAURANTS INC	9.3%	10.7%	6	1	0.857
September	ACXM	ACXIOM CORP	7.6%	14.8%	12	2	0.857
September	COX	COX COMMUNICATIONS INC DE	7.5%	11.4%	6	1	0.857
September	LMT	LOCKHEED MARTIN CORP	7.4%	9.3%	6	1	0.857
September	OCA	ORTHODONTIC CENTERS OF AMERICA INC	6.8%	9.3%	6	1	0.857
September	IDNX	IDENTIX INC	16.0%	24.5%	11	2	0.846
September	DVN	DEVON ENERGY CORP DE	5.1%	11.7%	11	2	0.846
September	NBIX	NEUROCRINE BIOSCIENCES INC	21.4%	23.4%	5	1	0.833
September	SBC	SBC COMMUNICATIONS INC	6.2%	7.4%	13	3	0.813
September	ESRX	EXPRESS SCRIPTS INC	8.5%	8.9%	8	2	0.800
September	OHI	OMEGA HEALTHCARE INVESTORS INC	5.2%	4.4%	8	2	0.800
September	CRY	CRYOLIFE INC	9.5%	13.1%	7	2	0.778
September	ISYS	INTEGRAL SYSTEMS INC	7.8%	9.3%	7	2	0.778
September	STU	STUDENT LOAN CORP	2.6%	6.0%	7	2	0.778
September	PSSI	PSS WORLD MEDICAL INC	8.9%	24.5%	6	2	0.750
September	COT	COTT CORP CN	12.0%	10.3%	7	3	0.700

(Continued)

Table 4.8 (Continued)

Month	Sym.	Name	Mean Chg.	Std. Dev.	Mos. Up	Mos. Dwn	Batting Avg.
October	CTSH	COGNIZANT TECHNOLOGY SOLUTIONS CORP	32.4%	20.7%	4	0	1.000
October	CLS	CELESTICA INC	25.2%	20.7%	4	0	1.000
October	UWN	NEVADA GOLD & CASINOS INC	23.4%	11.1%	4	0	1.000
October	TSM	TAIWAN SEMICONDUCTOR MFG CO LTD	23.0%	17.0%	4	0	1.000
October	MRCY	MERCURY COMPUTER SYSTEMS INC	21.5%	13.3%	4	0	1.000
October	APWR	ASTROPOWER INC	20.5%	14.3%	4	0	1.000
October	DOX	AMDOCS LTD	15.2%	12.4%	4	0	1.000
October	EDS	ELECTRONIC DATA SYSTEMS CORP	13.8%	6.3%	5	0	1.000
October	FTE	FRANCE TELECOM	13.7%	9.7%	4	0	1.000
October	CERS	CERUS CORP	13.5%	10.6%	5	0	1.000
October	MLNM	MILLENNIUM PHARMACEUTICALS INC	13.2%	19.4%	6	0	1.000
October	SCMM	SCM MICROSYSTEMS INC	13.0%	16.1%	4	0	1.000
October	CEFT	CONCORD EFS INC	12.7%	8.4%	7	0	1.000
October	OTL	OCTEL CORP	11.8%	11.9%	4	0	1.000
October	BCS	BARCLAYS PLC	11.2%	15.2%	4	0	1.000
October	LIN	LINENS N THINGS INC	9.9%	5.2%	5	0	1.000
October	ROAD	ROADWAY CORP	9.4%	10.6%	6	0	1.000
October	LLL	L 3 COMMUNICATIONS HOLDINGS INC	9.1%	4.0%	4	0	1.000
October	WDR	WADDELL & REED FINANCIAL INC	6.6%	3.3%	4	0	1.000
October	CPO	CORN PRODUCTS INTERNATIONAL INC	6.4%	4.8%	4	0	1.000
October	UNFI	UNITED NATURAL FOODS INC	6.4%	6.3%	5	0	1.000
October	STU	STUDENT LOAN CORP	6.0%	5.6%	9	0	1.000
October	RHD	R H DONNELLEY CORP	5.2%	5.8%	4	0	1.000

Month	Ticker	Company					
October	CNI	CANADIAN NATIONAL RAILWAY CO	4.3%	5.2%	5	0	1.000
October	FNFG	FIRST NIAGARA FINANCIAL GROUP INC	3.9%	5.5%	4	0	1.000
October	MTD	METTLER TOLEDO INTERNATIONAL INC	3.8%	5.9%	4	0	1.000
October	PNP	PAN PACIFIC RETAIL PROPERTIES INC	2.8%	2.8%	5	0	1.000
October	FLIR	FLIR SYSTEMS INC	5.9%	9.8%	8	1	0.889
October	AMSY	AMERICAN MANAGEMENT SYSTEMS INC	7.4%	14.1%	14	2	0.875
October	CPB	CAMPBELL SOUP CO	4.2%	8.3%	14	2	0.875
October	G	GILLETTE CO	3.6%	10.2%	14	2	0.875
October	OSBC	OLD SECOND BANCORP INC	3.2%	4.3%	7	1	0.875
October	PEP	PEPSICO INC	2.7%	7.5%	14	2	0.875
October	XPRSA	U S XPRESS ENTERPRISES INC	13.4%	16.4%	6	1	0.857
October	PMI	PMI GROUP INC	6.7%	10.5%	6	1	0.857
October	CTXS	CITRIX SYSTEMS INC	14.0%	16.3%	5	1	0.833
October	MAIR	MESABA HOLDINGS INC	11.9%	12.1%	10	2	0.833
October	STRA	STRAYER EDUCATION INC	10.8%	14.2%	5	1	0.833
October	AXA	AXA	9.8%	11.8%	5	1	0.833
October	GPS	GAP INC	8.1%	8.0%	10	2	0.833
October	CXR	COX RADIO INC	6.9%	13.8%	5	1	0.833
October	RY	ROYAL BANK OF CANADA	6.4%	7.3%	5	1	0.833
October	IPCR	IPC HOLDINGS LTD	5.4%	10.5%	5	1	0.833
October	BMY	BRISTOL MYERS SQUIBB CO	3.3%	6.3%	13	3	0.813
October	DYII	DYNACQ INTERNATIONAL INC	7.8%	8.5%	4	1	0.800
October	AC	ALLIANCE CAPITAL MANAGEMENT HOLDING L P	3.9%	7.5%	11	3	0.786
October	CFCP	COASTAL FINANCIAL CORP DE	7.7%	11.1%	7	2	0.778
October	ORLY	O REILLY AUTOMOTIVE INC	6.8%	11.0%	7	2	0.778
October	CGI	COMMERCE GROUP INC	5.1%	12.0%	6	2	0.750

(Continued)

Table 4.8 *(Continued)*

Month	Sym.	Name	Mean Chg.	Std. Dev.	Mos. Up	Mos. Dwn	Batting Avg.
November	BEBE	BEBE STORES INC	29.3%	25.8%	4	0	1.000
November	RADS	RADIANT SYSTEMS INC	23.3%	22.0%	5	0	1.000
November	HCOW	HORIZON ORGANIC HOLDING CORP	21.5%	3.3%	4	0	1.000
November	SONO	SONOSITE INC	19.9%	12.7%	4	0	1.000
November	ELBO	ELECTRONICS BOUTIQUE HOLDINGS CORP	16.0%	15.4%	4	0	1.000
November	PHCC	PRIORITY HEALTHCARE CORP	14.5%	13.7%	5	0	1.000
November	ISCA	INTERNATIONAL SPEEDWAY CORP	13.3%	9.9%	5	0	1.000
November	GDT	GUIDANT CORP	12.0%	5.4%	7	0	1.000
November	MTD	METTLER TOLEDO INTERNATIONAL INC	11.9%	10.1%	4	0	1.000
November	TIER	TIER TECHNOLOGIES INC	11.8%	8.2%	4	0	1.000
November	NCOG	NCO GROUP INC	11.5%	6.0%	5	0	1.000
November	LXK	LEXMARK INTERNATIONAL INC	10.4%	4.5%	6	0	1.000
November	FWRD	FORWARD AIR CORP	9.5%	7.5%	8	0	1.000
November	SJR	SHAW COMMUNICATIONS INC	8.5%	3.4%	4	0	1.000
November	IFS	INSIGNIA FINANCIAL GROUP INC NEW	8.2%	3.6%	4	0	1.000
November	ARE	ALEXANDRIA REAL ESTATE EQUITIES INC	8.1%	5.7%	5	0	1.000
November	GBBK	GREATER BAY BANCORP	7.6%	4.8%	6	0	1.000
November	RACN	RACING CHAMPIONS ERTL CORP	7.2%	6.2%	4	0	1.000
November	SLG	SL GREEN REALTY CORP	6.5%	5.8%	5	0	1.000
November	SSP	E W SCRIPPS CO OH	4.7%	6.7%	5	0	1.000
November	STJ	ST JUDE MEDICAL INC	4.7%	2.7%	4	0	1.000
November	RAS	RAIT INVESTMENT TRUST	4.4%	3.3%	4	0	1.000

Month	Ticker	Company Name					
November	RTN	RAYTHEON CO NEW	3.1%	3.4%	4	0	1.000
November	BUSE	FIRST BUSEY CORP	2.7%	2.6%	4	0	1.000
November	BOL	BAUSCH & LOMB INC	6.3%	8.7%	15	1	0.938
November	LLTC	LINEAR TECHNOLOGY CORP	7.7%	17.1%	9	1	0.900
November	AOT	APOGENT TECHNOLOGIES INC	5.9%	6.9%	9	1	0.900
November	POS	CATALINA MARKETING CORP	5.8%	9.1%	9	1	0.900
November	IMCL	IMCLONE SYSTEMS INC	21.9%	32.5%	7	1	0.875
November	MAPS	MAPINFO CORP	18.3%	21.4%	7	1	0.875
November	QTRN	QUINTILES TRANSNATIONAL CORP	10.6%	11.0%	7	1	0.875
November	BTH	BLYTH INC	8.0%	8.3%	7	1	0.875
November	ACAI	ATLANTIC COAST AIRLINES HOLDINGS INC	7.8%	10.7%	7	1	0.875
November	CK	CROMPTON CORP	5.5%	6.4%	14	2	0.875
November	MRK	MERCK & CO INC	5.4%	5.4%	14	2	0.875
November	CPB	CAMPBELL SOUP CO	5.0%	5.9%	14	2	0.875
November	GPK	GRAPHIC PACKAGING INTERNATIONAL CORP	4.9%	10.4%	7	1	0.875
November	EMN	EASTMAN CHEMICAL CO	2.7%	7.8%	7	1	0.875
November	OSBC	OLD SECOND BANCORP INC	1.3%	3.8%	7	1	0.875
November	HRH	HILB ROGAL & HAMILTON CO	5.8%	7.3%	13	2	0.867
November	DST	DST SYSTEMS INC	8.6%	6.5%	5	1	0.833
November	CLTK	CELERITEK INC	7.9%	8.5%	5	1	0.833
November	PROV	PROVIDENT FINANCIAL HOLDINGS INC	5.9%	6.4%	5	1	0.833
November	RDA	READER S DIGEST ASSOCIATION INC	4.9%	8.6%	10	2	0.833
November	PHSB	PHSB FINANCIAL CORP	2.3%	2.7%	4	1	0.800
November	ATR	APTARGROUP INC	5.2%	7.3%	7	2	0.778
November	EQY	EQUITY ONE INC	3.8%	2.7%	3	1	0.750

(Continued)

Table 4.8 *(Continued)*

Month	Sym.	Name	Mean Chg.	Std. Dev.	Mos. Up	Mos. Dwn	Batting Avg.
December	GLGC	GENE LOGIC INC	76.1%	126.0%	5	0	1.000
December	SRDX	SURMODICS INC	43.3%	22.4%	4	0	1.000
December	CWST	CASELLA WASTE SYSTEMS INC	38.2%	50.4%	5	0	1.000
December	ICPT	INTERCEPT INC GA	34.2%	26.7%	4	0	1.000
December	NTAP	NETWORK APPLIANCE INC	33.6%	12.8%	6	0	1.000
December	IHI	INFORMATION HOLDINGS INC	32.5%	18.2%	4	0	1.000
December	KG	KING PHARMACEUTICALS INC	26.7%	32.0%	4	0	1.000
December	ISSX	INTERNET SECURITY SYSTEMS INC DE	26.5%	27.2%	4	0	1.000
December	CSGP	COSTAR GROUP INC	22.5%	12.4%	4	0	1.000
December	BSTE	BIOSITE INC	19.4%	14.9%	5	0	1.000
December	CPS	CHOICEPOINT INC	19.3%	9.5%	5	0	1.000
December	ADVP	ADVANCEPCS	18.5%	18.2%	6	0	1.000
December	OTEX	OPEN TEXT CORP	17.8%	12.9%	6	0	1.000
December	PSTI	PER SE TECHNOLOGIES INC	17.7%	9.0%	11	0	1.000
December	GNSS	GENESIS MICROCHIP INC	17.2%	11.6%	4	0	1.000
December	BFT	BALLY TOTAL FITNESS HOLDING CORP	17.2%	17.9%	6	0	1.000
December	AMG	AFFILIATED MANAGERS GROUP INC	16.1%	9.5%	5	0	1.000
December	LMC..B	LIBERTY MEDIA CORP NEW	15.5%	14.6%	7	0	1.000
December	MTA	HUNGARIAN TELECOMMUNICATIONS CO LTD	15.0%	10.3%	5	0	1.000
December	ECLP	ECLIPSYS CORP	14.8%	17.0%	4	0	1.000
December	ICLR	ICON PLC	14.7%	7.5%	4	0	1.000
December	FBR	FRIEDMAN BILLINGS RAMSEY GROUP INC	14.6%	13.1%	4	0	1.000
December	GETY	GETTY IMAGES INC	14.5%	7.1%	4	0	1.000

Month	Ticker	Company					
December	JDAS	JDA SOFTWARE GROUP INC	14.4%	11.2%	6	0	1.000
December	SCM	SWISSCOM AG	13.4%	10.7%	4	0	1.000
December	TP	TPG NV	12.8%	12.4%	4	0	1.000
December	VCI	VALASSIS COMMUNICATIONS INC	11.9%	6.6%	10	0	1.000
December	KEYS	KEYSTONE AUTOMOTIVE INDUSTRIES INC	11.5%	8.8%	6	0	1.000
December	FCEL	FUELCELL ENERGY INC	11.3%	7.9%	5	0	1.000
December	CVG	CONVERGYS CORP	11.1%	4.7%	4	0	1.000
December	CECO	CAREER EDUCATION CORP	11.1%	3.9%	4	0	1.000
December	LFIN	LOCAL FINANCIAL CORP NEW	10.9%	10.1%	4	0	1.000
December	CXP	CENTEX CONSTRUCTION PRODUCTS INC	10.7%	7.8%	8	0	1.000
December	ABV	COMPANHIA DE BEBIDAS DAS AMERICAS	10.7%	7.5%	5	0	1.000
December	V	VIVENDI UNIVERSAL SA	10.2%	4.7%	4	0	1.000
December	PLT	PLANTRONICS INC DE	9.9%	7.9%	8	0	1.000
December	CPO	CORN PRODUCTS INTERNATIONAL INC	9.7%	7.5%	4	0	1.000
December	IFIN	INVESTORS FINANCIAL SERVICES CORP	8.7%	10.5%	7	0	1.000
December	SUR	CNA SURETY CORP	8.1%	8.5%	5	0	1.000
December	AXTI	AXT INC	7.9%	4.8%	4	0	1.000
December	HERB	HERBALIFE INTERNATIONAL INC	7.9%	6.7%	4	0	1.000
December	FII	FEDERATED INVESTORS INC	7.8%	3.9%	4	0	1.000
December	DSWT	DURASWITCH INDUSTRIES INC	7.8%	10.3%	4	0	1.000
December	USON	US ONCOLOGY INC	22.7%	13.6%	6	1	0.857
December	MBRS	MEMBERWORKS INC	18.0%	16.0%	5	1	0.833
December	RADS	RADIANT SYSTEMS INC	24.9%	31.5%	4	1	0.800
December	MVSN	MACROVISION CORP	23.6%	31.6%	4	1	0.800
December	SWBT	SOUTHWEST BANCORPORATION OF TEXAS INC	8.1%	8.9%	4	1	0.800
December	HEI.A	HEICO CORP	17.9%	20.2%	3	1	0.750
December	FLYR	NAVIGANT INTERNATIONAL INC	16.1%	14.6%	3	1	0.750

Source: Camelback Research Alliance.

205

Table 4.9 HiMARQ Shorts—Best Short Candidates Historically by Month*

Month	Sym.	Name	Mean Chg.	Std. Dev.	Mos. Up	Mos. Dwn	Batting Avg.
January	CWST	CASELLA WASTE SYSTEMS INC	-18.4%	10.0%	0	4	0.000
January	IBA	BACHOCO INDUSTRIES	-18.0%	4.3%	0	4	0.000
January	TSA	SPORTS AUTHORITY INC	-17.0%	4.7%	0	5	0.000
January	MOVI	MOVIE GALLERY INC	-14.1%	11.4%	0	4	0.000
January	BRLI	BIO REFERENCE LABORATORIES INC	-14.1%	15.4%	0	4	0.000
January	CPS	CHOICEPOINT INC	-12.9%	5.6%	0	4	0.000
January	UWN	NEVADA GOLD & CASINOS INC	-11.4%	5.5%	0	4	0.000
January	AMH	AMERUS GROUP CO	-10.3%	2.4%	0	4	0.000
January	RSLN	ROSLYN BANCORP INC	-10.2%	1.8%	0	4	0.000
January	IDR	INTRAWEST CORP	-8.2%	10.6%	0	4	0.000
January	CGI	COMMERCE GROUP INC	-8.0%	7.7%	0	8	0.000
January	MOSS	MOSSIMO INC	-8.0%	9.4%	0	4	0.000
January	RAH	RALCORP HOLDINGS INC NEW	-7.6%	11.7%	0	4	0.000
January	KRC	KILROY REALTY CORP	-6.5%	5.1%	0	4	0.000
January	BF	BASF AG	-6.5%	4.5%	0	5	0.000
January	IRM	IRON MOUNTAIN INC PA	-6.4%	5.6%	0	5	0.000
January	CAM	COOPER CAMERON CORP	-6.4%	4.7%	0	6	0.000
January	ERIE	ERIE INDEMNITY CO	-6.1%	4.4%	0	6	0.000
January	HSIC	HENRY SCHEIN INC	-5.8%	3.0%	0	6	0.000
January	NAT	NORDIC AMERICAN TANKER SHIPPING LTD	-5.4%	2.9%	0	4	0.000
January	ATR	APTARGROUP INC	-5.1%	3.4%	0	8	0.000
January	CEM	CHEMFIRST INC	-4.3%	3.1%	0	5	0.000

*Constraints: At start of historical month, split-adjusted price greater than $2. Also, minimum price in June 2002 greater than $5 and average daily volume greater than 25,000.

January	TESOF	TESCO CORP	-4.3%	4.6%	0	5	0.000
January	BNN	BRASCAN CORP	-3.7%	1.8%	0	4	0.000
January	FR	FIRST INDUSTRIAL REALTY TRUST INC	-2.7%	2.0%	0	7	0.000
January	FNBP	FNB CORP VA	-2.0%	0.7%	0	4	0.000
January	OCR	OMNICARE INC	-6.3%	5.4%	1	11	0.083
January	ACF	AMERICREDIT CORP	-7.2%	13.7%	1	10	0.091
January	CKH	SEACOR SMIT INC	-5.4%	6.3%	1	8	0.111
January	BBOX	BLACK BOX CORP	-3.0%	13.8%	1	8	0.111
January	NBTB	NBT BANCORP INC	-2.0%	8.1%	1	8	0.111
January	BKST	BROOKSTONE INC	-8.4%	12.6%	1	7	0.125
January	TLB	TALBOTS INC	-8.1%	11.0%	1	7	0.125
January	VCI	VALASSIS COMMUNICATIONS INC	-7.6%	8.1%	1	7	0.125
January	MEDI	MEDIMMUNE INC	-7.3%	8.8%	1	7	0.125
January	CTEC	CHOLESTECH CORP	-7.0%	7.1%	1	7	0.125
January	GYMB	GYMBOREE CORP	-6.5%	14.2%	1	7	0.125
January	RGA	REINSURANCE GROUP OF AMERICA INC	-6.2%	6.7%	1	7	0.125
January	CPT	CAMDEN PROPERTY TRUST	-3.5%	2.2%	1	7	0.125
January	CRE	CARRAMERICA REALTY CORP	-2.8%	3.6%	1	7	0.125
January	CPG	CHELSEA PROPERTY GROUP INC	-2.5%	4.0%	1	7	0.125
January	SUI	SUN COMMUNITIES INC	-2.2%	3.5%	1	7	0.125
January	MEDW	MEDIWARE INFORMATION SYSTEMS INC	-14.7%	15.4%	1	6	0.143
January	HNP	HUANENG POWER INTERNATIONAL INC	-8.9%	12.3%	1	6	0.143
January	SRZ	SUNRISE ASSISTED LIVING INC	-10.5%	8.9%	1	4	0.200
January	ADVP	ADVANCEPCS	-8.6%	5.9%	1	4	0.200
January	HH	HOOPER HOLMES INC	-6.6%	10.5%	1	4	0.200
January	CDIS	CAL DIVE INTERNATIONAL INC	-9.4%	11.4%	1	3	0.250

(Continued)

Table 4.9 *(Continued)*

Month	Sym.	Name	Mean Chg.	Std. Dev.	Mos. Up	Mos. Dwn	Batting Avg.
February	CWST	CASELLA WASTE SYSTEMS INC	-23.0%	23.0%	0	4	0.000
February	SYKE	SYKES ENTERPRISES INC	-19.5%	11.5%	0	5	0.000
February	ETT	ELDERTRUST	-14.9%	13.5%	0	4	0.000
February	WSTC	WEST CORP	-13.8%	10.7%	0	5	0.000
February	LCRY	LECROY CORP	-12.9%	13.1%	0	6	0.000
February	MEDW	MEDIWARE INFORMATION SYSTEMS INC	-11.7%	10.1%	0	6	0.000
February	KEP	KOREA ELECTRIC POWER CORP	-9.1%	7.4%	0	7	0.000
February	KEYS	KEYSTONE AUTOMOTIVE INDUSTRIES INC	-7.1%	3.0%	0	5	0.000
February	WXH	WINSTON HOTELS INC	-6.2%	6.8%	0	4	0.000
February	IBA	BACHOCO INDUSTRIES	-5.8%	6.5%	0	4	0.000
February	NTT	NIPPON TELEGRAPH & TELEPHONE CORP	-4.4%	3.4%	0	7	0.000
February	WRP	WELLSFORD REAL PROPERTIES INC	-3.9%	2.4%	0	4	0.000
February	HIW	HIGHWOODS PROPERTIES INC	-3.0%	2.9%	0	7	0.000
February	SCHL	SCHOLASTIC CORP	-9.5%	15.9%	1	8	0.111
February	MRNT	MERANT PLC	-7.1%	10.5%	1	8	0.111
February	CSAR	CARAUSTAR INDUSTRIES INC	-7.0%	10.9%	1	8	0.111
February	ARA	ARACRUZ CELULOSE SA	-5.9%	7.1%	1	8	0.111
February	ULTE	ULTIMATE ELECTRONICS INC	-10.7%	10.1%	1	7	0.125
February	SCHN	SCHNITZER STEEL INDUSTRIES INC	-5.8%	9.3%	1	7	0.125
February	ROCK	GIBRALTAR STEEL CORP	-2.4%	8.1%	1	7	0.125
February	BRG	BG GROUP PLC	-3.5%	7.4%	2	13	0.133

Month	Ticker	Company					
February	UHAL	AMERCO	-12.4%	13.4%	1	6	0.143
February	GBX	GREENBRIER COS INC	-6.4%	8.5%	1	6	0.143
February	RYN	RAYONIER INC	-3.8%	4.0%	1	6	0.143
February	O	REALTY INCOME CORP	-3.4%	4.8%	1	6	0.143
February	CLI	MACK CALI REALTY CORP	-2.6%	3.7%	1	6	0.143
February	AVB	AVALONBAY COMMUNITIES INC	-0.9%	1.2%	1	6	0.143
February	IDXC	IDX SYSTEMS CORP	-10.8%	18.7%	1	5	0.167
February	LTRE	LEARNING TREE INTERNATIONAL INC	-10.3%	11.5%	1	5	0.167
February	USON	US ONCOLOGY INC	-8.7%	19.0%	1	5	0.167
February	HWD	HOLLYWOOD CASINO CORP	-8.4%	10.3%	1	5	0.167
February	TQNT	TRIQUINT SEMICONDUCTOR INC	-7.2%	38.1%	1	5	0.167
February	APU	AMERIGAS PARTNERS L P	-4.3%	4.6%	1	5	0.167
February	CMIN	COMMONWEALTH INDUSTRIES INC DE	-3.0%	4.2%	1	5	0.167
February	HTCO	HICKORY TECH CORP	-2.4%	3.8%	1	5	0.167
February	RA	RECKSON ASSOCIATES REALTY CORP	-2.4%	3.1%	1	5	0.167
February	MYGN	MYRIAD GENETICS INC	11.8%	60.3%	1	5	0.167
February	BEAV	BE AEROSPACE INC	-3.0%	12.3%	2	9	0.182
February	LKFN	LAKELAND FINANCIAL CORP	-24.1%	43.0%	1	4	0.200
February	CSR	CREDIT SUISSE GROUP	-22.5%	44.8%	1	4	0.200
February	CURE	CURATIVE HEALTH SERVICES INC	-15.6%	18.8%	2	8	0.200
February	BRLI	BIO REFERENCE LABORATORES INC	-13.1%	11.3%	1	4	0.200
February	SLFI	STERLING FINANCIAL CORP	-5.8%	6.4%	1	4	0.200
February	FAB	FIRSTFED AMERICA BANCORP INC	-2.2%	2.2%	1	4	0.200
February	CVU	CPI AEROSTRUCTURES INC	-13.3%	17.7%	2	7	0.222
February	PGE	PRIME GROUP REALTY TRUST	-2.6%	2.7%	1	3	0.250
February	UHCO	UNIVERSAL AMERICAN FINANCIAL CORP	-5.0%	8.0%	3	7	0.300

(Continued)

Table 4.9 (*Continued*)

Month	Sym.	Name	Mean Chg.	Std. Dev.	Mos. Up	Mos. Dwn	Batting Avg.
March	GLGC	GENE LOGIC INC	-31.4%	24.4%	0	4	0.000
March	CRXA	CORIXA CORP	-29.5%	23.4%	0	4	0.000
March	ARQL	ARQULE INC	-24.1%	21.0%	0	5	0.000
March	PEGA	PEGASYSTEMS INC	-23.6%	16.4%	0	5	0.000
March	VWKS	VITALWORKS INC	-23.1%	20.1%	0	4	0.000
March	HYC	HYPERCOM CORP	-21.4%	15.7%	0	4	0.000
March	BREL	BIORELIANCE CORP	-20.2%	10.7%	0	4	0.000
March	VICL	VICAL INC	-20.0%	15.5%	0	8	0.000
March	TRMS	TRIMERIS INC	-19.9%	16.5%	0	4	0.000
March	NPSP	NPS PHARMACEUTICALS INC	-19.5%	17.3%	0	7	0.000
March	RMBS	RAMBUS INC	-18.0%	19.3%	0	4	0.000
March	AVGN	AVIGEN INC	-17.7%	14.6%	0	5	0.000
March	CXW	CORRECTIONS CORP OF AMERICA MD	-17.6%	11.4%	0	4	0.000
March	OSIS	OSI SYSTEMS INC	-17.3%	12.4%	0	4	0.000
March	SSYS	STRATASYS INC	-15.2%	8.5%	0	4	0.000
March	NBIX	NEUROCRINE BIOSCIENCES INC	-14.8%	13.3%	0	5	0.000
March	GLFD	GUILFORD PHARMACEUTICALS INC	-13.9%	10.8%	0	7	0.000
March	MEDC	MED DESIGN CORP	-13.3%	8.6%	0	6	0.000
March	AVCT	AVOCENT CORP	-13.0%	5.1%	0	5	0.000
March	NICE	NICE SYSTEMS LTD	-11.8%	9.9%	0	6	0.000
March	SCSC	SCANSOURCE INC	-10.3%	7.1%	0	7	0.000
March	JDEC	J D EDWARDS & CO	-10.2%	9.4%	0	4	0.000
March	HHLF	HURRICANE HYDROCARBONS LTD	-6.3%	2.3%	0	4	0.000

March	EAGL	EGL INC	-5.9%	6.4%	0	6	0.000
March	CBKN	CAPITAL BANK CORP	-5.8%	3.8%	0	4	0.000
March	SLGN	SILGAN HOLDINGS INC	-5.0%	6.1%	0	5	0.000
March	WPC	W P CAREY & CO L L C	-3.3%	0.9%	0	4	0.000
March	PRA	PROASSURANCE CORP	-5.6%	6.1%	1	9	0.100
March	AMLN	AMYLIN PHARMACEUTICALS INC	-19.7%	14.5%	1	8	0.111
March	PDLI	PROTEIN DESIGN LABS INC	-18.3%	24.0%	1	8	0.111
March	CEGE	CELL GENESYS INC	-13.3%	19.1%	1	8	0.111
March	RDB	READER S DIGEST ASSOCIATION INC	-5.0%	6.5%	1	8	0.111
March	MEDX	MEDAREX INC	-19.4%	24.0%	1	7	0.125
March	TFS	THREE FIVE SYSTEMS INC	-17.0%	12.0%	1	7	0.125
March	FSTW	FIRSTWAVE TECHNOLOGIES INC	-16.4%	19.0%	1	7	0.125
March	NMRX	NUMEREX CORP PA	-11.7%	10.6%	1	7	0.125
March	HGSI	HUMAN GENOME SCIENCES INC	-10.4%	23.6%	1	7	0.125
March	CTEC	CHOLESTECH CORP	-9.4%	13.3%	1	7	0.125
March	BNT	BENTLEY PHARMACEUTICALS INC	-6.7%	13.1%	2	11	0.154
March	ALXN	ALEXION PHARMACEUTICALS INC	-17.6%	15.3%	1	5	0.167
March	ZICA	ZI CORP	-15.8%	18.8%	1	5	0.167
March	KROL	KROLL INC	-10.6%	11.1%	1	4	0.200
March	WEDC	WHITE ELECTRONIC DESIGNS CORP	-5.0%	13.2%	2	8	0.200
March	CAC	CAMDEN NATIONAL CORP	-5.7%	6.0%	1	4	0.200
March	GNTA	GENTA INC	-15.2%	17.3%	2	7	0.222
March	PGNX	PROGENICS PHARMACEUTICALS INC	-20.5%	16.7%	1	3	0.250
March	CLRO	CLEARONE COMMUNICATIONS INC	-12.0%	11.6%	1	3	0.250
March	BED	BEDFORD PROPERTY INVESTORS INC	-2.8%	3.8%	4	12	0.250
March	DHOM	DOMINION HOMES INC	-9.8%	9.2%	2	5	0.286
March	MBHI	MIDWEST BANC HOLDINGS INC	-3.9%	4.9%	2	2	0.500

(Continued)

211

Table 4.9 *(Continued)*

Month	Sym.	Name	Mean Chg.	Std. Dev.	Mos. Up	Mos. Dwn	Batting Avg.
April	HBEK	HUMBOLDT BANCORP	-33.2%	45.2%	0	4	0.000
April	KVHI	KVH INDUSTRIES INC	-16.7%	10.7%	0	4	0.000
April	TKTX	TRANSKARYOTIC THERAPIES INC	-15.9%	17.9%	0	5	0.000
April	CCRD	CONCORD COMMUNICATIONS INC	-15.6%	7.6%	0	4	0.000
April	EEFT	EURONET WORLDWIDE INC	-10.1%	8.9%	0	5	0.000
April	VIBC	VIB CORP	-6.5%	4.2%	0	5	0.000
April	REMX	REMEDYTEMP INC	-6.1%	4.2%	0	5	0.000
April	ACMR	A C MOORE ARTS & CRAFTS INC	-4.7%	6.9%	0	4	0.000
April	TCR	CORNERSTONE REALTY INCOME TRUST INC	-4.4%	2.4%	0	4	0.000
April	CIV_A	CONECTIV INC	-2.5%	1.1%	0	4	0.000
April	APSG	APPLIED SIGNAL TECHNOLOGY INC	-12.6%	11.5%	1	8	0.111
April	FIMG	FISCHER IMAGING CORP	-8.5%	14.5%	1	8	0.111
April	CIMA	CIMA LABS INC	-12.2%	7.6%	1	6	0.143
April	FCEL	FUELCELL ENERGY INC	-12.3%	25.7%	1	5	0.167
April	SNAP	SYNAPTIC PHARMACEUTICAL CORP	-9.1%	14.0%	1	5	0.167
April	IFNY	INFINITY INC	-7.9%	10.0%	1	5	0.167
April	RNR	RENAISSANCERE HOLDINGS LTD	-5.7%	4.7%	1	5	0.167
April	RE	EVEREST RE GROUP LTD	-4.0%	3.6%	1	5	0.167
April	AACB	ALLIANCE ATLANTIS COMMUNICATIONS INC	-1.3%	8.6%	1	5	0.167
April	CLTK	CELERITEK INC	-0.2%	14.1%	1	5	0.167
April	MATR	MATRIA HEALTHCARE INC	4.1%	32.9%	1	5	0.167
April	TMI	TEAM INC	-5.0%	14.1%	2	9	0.182
April	SLE	SARA LEE CORP	-4.2%	6.2%	3	13	0.188
April	FRX	FOREST LABORATORIES INC	-4.1%	6.8%	3	13	0.188

April	GIS	GENERAL MILLS INC	-3.7%	4.6%	3	13	0.188
April	OSTE	OSTEOTECH INC	-12.9%	16.7%	2	8	0.200
April	NMTI	NMT MEDICAL INC	-12.6%	12.8%	1	4	0.200
April	TXCO	EXPLORATION CO OF DELAWARE INC	-10.1%	24.2%	3	12	0.200
April	ARQL	ARQULE INC	-9.9%	10.3%	1	4	0.200
April	PEGA	PEGASYSTEMS INC	-9.6%	11.2%	1	4	0.200
April	SEPR	SEPRACOR INC	-8.1%	15.6%	2	8	0.200
April	PRGS	PROGRESS SOFTWARE CORP	-7.5%	13.8%	2	8	0.200
April	NWRE	NEOWARE SYSTEMS INC	-7.2%	40.0%	1	4	0.200
April	SPRI	SPORTS RESORTS INTERNATIONAL INC	-7.1%	26.3%	1	4	0.200
April	CVD	COVANCE INC	-6.3%	13.5%	1	4	0.200
April	INFM	INFINIUM SOFTWARE INC	-5.9%	10.2%	1	4	0.200
April	NBIX	NEUROCRINE BIOSCIENCES INC	-5.8%	14.0%	1	4	0.200
April	SRCL	STERICYCLE INC	-5.2%	9.0%	1	4	0.200
April	ITY	IMPERIAL TOBACCO GROUP PLC	-4.6%	6.7%	1	4	0.200
April	PSAI	PEDIATRIC SERVICES OF AMERICA INC	-4.6%	6.2%	1	4	0.200
April	GNWR	GENESEE & WYOMING INC	-4.3%	5.1%	1	4	0.200
April	SCHL	SCHOLASTIC CORP	-3.8%	9.4%	2	8	0.200
April	CHKR	CHECKERS DRIVE IN RESTAURANTS INC	-3.5%	25.6%	2	8	0.200
April	WRLD	WORLD ACCEPTANCE CORP	-3.4%	7.0%	2	8	0.200
April	RAH	RALCORP HOLDINGS INC NEW	-3.4%	2.0%	1	4	0.200
April	NHHC	NATIONAL HOME HEALTH CARE CORP	-9.5%	8.6%	3	10	0.231
April	CNXS	CNS INC	-5.8%	9.0%	2	6	0.250
April	OCAS	OHIO CASUALTY CORP	-4.5%	6.0%	4	12	0.250
April	NEV	NUEVO ENERGY CO	-3.4%	9.6%	3	8	0.273
April	RPT	RAMCO GERSHENSON PROPERTIES TRUST	-2.4%	3.8%	4	9	0.308

(Continued)

Table 4.9 (Continued)

Month	Sym.	Name	Mean Chg.	Std. Dev.	Mos. Up	Mos. Dwn	Batting Avg.
May	PSO	PEARSON PLC	−34.9%	43.7%	0	4	0.000
May	UPM	UPM KYMMENE CORP	−26.3%	49.1%	0	4	0.000
May	DCLK	DOUBLECLICK INC	−23.6%	19.0%	0	4	0.000
May	LVLT	LEVEL 3 COMMUNICATIONS INC	−18.3%	4.3%	0	4	0.000
May	ARMHY	ARM HOLDINGS PLC	−14.2%	8.0%	0	4	0.000
May	SCMM	SCM MICROSYSTEMS INC	−13.9%	2.7%	0	4	0.000
May	NTBK	NET BANK INC	−13.3%	12.9%	0	4	0.000
May	AMZN	AMAZON COM INC	−12.9%	13.7%	0	4	0.000
May	NTAP	NETWORK APPLIANCE INC	−11.9%	8.3%	0	4	0.000
May	CSTR	COINSTAR INC	−11.5%	4.7%	0	4	0.000
May	MANH	MANHATTAN ASSOCIATES INC	−11.4%	6.4%	0	4	0.000
May	IBA	BACHOCO INDUSTRIES	−11.3%	6.1%	0	4	0.000
May	MRCY	MERCURY COMPUTER SYSTEMS INC	−11.1%	9.0%	0	4	0.000
May	SNIC	SONIC SOLUTIONS	−10.9%	10.8%	0	7	0.000
May	YHOO	YAHOO INC	−10.0%	4.4%	0	6	0.000
May	CHL	CHINA MOBILE HONG KONG LTD	−8.5%	4.0%	0	4	0.000
May	FCGI	FIRST CONSULTING GROUP INC	−8.2%	4.5%	0	4	0.000
May	SPOT	PANAMSAT CORP NEW	−7.1%	4.6%	0	6	0.000
May	CCRD	CONCORD COMMUNICATIONS INC	−7.0%	7.7%	0	4	0.000
May	CHH	CHOICE HOTELS INTERNATIONAL INC NEW	−7.0%	7.5%	0	4	0.000
May	BCS	BARCLAYS PLC	−5.8%	2.8%	0	4	0.000
May	RGX	RADIOLOGIX INC	−5.2%	2.1%	0	4	0.000
May	MTA	HUNGARIAN TELECOMMUNICATIONS CO LTD	−4.7%	3.1%	0	4	0.000
May	ETT	ELDERTRUST	−4.5%	3.6%	0	4	0.000
May	WEDC	WHITE ELECTRONIC DESIGNS CORP	−12.3%	14.4%	1	7	0.125

May	ALTR	ALTERA CORP	-9.5%	10.2%	1	7	0.125
May	ROCK	GIBRALTAR STEEL CORP	-6.3%	10.1%	1	7	0.125
May	ARXX	AEROFLEX INC	-7.0%	8.3%	1	6	0.143
May	LION	FIDELITY NATIONAL CORP GA	-6.0%	5.8%	1	6	0.143
May	ESI	ITT EDUCATIONAL SERVICES INC	-3.3%	5.0%	1	6	0.143
May	NTT	NIPPON TELEGRAPH & TELEPHONE CORP	-2.9%	10.9%	1	6	0.143
May	OTEX	OPEN TEXT CORP	-14.9%	13.6%	1	5	0.167
May	ZICA	ZI CORP	-12.7%	15.6%	1	5	0.167
May	DCTM	DOCUMENTUM INC	-8.2%	8.0%	1	5	0.167
May	AEOS	AMERICAN EAGLE OUTFITTERS INC NEW	-6.7%	13.5%	1	5	0.167
May	AEIS	ADVANCED ENERGY INDUSTRIES INC	-6.5%	26.6%	1	5	0.167
May	MVL	MARVEL ENTERPRISES INC	-5.8%	6.8%	1	5	0.167
May	PCU	SOUTHERN PERU COPPER COEP	-5.0%	8.5%	1	5	0.167
May	ISIG	INSIGNIA SYSTEMS INC	-5.0%	14.5%	1	5	0.167
May	DO	DIAMOND OFFSHORE DRILLING INC	-4.7%	9.4%	1	5	0.167
May	PHTN	PHOTON DYNAMICS INC	-3.7%	21.1%	1	5	0.167
May	NEOL	NEOPHARM INC	-3.7%	9.2%	1	5	0.167
May	ZRAN	ZORAN CORP	-3.6%	32.7%	1	5	0.167
May	DORL	DORAL FINANCIAL CORP	-4.6%	7.9%	2	7	0.222
May	FBP	FIRST BANCORP PR	-4.2%	7.4%	2	7	0.222
May	SSFT	SCANSOFT INC	-16.5%	12.9%	1	3	0.250
May	ABV	COMPANHIA DE BEBIDAS DAS AMERICAS	-7.8%	5.6%	1	3	0.250
May	TCT	TOWN & COUNTRY TRUST	-3.2%	2.7%	2	6	0.250
May	IIVI	II VI INC	-5.0%	7.3%	2	5	0.286
May	FMBN	F&M BANCORP	-3.0%	5.0%	3	7	0.300
May	VESC	VESTCOM INTERNATIONAL INC	-14.7%	17.9%	0	4	0.000

(Continued)

Table 4.9 (Continued)

Month	Sym.	Name	Mean Chg.	Std. Dev.	Mos. Up	Mos. Dwn	Batting Avg.
June	DOCC	DOCUCORP INTERNATIONAL INC	-12.7%	6.7%	0	4	0.000
June	SNIC	SONIC SOLUTIONS	-12.0%	9.7%	0	7	0.000
June	MDS	MIDAS INC	-11.5%	9.5%	0	4	0.000
June	CCJ	CAMECO CORP	-8.7%	6.1%	0	6	0.000
June	AKO_B	ANDINA BOTTLING CO INC	-8.1%	2.1%	0	5	0.000
June	OTL	OCTEL CORP	-7.2%	4.3%	0	4	0.000
June	WPC	W P CAREY & CO L L C	-5.3%	4.8%	0	4	0.000
June	MAR	MARRIOTT INTERNATIONAL INC NEW	-4.4%	4.9%	0	4	0.000
June	MCBC	MACATAWA BANK CORP	-3.6%	1.5%	0	4	0.000
June	PGE	PRIME GROUP REALTY TRUST	-3.6%	6.2%	0	4	0.000
June	DECC	D & E COMMUNICATIONS INC	-2.2%	2.4%	0	5	0.000
June	SUN	SUNOCO INC	-6.0%	5.1%	1	15	0.063
June	AHC	AMERADA HESS CORP	-4.2%	3.1%	1	15	0.063
June	MVK	MAVERICK TUBE CORP	-9.0%	14.2%	1	10	0.091
June	FCH	FELCOR LODGING TRUST INC	-3.5%	3.9%	1	6	0.143
June	BR	BURLINGTON RESOURCES INC	-4.1%	8.1%	2	11	0.154
June	PTEK	PTEK HOLDINGS INC	-21.7%	26.0%	1	5	0.167
June	CAM	COOPER CAMERON CORP	-6.9%	9.4%	1	5	0.167
June	MLNM	MILLENNIUM PHARMACEUTICALS INC	-5.8%	20.5%	1	5	0.167
June	PAL	NORTH AMERICAN PALLADIUM LTD	-5.0%	14.7%	1	5	0.167
June	CMH	CLAYTON HOMES INC	-4.9%	6.9%	2	10	0.167

216

June	PCU	SOUTHERN PERU COPPER CORP	−2.6%	7.9%	1	5	0.167
June	ALXN	ALEXION PHARMACEUTICALS INC	8.1%	41.7%	1	5	0.167
June	BJS	BJ SERVICES CO	−8.0%	9.7%	2	9	0.182
June	AMD	ADVANCED MICRO DEVICES INC	−10.6%	13.6%	3	13	0.188
June	TEX	TEREX CORP	−5.9%	11.0%	3	13	0.188
June	P	PHILLIPS PETROLEUM CO	−5.3%	4.5%	3	13	0.188
June	NSH	NASHUA CORP	−4.4%	9.3%	3	13	0.188
June	MRO	MARATHON OIL CORP	−3.9%	5.2%	3	13	0.188
June	TKR	TIMKEN CO	−3.9%	6.8%	3	13	0.188
June	OXY	OCCIDENTAL PETROLEUM CORP	−3.1%	5.3%	3	13	0.188
June	OPTN	OPTION CARE INC	−6.3%	21.1%	2	8	0.200
June	ISCA	INTERNATIONAL SPEEDWAY CORP	−2.7%	1.6%	1	4	0.200
June	SHRP	SHARPER IMAGE CORP	−6.3%	8.4%	3	11	0.214
June	RNT	AARON RENTS INC	−3.4%	6.6%	2	7	0.222
June	MERCS	MERCER INTERNATIONAL INC	−4.7%	11.8%	3	10	0.231
June	TENT	TOTAL ENTERTAINMENT RESTAURANT CORP	−10.3%	9.5%	1	3	0.250
June	BONZ	INTERPORE INTERNATIONAL	−7.8%	17.3%	2	6	0.250
June	JOSB	JOS A BANK CLOTHIERS INC	−7.8%	9.2%	2	6	0.250
June	BREL	BIORELIANCE CORP	−6.6%	10.3%	1	3	0.250
June	MAG	MAGNETEK INC	−4.7%	4.2%	3	9	0.250
June	CMM	CRIIMI MAE INC	−3.9%	4.2%	3	9	0.250
June	PPP	POGO PRODUCING CO	−3.4%	5.8%	4	12	0.250
June	GMCR	GREEN MOUNTAIN COFFEE INC	−3.2%	9.1%	2	6	0.250
June	VANS	VANS INC	−4.7%	11.6%	3	7	0.300
June	PDE	PRIDE INTERNATIONAL INC DE	−8.1%	11.7%	4	9	0.308

(Continued)

Table 4.9 (Continued)

Month	Sym.	Name	Mean Chg.	Std. Dev.	Mos. Up	Mos. Dwn	Batting Avg.
July	CRXA	CORIXA CORP	−22.8%	5.4%	0	4	0.000
July	NWRE	NEOWARE SYSTEMS INC	−20.5%	13.9%	0	6	0.000
July	NTBK	NET BANK INC	−18.4%	17.7%	0	4	0.000
July	ZICA	ZI CORP	−18.0%	10.3%	0	7	0.000
July	NUS	NU SKIN ENTERPRISES INC	−16.9%	12.4%	0	5	0.000
July	DRQ	DRIL QUIP INC	−16.8%	13.5%	0	4	0.000
July	ARTI	ARTISAN COMPONENTS INC	−16.2%	7.7%	0	4	0.000
July	NPSI	NORTH PITTSBURGH SYSTEMS INC	−14.9%	5.2%	0	5	0.000
July	CPTS	CONCEPTUS INC	−14.1%	21.0%	0	4	0.000
July	CSGS	CSG SYSTEMS INTERNATIONAL INC	−13.6%	9.0%	0	6	0.000
July	JDEC	J D EDWARDS & CO	−13.5%	4.5%	0	4	0.000
July	TSIC	TROPICAL SPORTSWEAR INTERNATIONAL CORP	−12.9%	21.8%	0	4	0.000
July	HOFF	HORIZON OFFSHORE INC	−12.9%	11.9%	0	4	0.000
July	VLO	VALERO ENERGY CORP NEW	−12.7%	12.2%	0	4	0.000
July	ASF	ADMINISTAFF INC	−12.4%	7.6%	0	5	0.000
July	BSTE	BIOSITE INC	−12.1%	8.3%	0	5	0.000
July	VRSN	VERISIGN INC	−11.8%	2.8%	0	4	0.000
July	FBR	FRIEDMAN BILLINGS RAMSEY GROUP INC	−11.7%	12.1%	0	4	0.000
July	RSTI	ROFIN SINAR TECHNOLOGIES INC	−11.7%	7.9%	0	5	0.000
July	TMG	TRANSMONTAIGNE INC	−11.4%	8.6%	0	6	0.000
July	DCLK	DOUBLECLICK INC	−11.3%	7.0%	0	4	0.000
July	GETY	GETTY IMAGES INC	−11.3%	13.2%	0	4	0.000
July	RST	BOCA RESORTS INC	−11.2%	7.6%	0	5	0.000

July	GNSS	GENESIS MICROCHIP INC	-10.0%	2.6%	0	4	0.000
July	KMX	CIRCUIT CITY STORES CARMAX GROUP	-9.8%	10.4%	0	5	0.000
July	KNDL	KENDLE INTERNATIONAL INC	-9.3%	4.7%	0	4	0.000
July	TCC	TRAMMELL CROW CO	-9.1%	6.1%	0	4	0.000
July	CACI	CACI INTERNATIONAL INC	-9.0%	7.7%	0	10	0.000
July	EL	ESTEE LAUDER COS INC	-8.0%	1.9%	0	6	0.000
July	BLDP	BALLARD POWER SYSTEMS INC	-7.9%	8.0%	0	6	0.000
July	FTE	FRANCE TELECOM	-7.9%	5.1%	0	4	0.000
July	CCCG	CCC INFORMATION SERVICES GROUP INC	-7.8%	7.7%	0	5	0.000
July	DVD	DOVER MOTORSPORTS INC	-7.8%	6.5%	0	5	0.000
July	PLB	AMERICAN ITALIAN PASTA CO	-7.2%	1.5%	0	4	0.000
July	RCI	RENAL CARE GROUP INC	-7.2%	4.3%	0	6	0.000
July	MCH	MILLENNIUM CHEMICALS INC	-7.0%	7.3%	0	5	0.000
July	WXH	WINSTON HOTELS INC	-7.0%	3.5%	0	4	0.000
July	DEL	DELTIC TIMBER CORP	-6.8%	1.6%	0	5	0.000
July	FMX	FOMENTO ECONOMICO MEXICANO SA DE CV NEW	-6.8%	5.8%	0	4	0.000
July	WDR	WADDELL & REED FINANCIAL INC	-6.6%	3.4%	0	4	0.000
July	REFR	RESEARCH FRONTIERS INC	-6.1%	7.1%	0	4	0.000
July	SUR	CNA SURETY CORP	-4.9%	4.2%	0	4	0.000
July	CIV_A	CONECTIV INC	-4.4%	3.3%	0	4	0.000
July	PCU	SOUTHERN PERU COPPER CORP	-3.7%	1.0%	0	6	0.000
July	CPS	CHOICEPOINT INC	-3.6%	2.5%	0	4	0.000
July	GG	GOLDCORP INC NEW	-7.1%	4.7%	1	7	0.125
July	DPMI	DUPONT PHOTOMASKS INC	-8.6%	6.2%	1	5	0.167
July	SKP	SCPIE HOLDINGS INC	-4.4%	3.3%	1	4	0.200
July	SIL	APEX SILVER MINES LTD	-5.6%	5.3%	1	3	0.250

(Continued)

Table 4.9 *(Continued)*

Month	Sym.	Name	Mean Chg.	Std. Dev.	Mos. Up	Mos. Dwn	Batting Avg.
August	RINO	BLUE RHINO CORP	−31.3%	17.9%	0	4	0.000
August	CSGP	COSTAR GROUP INC	−23.6%	11.6%	0	4	0.000
August	HAKI	HALL KINION & ASSOCIATES INC	−17.4%	6.2%	0	4	0.000
August	MTA	HUNGARIAN TELECOMMUNICATIONS CO LTD	−15.7%	15.4%	0	4	0.000
August	RACN	RACING CHAMPIONS ERTL CORP	−14.6%	6.8%	0	4	0.000
August	INOC	INNOTRAC CORP	−13.4%	13.3%	0	4	0.000
August	TTIL	TTI TEAM TELECOM INTERNATIONAL LTD	−13.2%	6.7%	0	5	0.000
August	SRDX	SURMODICS INC	−12.5%	11.7%	0	4	0.000
August	FRN	FRIENDLY ICE CREAM CORP	−12.2%	8.4%	0	4	0.000
August	RYAAY	RYANAIR HOLDINGS PLC	−11.7%	8.3%	0	5	0.000
August	HC	HANOVER COMPRESSOR CO	−11.7%	11.1%	0	5	0.000
August	MRCY	MERCURY COMPUTER SYSTEMS INC	−11.6%	9.8%	0	4	0.000
August	CVD	COVANCE INC	−11.2%	5.2%	0	5	0.000
August	PLB	AMERICAN ITALIAN PASTA CO	−11.2%	9.8%	0	4	0.000
August	CRAI	CHARLES RIVER ASSOCIATES INC	−11.0%	3.0%	0	4	0.000
August	PRBZ	PROBUSINESS SERVICES INC	−10.9%	4.4%	0	4	0.000
August	CPV	CORRECTIONAL PROPERTIES TRUST	−10.9%	6.8%	0	4	0.000
August	SCS	STEELCASE INC	−10.7%	4.7%	0	4	0.000
August	PGEO	PARADIGM GEOPHYSICAL LTD	−10.7%	13.0%	0	4	0.000
August	AXM	APEX MORTGAGE CAPITAL INC	−10.3%	5.9%	0	4	0.000
August	GPI	GROUP 1 AUTOMOTIVE INC	−10.3%	2.9%	0	4	0.000
August	KEA	KEANE INC	−10.0%	4.4%	0	4	0.000
August	FLYR	NAVIGANT INTERNATIONAL INC	−9.9%	4.3%	0	4	0.000

August	VTAL	VITAL IMAGES INC	-9.8%	12.2%	0	4	0.000
August	TWR	TOWER AUTOMOTIVE INC	-9.6%	6.4%	0	7	0.000
August	OHB	ORLEANS HOMEBUILDERS INC	-9.5%	6.0%	0	7	0.000
August	NCEN	NEW CENTURY FINANCIAL CORP	-9.5%	2.0%	0	5	0.000
August	FII	FEDERATED INVESTORS INC	-9.2%	8.5%	0	4	0.000
August	ALS	ALSTOM SA	-8.5%	8.6%	0	4	0.000
August	SJR	SHAW COMMUNICATIONS INC	-7.6%	3.8%	0	4	0.000
August	IRE	BANK OF IRELAND	-7.6%	9.2%	0	5	0.000
August	IT	GARTNER INC	-7.5%	4.8%	0	8	0.000
August	ICLR	ICON PLC	-7.2%	6.7%	0	4	0.000
August	RBA	RITCHIE BROS AUCTIONEERS INC	-7.1%	3.2%	0	4	0.000
August	ABV	COMPANHIA DE BEBIDAS DAS AMERICAS	-7.0%	4.7%	0	5	0.000
August	CNI	CANADIAN NATIONAL RAILWAY CO	-6.5%	3.5%	0	5	0.000
August	CLRO	CLEARONE COMMUNICATIONS INC	-6.3%	2.7%	0	5	0.000
August	OZRK	BANK OF THE OZARKS INC	-6.3%	5.1%	0	5	0.000
August	MMS	MAXIMUS INC	-5.9%	5.0%	0	5	0.000
August	RIV	RIVIERA HOLDINGS CORP	-5.9%	3.5%	0	5	0.000
August	SAH	SONIC AUTOMOTIVE INC	-4.6%	3.1%	0	4	0.000
August	BMHC	BUILDING MATERIALS HOLDING CORP	-5.4%	4.9%	1	9	0.100
August	WSTC	WEST CORP	-7.9%	6.3%	1	4	0.200
August	CEM	CHEMFIRST INC	-4.6%	4.1%	1	4	0.200
August	CDCY	COMPUDYNE CORP	-7.3%	6.3%	2	7	0.222
August	RSG	REPUBLIC SERVICES INC	-15.1%	13.8%	1	3	0.250
August	TENT	TOTAL ENTERTAINMENT RESTAURANT CORP	-9.0%	6.1%	1	3	0.250
August	URI	UNITED RENTALS INC NEW	-8.4%	10.5%	1	3	0.250
August	UU	UNITED UTILITIES PLC	-5.1%	4.4%	1	3	0.250
August	ALLE	ALLEGIANT BANCORP INC NEW	-4.9%	4.1%	2	4	0.333

(Continued)

221

Table 4.9 (*Continued*)

Month	Sym.	Name	Mean Chg.	Std. Dev.	Mos. Up	Mos. Dwn	Batting Avg.
September	ROS	AO ROSTELECOM	−35.2%	8.5%	0	4	0.000
September	CYMI	CYMER INC	−24.4%	17.9%	0	5	0.000
September	FSCI	FISHER COMMUNICATIONS INC	−21.6%	39.0%	0	6	0.000
September	RSTO	RESTORATION HARDWARE INC	−21.0%	14.1%	0	4	0.000
September	TNT	TATNEFT JSC	−20.7%	13.1%	0	4	0.000
September	YBTVA	YOUNG BROADCASTING INC	−15.8%	13.8%	0	7	0.000
September	RSTI	ROFIN SINAR TECHNOLOGIES INC	−14.0%	14.3%	0	5	0.000
September	MAR	MARRIOTT INTERNATIONAL INC NEW	−12.8%	8.5%	0	4	0.000
September	FCGI	FIRST CONSULTING GROUP INC	−12.7%	9.9%	0	4	0.000
September	RBK	REEBOK INTERNATIONAL LTD	−12.7%	9.0%	0	4	0.000
September	NUTR	NUTRACEUTICAL INTERNATIONAL CORP	−11.6%	13.2%	0	4	0.000
September	CTV	COMMSCOPE INC	−11.4%	7.9%	0	5	0.000
September	RL	POLO RALPH LAUREN CORP	−10.9%	8.1%	0	5	0.000
September	SRI	STONERIDGE INC	−10.6%	7.5%	0	4	0.000
September	MGM	METRO GOLDWYN MAYER INC NEW	−9.6%	8.1%	0	4	0.000
September	DAKT	DAKTRONICS INC	−9.6%	7.1%	0	4	0.000
September	RG	ROGERS COMMUNICATIONS INC	−9.3%	4.6%	0	7	0.000
September	EDS	ELECTRONIC DATA SYSTEMS CORP	−5.7%	6.4%	0	5	0.000
September	FLBK	FLORIDA BANKS INC	−5.7%	4.1%	0	4	0.000
September	DGX	QUEST DIAGNOSTICS INC	−4.1%	3.9%	0	5	0.000
September	CARS	CAPITAL AUTOMOTIVE REIT	−3.0%	2.5%	0	4	0.000
September	UBP_A	URSTADT BIDDLE PROPERTIES INC	−2.1%	1.4%	0	4	0.000
September	TMM	GRUPO TMM SA DE CV	−8.9%	11.5%	1	9	0.100

September	RNT	AARON RENTS INC	-6.2%	5.0%	1	8	0.111
September	CENT	CENTRAL GARDEN & PET CO	-4.8%	15.0%	1	8	0.111
September	CAKE	CHEESECAKE FACTORY INC	-4.7%	10.8%	1	8	0.111
September	BDK	BLACK & DECKER CORP	-7.6%	8.0%	2	14	0.125
September	JBHT	J B HUNT TRANSPORT SERVICES INC	-7.5%	11.4%	2	14	0.125
September	STK	STORAGE TECHNOLOGY CORP	-7.0%	15.1%	2	14	0.125
September	MNC	MONACO COACH CORP	-6.0%	12.4%	1	7	0.125
September	GM	GENERAL MOTORS CORP	-5.7%	6.1%	2	14	0.125
September	DNY	R R DONNELLEY & SONS CO	-3.8%	5.2%	2	14	0.125
September	OII	OCEANEERING INTERNATIONAL INC	-2.6%	16.9%	2	13	0.133
September	USAP	UNIVERSAL STAINLESS & ALLOY PRODUCTS INC	-11.9%	13.9%	1	6	0.143
September	AHG	APRIA HEALTHCARE GROUP INC	-10.5%	11.7%	1	6	0.143
September	JS	JEFFERSON SMURFIT GROUP PLC	-9.7%	9.9%	1	6	0.143
September	AIN	ALBANY INTERNATIONAL CORP	-6.5%	8.6%	2	12	0.143
September	DUCK	DUCKWALL ALCO STORES INC	-5.5%	9.5%	1	6	0.143
September	PHHM	PALM HARBOR HOMES INC	-5.2%	10.3%	1	6	0.143
September	BW	BRUSH ENGINEERED MATERIALS INC	-6.6%	6.8%	3	13	0.188
September	AKO_B	ANDINA BOTTLING CO INC	-4.3%	7.7%	1	4	0.200
September	WPPGY	WPP GROUP PLC	-8.7%	10.0%	3	11	0.214
September	HEI_A	HEICO CORP	-12.5%	12.4%	1	3	0.250
September	HAFC	HANMI FINANCIAL CORP	-5.7%	6.6%	1	3	0.250
September	NMRX	NUMEREX CORP PA	-4.8%	8.3%	2	6	0.250
September	LFIN	LOCAL FINANCIAL CORP NEW	-3.8%	3.1%	1	3	0.250
September	FNFN	FRANKLIN FINANCIAL CORP TENNESSEE	-3.0%	2.2%	1	3	0.250
September	OLP	ONE LIBERTY PROPERTIES INC	-4.3%	6.4%	5	11	0.313

(Continued)

223

Table 4.9 (Continued)

Month	Sym.	Name	Mean Chg.	Std. Dev.	Mos. Up	Mos. Dwn	Batting Avg.
October	FNFN	FRANKLIN FINANCIAL CORP TENNESSEE	−51.6%	56.0%	0	4	0.000
October	DSWT	DURASWITCH INDUSTRIES INC	−16.3%	8.3%	0	4	0.000
October	CCCG	CCC INFORMATION SERVICES GROUP INC	−15.6%	4.9%	0	6	0.000
October	RADS	RADIANT SYSTEMS INC	−14.0%	13.1%	0	5	0.000
October	NHR	NATIONAL HEALTH REALTY INC	−12.0%	7.8%	0	4	0.000
October	AHR	ANTHRACITE CAPITAL INC	−11.3%	14.3%	0	4	0.000
October	VNT	NATIONAL TELEPHONE CO OF VENEZUELA CANTV	−11.1%	9.8%	0	5	0.000
October	PGEO	PARADIGM GEOPHYSICAL LTD	−10.8%	5.9%	0	4	0.000
October	GES	GUESS ? INC	−10.4%	13.5%	0	6	0.000
October	UAG	UNITED AUTO GROUP INC	−9.8%	6.4%	0	5	0.000
October	NWPX	NORTHWEST PIPE CO	−9.3%	2.6%	0	6	0.000
October	WRP	WELLSFORD REAL PROPERTIES INC	−8.4%	3.2%	0	5	0.000
October	PGE	PRIME GROUP REALTY TRUST	−7.8%	6.5%	0	4	0.000
October	PP	PRENTISS PROPERTIES TRUST	−7.5%	4.6%	0	5	0.000
October	SLG	SL GREEN REALTY CORP	−7.0%	3.5%	0	5	0.000
October	EOP	EQUITY OFFICE PROPERTIES TRUST	−7.0%	5.3%	0	5	0.000
October	AKO_A	ANDINA BOTTLING CO INC	−6.9%	2.5%	0	5	0.000
October	NLY	ANNALY MORTGAGE MANAGEMENT INC	−6.8%	2.1%	0	4	0.000
October	ARI	ARDEN REALTY INC	−6.4%	2.9%	0	5	0.000
October	BFAM	BRIGHT HORIZONS FAMILY SOLUTIONS INC	−6.4%	4.8%	0	4	0.000
October	LNR	LNR PROPERTY CORP	−6.3%	1.4%	0	4	0.000
October	PRFS	PENNROCK FINANCIAL SERVICES CORP	−6.2%	5.4%	0	5	0.000
October	SMT	SUMMIT PROPERTIES INC	−6.0%	4.7%	0	8	0.000

October	AMB	AMB PROPERTY CORP	-6.0%	3.7%	0	4	0.000
October	GLH	GALLAHER GROUP PLC	-5.6%	4.5%	0	5	0.000
October	NAT	NORDIC AMERICAN TANKER SHIPPING LTD	-5.4%	4.7%	0	5	0.000
October	WTFC	WINTRUST FINANCIAL CORP	-5.2%	5.1%	0	5	0.000
October	KRC	KILROY REALTY CORP	-4.6%	2.6%	0	5	0.000
October	WXH	WINSTON HOTELS INC	-4.3%	4.6%	0	5	0.000
October	SRE	SEMPRA ENERGY	-3.8%	4.3%	0	4	0.000
October	FNBP	FNB CORP VA	-3.8%	2.9%	0	5	0.000
October	CLI	MACK CALI REALTY CORP	-3.2%	2.4%	0	8	0.000
October	ARE	ALEXANDRIA REAL ESTATE EQUITIES INC	-2.6%	1.1%	0	5	0.000
October	FTBK	FRONTIER FINANCIAL CORP WASHINGTON	-2.5%	1.7%	0	4	0.000
October	GL	GREAT LAKES REIT INC	-2.4%	1.4%	0	5	0.000
October	MWRK	MOTHERS WORK INC	-10.2%	23.3%	1	8	0.111
October	TUTR	PLATO LEARNING INC	-9.9%	14.2%	1	8	0.111
October	GEM	PEPSI GEMEX SA DE CV	-12.4%	7.4%	1	7	0.125
October	ATMI	ATMI INC	-11.3%	18.4%	1	7	0.125
October	MTEC	MERIDIAN MEDICAL TECHNOLOGIES INC	-10.4%	16.0%	2	14	0.125
October	PYX	PLAYTEX PRODUCTS INC	-8.0%	8.7%	1	7	0.125
October	FRC	FIRST REPUBLIC BANK	-7.1%	7.1%	2	14	0.125
October	CIMA	CIMA LABS INC	-6.6%	8.9%	1	7	0.125
October	RPT	RAMCO GERSHENSON PROPERTIES TRUST	-3.2%	5.9%	2	11	0.154
October	BXP	BOSTON PROPERTIES INC	-4.8%	3.6%	1	4	0.200
October	FMBN	F&M BANCORP	-2.0%	2.2%	2	8	0.200
October	CIV_A	CONECTIV INC	-10.9%	15.9%	1	3	0.250
October	CITZ	CFS BANCORP INC	-2.5%	3.4%	1	3	0.250
October	UBP_A	URSTADT BIDDLE PROPERTIES INC	-0.9%	0.6%	1	3	0.250

(Continued)

Table 4.9 *(Continued)*

Month	Sym.	Name	Mean Chg.	Std. Dev.	Mos. Up	Mos. Dwn	Batting Avg.
November	MOSS	MOSSIMO INC	-22.2%	8.1%	0	4	0.000
November	VSAT	VIASAT INC	-16.6%	16.7%	0	5	0.000
November	DAVE	FAMOUS DAVE S OF AMERICA INC	-15.5%	9.3%	0	4	0.000
November	VBAC	VIRBAC CORP	-10.9%	10.1%	0	4	0.000
November	PDS	PRECISION DRILLING CORP	-10.5%	6.6%	0	5	0.000
November	RBA	RITCHIE BROS AUCTIONEERS INC	-10.1%	7.7%	0	4	0.000
November	DOM	DOMINION RESOURCES BLACK WARRIOR TRUST	-6.6%	2.9%	0	8	0.000
November	HC	HANOVER COMPRESSOR CO	-6.4%	2.3%	0	5	0.000
November	WCNX	WASTE CONNECTIONS INC	-6.2%	8.4%	0	4	0.000
November	APU	AMERIGAS PARTNERS L P	-4.9%	5.7%	0	7	0.000
November	BBX	BANKATLANTIC BANCORP INC	-4.9%	4.8%	0	6	0.000
November	KMP	KINDER MORGAN ENERGY PARTNERS L P	-4.3%	2.3%	0	10	0.000
November	RIV	RIVIERA HOLDINGS CORP	-4.1%	1.4%	0	5	0.000
November	CPV	CORRECTIONAL PROPERTIES TRUST	-2.5%	2.9%	0	4	0.000
November	CRK	COMSTOCK RESOURCES INC	-11.3%	12.3%	1	12	0.077
November	TMA	THORNBURG MORTGAGE INC	-2.3%	5.8%	1	8	0.111
November	MHR	MAGNUM HUNTER RESOURCES INC	-9.5%	8.8%	1	7	0.125
November	ORPH	ORPHAN MEDICAL INC	-8.0%	10.1%	1	7	0.125
November	REPB	REPUBLIC BANCSHARES INC	-5.2%	8.6%	1	7	0.125
November	NTT	NIPPON TELEGRAPH & TELEPHONE CORP	-1.3%	8.3%	1	7	0.125
November	KDE	4 KIDS ENTERTAINMENT INC	-11.6%	30.9%	1	6	0.143
November	TTEN	3TEC ENERGY CORP	1.7%	16.3%	1	6	0.143
November	CLHB	CLEAN HARBORS INC	-8.8%	9.5%	2	11	0.154

November	UAG	UNITED AUTO GROUP INC	-13.5%	17.9%	1	5	0.167
November	ARTC	ARTHROCARE CORP	-11.3%	12.3%	1	5	0.167
November	RGLD	ROYAL GOLD INC	-8.8%	8.1%	2	10	0.167
November	PETD	PETROLEUM DEVELOPMENT CORP	-8.0%	7.8%	1	5	0.167
November	TMG	TRANSMONTAIGNE INC	-7.2%	21.8%	1	5	0.167
November	PANL	UNIVERSAL DISPLAY CORP PA	-6.0%	25.2%	1	5	0.167
November	BVN	BUENAVENTURA MINING CO INC	-5.0%	6.1%	1	5	0.167
November	NWPX	NORTHWEST PIPE CO	-4.9%	6.8%	1	5	0.167
November	CRN	CORNELL COS INC	-4.9%	9.0%	1	5	0.167
November	WG	WILLBROS GROUP INC	-3.7%	9.9%	1	5	0.167
November	SPH	SUBURBAN PROPANE PARTNERS L P	-3.4%	3.3%	1	5	0.167
November	DECC	D & E COMMUNICATIONS INC	-3.3%	11.6%	1	5	0.167
November	BOY	BOYKIN LODGING CO	-3.2%	3.0%	1	5	0.167
November	USNA	USANA HEALTH SCIENCES INC	-9.1%	8.6%	1	4	0.200
November	ALR	ALLIED RESEARCH CORP	-7.6%	8.5%	3	12	0.200
November	GMRK	GULFMARK OFFSHORE INC	-7.6%	7.1%	1	4	0.200
November	GRKA	GREKA ENERGY CORP	-9.4%	21.9%	2	7	0.222
November	SPN	SUPERIOR ENERGY SERVICES INC	-6.0%	8.8%	2	7	0.222
November	OPTN	OPTION CARE INC	-5.8%	6.6%	2	7	0.222
November	RSCR	RES CARE INC KY	-5.0%	9.0%	2	7	0.222
November	AACE	ACE CASH EXPRESS INC	-4.1%	6.8%	2	7	0.222
November	FNIS	FIDELITY NATIONAL INFORMATION SOLNS INC	-11.5%	19.9%	2	6	0.250
November	ANH	ANWORTH MORTGAGE ASSET CORP	-4.7%	3.8%	1	3	0.250
November	BPFH	BOSTON PRIVATE FINANCIAL HOLDINGS INC	-2.4%	8.0%	2	6	0.250
November	EVG	EVERGREEN RESOURCES INC	-7.2%	9.9%	5	11	0.313
November	PHLY	PHILADELPHIA CONSOLIDATED HOLDING CORP	-5.1%	11.3%	3	6	0.333
November	STCO	SIGNAL TECHNOLOGY CORP	-8.6%	13.0%	3	5	0.375

(Continued)

Table 4.9 (*Continued*)

Month	Sym.	Name	Mean Chg.	Std. Dev.	Mos. Up	Mos. Dwn	Batting Avg.
December	TSA	SPORTS AUTHORITY INC	-13.2%	9.0%	0	7	0.000
December	USNA	USANA HEALTH SCIENCES INC	-13.1%	9.3%	0	4	0.000
December	SPRI	SPORTS RESORTS INTERNATIONAL INC	-12.9%	8.0%	0	6	0.000
December	IART	INTEGRA LIFESCIENCES HOLDINGS CORP	-10.0%	8.0%	0	7	0.000
December	TRDO	INTRADO INC	-9.0%	7.4%	0	4	0.000
December	RTN	RAYTHEON CO NEW	-8.5%	6.0%	0	4	0.000
December	RAS	RAIT INVESTMENT TRUST	-7.6%	7.9%	0	4	0.000
December	CMIN	COMMONWEALTH INDUSTRIES INC DE	-7.5%	5.9%	0	7	0.000
December	WLSN	WILSONS THE LEATHER EXPERTS INC	-6.2%	5.5%	0	5	0.000
December	WXH	WINSTON HOTELS INC	-5.9%	4.7%	0	5	0.000
December	FNC	FIRST NATIONAL CORP SC	-4.2%	3.7%	0	5	0.000
December	RAM	ROYAL APPLIANCE MFG CO	-9.3%	14.6%	1	10	0.091
December	FIMG	FISCHER IMAGING CORP	-11.4%	9.9%	1	9	0.100
December	MCRI	MONARCH CASINO & RESORT INC	-10.6%	14.2%	1	8	0.111
December	ATN	ACTION PERFORMANCE COS INC	-7.0%	18.1%	1	8	0.111
December	APSG	APPLIED SIGNAL TECHNOLOGY INC	-6.9%	13.1%	1	8	0.111
December	CNJ	COLE NATIONAL CORP	-5.0%	9.0%	1	7	0.125
December	USV	U S RESTAURANT PROPERTIES INC	-3.0%	7.0%	2	14	0.125
December	MAXS	MAXWELL SHOE CO INC	-2.9%	12.9%	1	7	0.125
December	ANL	AMERICAN LAND LEASE INC	-6.6%	8.1%	2	13	0.133

December	FBAY	FRISCO BAY INDUSTRIES LTD	-11.9%	12.1%	1	6	0.143
December	TRKN	TRIKON TECHNOLOGIES INC	-15.2%	22.0%	1	5	0.167
December	WTSLA	WET SEAL INC	-11.0%	12.2%	2	10	0.167
December	ANST	ANSOFT CORP	-8.7%	12.9%	1	5	0.167
December	KNSY	KENSEY NASH CORP	-7.8%	7.8%	1	5	0.167
December	INFM	INFINIUM SOFTWARE INC	-6.8%	24.2%	1	5	0.167
December	IM	INGRAM MICRO INC	-6.8%	11.3%	1	5	0.167
December	IDT	IDT CORP	-5.1%	27.4%	1	5	0.167
December	CNI	CANADIAN NATIONAL RAILWAY CO	-5.0%	8.0%	1	5	0.167
December	PETD	PETROLEUM DEVELOPMENT CORP	-4.8%	15.5%	1	5	0.167
December	SSNC	SS&C TECHNOLOGIES INC	-4.7%	10.6%	1	5	0.167
December	JOF	JAPAN SMALLER CAPITALIZATION FUND INC	-4.2%	6.5%	2	10	0.167
December	PICO	PICO HOLDINGS INC	-9.6%	9.8%	2	9	0.182
December	EMBX	EMBREX INC	-2.8%	13.8%	2	9	0.182
December	POSS	POSSIS MEDICAL INC	-8.4%	14.0%	3	13	0.188
December	TOY	TOYS R US INC NEW	-5.4%	9.6%	3	13	0.188
December	KVHI	KVH INDUSTRIES INC	-11.8%	15.2%	1	4	0.200
December	PLCE	CHILDREN S PLACE RETAIL STORES INC	-10.6%	24.6%	1	4	0.200
December	CTEC	CHOLESTECH CORP	-9.8%	11.4%	2	8	0.200
December	SMAN	STANDARD MANAGEMENT CORP	-8.9%	9.4%	2	7	0.222
December	MODT	MODTECH HOLDINGS INC	-7.8%	9.1%	2	7	0.222
December	TCHC	21ST CENTURY HOLDING CO	-4.3%	4.7%	1	3	0.250
December	BNP	BNP RESIDENTIAL PROPERTIES INC	-3.4%	4.3%	4	11	0.267
December	ISIG	INSIGNIA SYSTEMS INC	-8.5%	17.1%	2	5	0.286

Source: Camelback Research Alliance.

Chapter 5

RICHARD RHODES
The Macroeconomic Trend Trader

As a teenager growing up in Memphis, Tennessee, Richard Rhodes loved nothing more than to get up at 3:30 A.M., brew strong coffee, then join friends for a morning of duck hunting from a blind in a secret spot near the Mississippi River. He never shot down many birds with his double-barreled over-and-under shotgun, but he enjoyed the crisp morning air, watching the sun rise, the camaraderie of close companions—and maybe a clandestine shot or two of Jack Daniels.

You could say that Rhodes, now a swing trader and newsletter publisher based in Chicago, was born and bred to go with the flow. Raised a few miles from the mighty Mississippi, he spent 20 years in blues country before moving to the booming oil patch in Houston in the early 1980s. He earned a bachelor's degree in Russian Studies from the University of Houston and went on to open successful restaurants in the southern Texas town. But after a while he felt that he needed an advanced business degree, so he headed for Arizona to study at the American Graduate School of International Management—better known as Thunderbird—in 1994.

After graduating, he spread his wings and flew to Russia to help direct Thunderbird's training and consulting practice in Moscow for a few years, then in 1999 returned to the United States to perch in Chicago with a job as a strategic planner at one-time telecom giant WorldCom.

All the while, however, Rhodes' passion was equity and commodity trading. His initial interest in the market came from inheriting shares in the regional bank Union Planters in 1983. Not long after, his father, a Tennessee banker, recommended that he buy a few shares of IBM. That was a pretty dull idea, but his interest was piqued—and soon the restaurateur turned Russian scholar began an intense study of technical analysis and global commodities. By the mid-1980s, he was trading currency, bond, and oil futures every day before work, and studying world markets and charts at night. He began publishing *The Rhodes Report* newsletter on global economics, stocks, and commodities for a few friends, but word got around and it grew in popularity. He's comfortable with this role now: hooked by the continual emotional, intellectual, and physical challenge of matching his wits with traders around the world.

Until 2000 Rhodes' work on swing trading was known only by a select few. But his reputation advanced when he launched a weekly column on the pioneering website StockCharts.com, as he offered one winning idea after another—mostly short—in his uniquely sober and thoughtful way. In 2001 and 2002 I invited him to battle with two sets of five professionals in the Strategy Lab competition at CNBC on MSN Money, and he annihilated the field twice with steady, brilliant campaigns of strategic bearishness balanced by tactical longs and shorts. Let's see how he works.

A Simplified Macroeconomic Trading Approach

Rhodes says that if there is anything that he has learned in more than two decades of trading, it's that simple works best. Those who need to rely upon complex stochastics, linear-weighted moving averages, smoothing techniques, and Fibonacci numbers, he says, usually find that they have so many things rolling around in their heads that they cannot make a rational decision. One technique says buy, another says sell, a third says sit tight, while another says add to the trade. It sounds like a cliché, but the more straightforward the better.

So from a simplification point of view, the ideal swing-trading strategy for him focuses on forecasting intermediate-term moves in stocks, either up or down, that will lead to trades of three weeks to six months in duration, or possibly longer if the trend becomes well ingrained.

Rhodes takes a three-pronged approach: First, he develops a macroeconomic stance on world economic fundamentals by studying a variety of journals and government statistics for clues on United States and European monetary policy, employment, manufacturing, and services strength. Then, he uses a couple of technical indicators to pick stocks. If he is fundamentally bullish on world economic trends, then he looks for ways to be long U.S. stocks. If he is fundamentally bearish on world economic trends, then he focuses on ways to be short U.S. stocks.

Here's the strategy in a nutshell:

- *Fundamental analysis.* Determine the overriding intermediate economic trend, which allows one to confidently hold trades longer.
- *Technical analysis.* Determine infrequent timing signals that minimize the number of in and out trades, enhancing the probability of success.
- *Position management.* Use explicit trading rules to provide structure to swing trades and mitigate errors in judgment.

Rhodes' technical resources are a small array of trendlines, moving averages, and chart patterns. About the most esoteric he ever gets is in using different moving averages for different equities, as he believes that each marches to the beat of its own drummer; no single moving average fits them all. He also uses a single oscillator—the 20-day stochastic—for its often-uncanny ability to spotlight changes in the intermediate trends in stocks.

Finally, and most importantly, he uses a set of trading rules inherited from a mentor to manage his positions and to protect himself from errors in judgment. He believes that if you follow these rules, breaking them as infrequently as possible, you will make money year in and year out. The 18 rules are simple, but adhering to them is difficult. Here they are:

1. *In bull markets, a trader should be long.* This may sound obvious, but every trader will admit that he or she has sold the first rally in a bull market, believing that it has moved too far, too fast—and thus has not fully taken advantage of their original bullish outlook. In a bull market, one can be only long or on the sidelines.
2. *Buy strength; sell weakness.* The public continues to buy when prices have fallen. The professional buys because prices have ral-

lied. The difference may not sound logical, but buying strength works. The rule of survival is not to "buy low, sell high," but to "buy higher and sell higher." Furthermore, when comparing various stocks within a group, buy only the strongest and sell the weakest.

3. *Enter every trade as if it has the potential to be the biggest trade of the year.* Don't enter a trade until it has been well thought out, with a campaign devised for additions and exit.

4. *On minor corrections against the major trend, add to trades.* In bull markets, add to the trade on minor corrections back into support levels. In bear markets, add to short sales on corrections into resistance. Use either the 33 percent to 50 percent corrections level of the previous movement, or the appropriate moving average, as a first point in which to add.

5. *Be patient.* If you miss a trade, wait for a correction to occur before putting the trade on.

6. *Be patient.* Once a trade is put on, allow it time to develop, and give it time to create the profits you expected.

7. *Be patient.* The cliché that "you never go broke taking a profit" is worthless. Taking small profits is the surest way to ultimate loss, for small profits are never allowed to develop into enormous profits. The real money in trading is made from the one, two, or three large trades that develop each year. You must develop the ability to patiently stay with winning trades to allow them to develop into something important.

8. *Be patient.* Once a trade is put on, give it time to work; give it time to insulate itself from random noise; give it time for others to see the merit of what you saw earlier than they.

9. *Be impatient.* As always, small losses and quick losses are the best losses. It is not the loss of money that is important. Rather, it is the mental capital that is used up when you sit with a losing trade that is important.

10. *Never, ever add to a losing trade, or "average" into a position.* If you are buying, then each new buy price must be higher than the previous buy price. If you are shorting, then each new selling price must be lower. This rule is to be adhered to without question.

11. *Do more of what is working for you, and less of what's not.* Each day, look at the various positions you are holding and try to add to

the trade that has the most profit while subtracting from that trade that is either unprofitable or is showing the smallest profit. This is the basis of the adage Let your profits run.

12. *Don't trade until the technicals and the fundamentals agree.* This rule makes pure technicians cringe. Yet Rhodes will not trade until he is sure that the simple technical rules he follows, and his fundamental analyses, are running in tandem. Then he can act with authority, and with certainty, and patiently sit tight.

13. *When sharp losses are experienced, take time off.* Close all trades and stop trading for several days. The mind can play games with itself following sharp, quick losses. The urge to get the money back is extreme, and should not be indulged.

14. *When trading well, trade somewhat larger.* Everyone experiences those incredible periods of time when all trades are profitable. When that happens, trade aggressively and trade larger. Make hay while the sun shines.

15. *When adding to a trade, add only one-fourth to one-half as much as currently held.* That is, if you are holding 400 shares of a stock, at the next point at which to add, add no more than 100 or 200 shares. That moves the average price of your holdings less than half of the distance moved, thus allowing you to sit through 50 percent corrections without touching your average price.

16. *Think like a guerrilla warrior.* Fight on the side of the market that is winning. Don't waste time and capital on futile efforts to buy the lows or sell the highs of some market movement. Your duty is to earn profits by fighting alongside the winning forces. If neither side is winning, then don't fight at all.

17. *Markets form their tops in violence; markets form their lows in quiet conditions.*

18. *The final 10 percent of the time of a bull run will usually encompass 50 percent or more of the price movement.* Thus, the first 50 percent of the price movement will take 90 percent of the time, will require the most backing and filling, and will be far more difficult to trade than the last 50 percent.

There is no special genius in these rules for swing traders. They are common sense and nothing else. But as Voltaire said, "Common sense is uncommon." When you trade contrary to common sense, you will lose. Perhaps not always, but enormously and eventually.

How to Define the Macroenvironment

Before downloading charts and thinking about individual stocks to swing-trade, Rhodes determines his current view of the big macroeconomic world picture. He looks at the world as a single integrated machine, with Japan, the rest of Asia, Europe, and the United States as separate cogs in a mechanism that cannot work well if it is not all working together.

Here is an outline of the way in which he views the fundamental world economic environment:

1. International spending
   - Asian business conditions
   - European business conditions
   - Latin American business conditions
2. U.S. monetary policy (The Federal Reserve)
   - Money supply figures
   - Currency movements
3. Consumer spending (66 percent of the economy)
   - Employment/jobless claims trends
   - Disposable income trends
   - Consumer credit trends
   - Retail sales trends
   - Mortgage Bankers Application Survey trends
4. Business investment spending (34 percent of the economy)
   - Corporate capital investment plans
   - Nondefense capital goods (durable goods report)

He always starts with Japan by reading the English-language website of the *Nihon Keizai Shimbun*, which is the country's equivalent of the *Wall Street Journal* (See Figure 5.1.) Rhodes points out that while Japan's stock market today is in shambles, it is still the second largest economy in the world. The people of Japan also have vast personal savings, making the country one of the greatest stores of wealth in the world. Any long-term view of the world economy, he believes, must take into consideration the generational issues of Japan's faltering consumer class. If these workers continue to lose confidence in themselves and their government, Rhodes believes, the rest of Asia will suffer—putting a drag on the world economy.

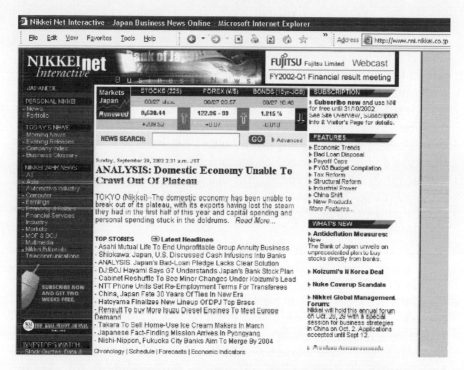

Figure 5.1 The *Nihon Keizai Shimbun*, Japan's leading daily business journal, publishes most of its contents on its English-language website at http://nni.nikkei.co.jp. News on the site ranges from domestic economics, commerce, and politics to pan-Asian economics, technology, and consumer trends.
Source: Copyright 2003 Nihon Keizai Shimbun, Inc. All rights reserved.

The issue isn't just academic. For if Asia fails to encourage more business investment, and its people fail to demand an increasing number of European and U.S. goods, then Americans and Europeans will have less money to buy *their* goods. It's a vicious cycle. Through late 2002, Rhodes believed that Asia will be weak for the foreseeable future with little demand for European and U.S. goods and services. However, he is always aware that he could be wrong, so he checks the Japanese currency every day. A sustained up move for the yen would signal that world money flow is supporting Japan and that it might be time to upgrade its economy in his mental checklist—and potentially even consider buying its stocks.

When he turns to Europe, Rhodes focuses on interest rates—for countries there generally run very rigid economies. That means they are highly regulated and beholden to the long-term wage restrictions of powerful labor-union movements. When interest rates drop, money flutters in the windows of the Continent's predominantly heavy industrial companies like a windfall. To switch metaphors, a decline in interest rates acts like the lowering of a lock on a dam. The lowered rates allow business investment to flood in much more quickly than a similar move in the United States. So Rhodes monitors the website of the European Central Bank at http://www.ecb.int to determine whether it is hiking or cutting rates, and why. (See Figure 5.2.) If it is dropping rates, it is supplying liquidity to the markets, and national banks will lend money in greater amounts to businesses, which will then begin to make more stuff for export.

To get a firm grip on Europe's prospects, Rhodes recommends just watching its currency, the euro. A falling euro often (though not always) signals trouble in Europe. If the euro is weak, Rhodes tends to want to avoid the shares of U.S. companies with heavy European exposure; if the euro is strong, he would tend to favor U.S. companies with heavy European exposure. Through the fall of 2002, the European economy was suffering a double whammy: slack domestic demand due in part to high interest rates and a weak currency. To further improve his view of European economic vitality, Rhodes regularly visits the website of the Bank of England, at http://bankofengland.co.uk, and the website of the Bank for International Settlements, at http://bis.org to read their impressive daily postings of speeches, reports, white papers, and press releases. (See Figure 5.3.)

As for the United States, Rhodes focuses on U.S. monetary policy, the strength of the dollar, and weekly economic reports by regularly reading and analyzing reports at the Dismal Scientist website at http://economy.com/dismal. (See Figure 5.4.) If nothing else, he says, watch the dollar. A strong dollar brings strong investment flows into the United States, which finance our bonds and support our stocks. A weak dollar does the opposite. Thus, investors generally prefer a strong dollar. Rhodes also looks at U.S. interest rates, particularly the 10-year Treasury note, the 5-year Treasury bill, and the 2-year Treasury bill. Early in the interest-rate cycle, as rates are high and heading lower, short-term and long-term rates fall in tandem and the decline has the most impactful effect on both businesses and consumers. Suddenly, consumers start to buy more homes and big-ticket items like cars, or refinance their homes and

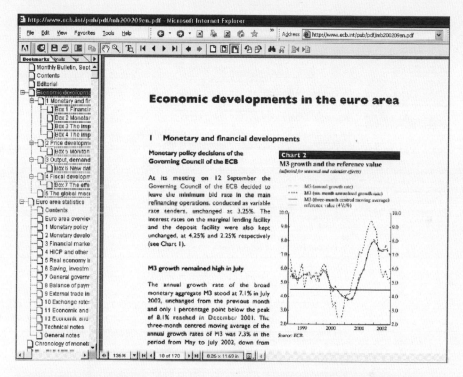

Figure 5.2 The European Central Bank's website offers a wealth of up-to-date, English-language commentary and statistics on the state of the euro zone. One of the most useful documents is the bank's Monthly Bulletin. To find it, visit the home page at http://www.ecb.int, find the Periodical Publications section, click the ECB Monthly Bulletin link, then choose the appropriate month's report on the following page. The lengthy report, which is in the Adobe PDF format, offers a relatively easy-to-read overview of economic trends throughout the Continent. Shown above is page 10 of the September 2002 bulletin.
Source: European Central Bank

take out cash to buy things. Likewise, for businesses the cost of investing in new projects declines. A factory or new store that would be unprofitable at a higher rate of borrowing—sometimes known as the "hurdle rate"—becomes profitable at a lower one. That has implications throughout the economy in businesses large and small, and helps define the macroenvironment.

The problem in the United States in 2001 and 2002, Rhodes believes, was that there was already so much debt that most businesses were not willing to take on new projects at any interest rate. Instead,

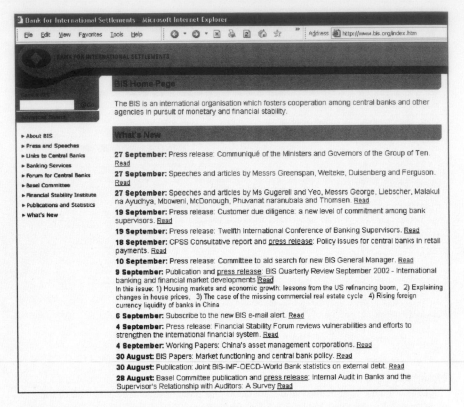

Figure 5.3 The Bank for International Settlements—an organization that seeks to foster cooperation among the world's central banks and other agencies in pursuit of monetary and financial stability—provides a tremendous set of economics resources at its website. To get an edge on traders who don't do their own homework and develop a personal global point of view, visit regularly to read speeches and press releases from central bankers, economists, and researchers. Most of the academic papers are current and insightful. To dig deeper into monetary policy at individual countries worldwide, click the Links to Central Banks button on the BIS home page, shown above.
Source: Bis.org.

they became interested in "reliquefying" their balance sheets—or using the lower rates to simply pay less to their lenders. That made for a declining business environment. When the country went through the up-thrust of this cycle, companies extrapolated fantastic revenues into the future and greatly expanded factory capacity and headcount. That left little to build when interest rates fell on the downthrust of the cycle, pri-

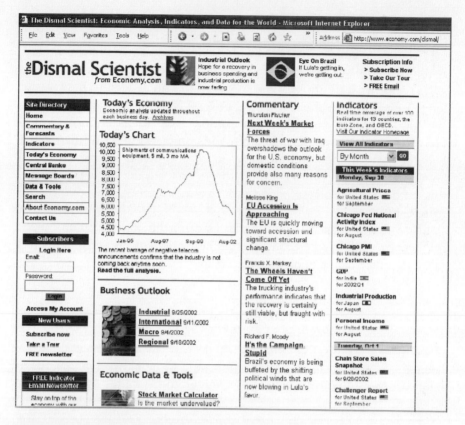

Figure 5.4 The Dismal Scientist (http://economy.com/dismal) offers an incredibly comprehensive and well-presented array of daily articles, columns, and statistics about the United States and world economies with lively charts and easy-to-download charts and tables of data.
Source: Economy.com, Inc.

marily because they did not receive a sufficient rate of return in the previously deployed capital.

One of the main reasons that Rhodes was able to emphatically get bearish in 2000 and hunt almost exclusively for shorts as a swing trader was the campaign of rising interest rates that the Federal Reserve had embarked upon, combined with rising oil prices. At the time, bulls said that interest rates didn't matter for technology stocks since they mostly carried no debt. But that was a massive red flag to this trader. He knew that the effect of interest rates on business was much easier to exploit as a short seller as they rise than as a long holder as they fall. When rates rise, they are very effective at slowing down business. As they fall, they're less capable of helping business improve. Thus, the rise in rates at the same time as extreme highs in overpriced stocks was, as he puts it, "a recipe to scare the hell out of anyone" who needed to hold stocks long. To learn more about what the Federal Reserve governors are saying and thinking, visit the organization website at http://federalreserve.gov. Pay special attention to reports on the minutes of the regular Federal Open Market Committee meetings, which are typically available from a link on the site's home page, or from the Monetary Policy link on the Press Release page (http://www.federalreserve.gov/pressreleases.htm).

Now that we can see how Rhodes assesses the macroeconomic environment by studying the economies of the world, currencies, and interest rates, let's take a look at his favorite setups.

Rhodes' Setups

Once Rhodes thinks he knows which way the world economy is headed, and which stock groups will benefit or be harmed, he begins to hunt for stocks that offer the most leverage to his beliefs. Let's review where we are:

- Once the *Fundamental* outlook is in place—either bullish or bearish—one should look to trade only from that perspective. If you are bullish, you should be looking to buy.
- Use the *Technicals* to time yourself into positions—both initially and when adding. If bullish, look to buy at support levels denoted by previous lows or moving averages.

Rhodes' favorite technical indicator is the 20-day Full Stochastics oscillator (use 20/10 for %K and 5 for %D as the Full Stochastics setting at StockCharts.com). His favorite price pattern is an "outside reversal" day or week, which means that the low of the period is lower than the low of the prior period, the high is higher than the prior high, and the close is at whichever extreme that would signal a reversal (at the top of the bar for a reversal to a downward trend; at the bottom of the bar for a reversal to an upward trend). The outside reversal signals an "exhaustion" in the previously dominant trend. Rhodes calls it "the most powerful tool" in his arsenal. "I will trade on it with almost blind faith," he says.

An excellent example for both in mid-2002 came in trading of mailing services powerhouse Pitney-Bowes (PBI). The company had made a terrific move from lows made after the September 11, 2001 terrorist attacks in New York and Washington, trending perfectly in such a way that each low touched an easily drawn trendline—adding more and more to bulls' confidence that the move had merit. (See Figure 5.5.) The stock had an easily identifiable target, which was the August 2001 high at $45.

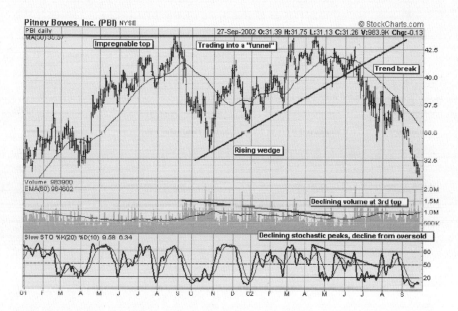

Figure 5.5 Shares of mailing services provider Pitney-Bowes rebounded from late-September lows like a champ following a series of postal-system anthrax scares. Traders could have played it as a long, as its uptrend became well-defined by February and the old high of $45 was easily definable as an upside target. However, it became an even better short for swing traders in March after it traded into a "funnel" by repeatedly failing to breach the old high on faltering momentum (as shown in declining stochastics peaks) and contracting volume. This "wedge" pattern would become an excellent short, however, only after it fell through the well-established upward trendline in mid-June at $41. Downside targets then were identifiable at previous support around $37.50, $36, and $32.50.
Source: StockCharts.com.

If it sliced through that high on good volume, it would be a huge win for bulls who sought an upside breakout. Yet prices stopped at $45 in March and again in April. In May, bulls tried again and it quickly began to appear the stock was trading into a "funnel" after running into an impregnable top. This wedge-shaped pattern is typically indicative of distribution. You have retracement of a former high, a second and third attempt, and selling each time as supply comes into the market. Something has to give.

And then in mid-June came an outside reversal week (see Figure 5.6) and a break of the trend to the downside that coincided with a decline from oversold in the 20/10 stochastic. Targets were previous support at $38 and $32, and then a test of lows in the mid-$20s. In a stock like this, Rhodes would pull the trigger at the open of the first trading day after the

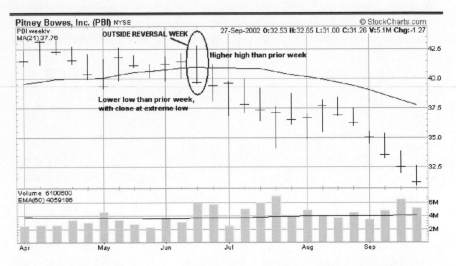

Figure 5.6   Once Rhodes' radar was tuned into Pitney-Bowes due to its failure to penetrate the $45 highs, the decline in momentum, and the contraction in volume, the last confirmation for a short sale came at the end of an "outside reversal week" around $40 in mid-June. In this pattern, the high of a weekly price bar is higher than the prior week's high, the low is lower than the prior week's low, and the close is at or very near the low. These are relatively rare but powerful patterns, and Rhodes hunts for them among all the stocks that catch his eye for other reasons. In this case, the reversal led to a string of declines that went on to take the stock into the low $30s by late September 2002.
Source: StockCharts.com.

conclusion of the outside reversal week. It's almost always seen at tops and bottoms, which by definition are rare. When they do occur, he says, you have an 80 percent chance of being correct that a real trend reversal is taking place.

As for his strategy on entering a trade, Rhodes advocates just going in at the market. "If I want to be short, I want to be short—good or bad fill, I don't care. I just want to be short when I see things going my way. I have enough confidence in the position that I don't worry about half a point, because we're not going for one to two points; we are going for a whole bucket of points."

Once in a trade, *position management* takes Rhodes' focus, as it forces him to bring structure to the exercise—protecting profits and minimizing losses. For instance, if he's bearish, he places a stop-loss order just above previous levels of resistance, allowing his position to be stopped out only upon a breakout and insulating it from every-day noise.

Managing a trade after entry is critical, as the real money is made by pyramiding into a correct idea. In a portfolio of $100,000, Rhodes would start his short of Pitney-Bowes with a 5 percent position, or $5,000. Then he would sit back and wait to see if support levels are broken. In this case, he started shorting at $41, and added additional 5 percent increments at $37 and $35. This is when holding the stock becomes ever more horrific for longs—a grinding-down period that Rhodes calls a "death-by-a-thousand-cuts decline." Every time it rallies, the longs try to come into the stock hoping it will hold, but if the short seller has made the correct call, the stock pushes lower and lower on heavier and heavier volume into multiyear support. Rhodes would stop adding to his short at the point that it becomes a 20 percent position because, at that point, in his words, "you're pretty damned exposed." Still, in this case, the market kept telling him he was right as he sold it short again and again at lower prices. Ultimately, the stock completely broke down into the low $30s by late September 2002. By then the new target was the three-year low in the mid-$20s.

The position that I most associate with Rhodes is his call in November 2000 to short communications semiconductor maker PMC-Sierra, which until that time had been one of the most sensational earnings-growth stories of the late 1990s bull market. Even fund managers who could not abide by the idea of owning momentum stocks like Amazon.com or Yahoo! during that time believed that the price of chip stocks like PMC-Sierra could be rationalized. Yet Rhodes believed that the plain fact that the Federal Reserve had begun raising interest rates would dampen demand for communications equipment of all kinds, and at the same time burst the bubble of demand for these stocks. He waited patiently through the summer and early fall of 2000, for signs that the stock might break, then he finally pounced. (See Figure 5.7.)

His argument for the short sale:

- PMCS had risen parabolically from 1998 through the beginning of 2000.
- A trendline drawn off the 1998–1999–2000 lows until that time showed several touches—proving the move's merit for longs.
- In September 2000, PMCS rose to test its previous highs at $255. The test failed, and that focused his attention on its relationship with its

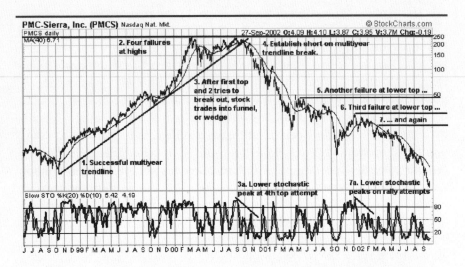

Figure 5.7 Shares of communications semiconductor maker PMC-Sierra were a momentum trader's delight from 1998 through the fall of 2000, but all good things come to an end. The safe trade for a risk-averse swing trader came from the short side when four attempts to rally through $255 failed as the stock traded into a wedge pattern. Something had to give, and the stock ultimately crashed through its multiyear trendline at $198 at the start of a long journey to $3.50. Several additional entry points were presented on weak attempts to rally through intermediate highs on the way down, as shown in the above log chart.
Source: StockCharts.com.

rising trendline. Now prices would be trading into a funnel, as we saw with Pitney-Bowes, in Figure 5.6.

- The trendline was broken the first week of October 2000. In conjunction with action in the 20-week stochastic, which turned lower from lower highs, this was a very negative development for bulls.
- Following the plethora of technical breakdowns, Rhodes went short "two units," or 10 percent of his portfolio, of PMC-Sierra at about $198. He placed his stop loss at $235.
- Three weeks later, the stock broke down through its 40-week moving average, while an outside reversal day formed. Those were two additional negative confirming indicators on top of the already negative trendline break. He added another unit, or 5 percent, to his position at $157. He also lowered his stop loss to $220.
- Upon the break of previous support at $115 he added a fourth unit at $108—meaning he now had 20 percent of his tradable funds in this one play. His stop loss was then dropped to $170.
- Prices and stop-loss levels continued to move lower in the trend to $18, but he was stopped out at $38 in April 2001, during the spike move from $18 to $40.
- His average selling price for the four units of shorts totaled about $165. The gain was 77 percent after the stop at $38.
- By late September 2002, the stock had traded down to $3.50.

Another excellent example of combining fundamentals and technicals for a multimonth swing trade came in a speech that Rhodes gave on August 23 at the San Francisco Money Show. I attended the presentation with about 150 other people, and the trader proposed this idea: Despite the rally that had occurred from July 24 lows, short the S&P 500 immediately. Here's how he came to the suggestion.

Fundamental Outlook: Negative
- Wages and salaries are growing, but employment costs are rising even faster. This puts a drag on disposable income.
- Consumer spending is slowly declining.
     Radio Shack announcement of plunging August sales.
     Wal-Mart indicates sales at lower end of their estimated range.
- Existing and new housing sales are slowly declining.
     Continued strength, but relatively weak to past months—even with the recent "refinancing boom."

Technical Outlook: Mixed

- Chart patterns are negative. "Rising wedge" predominates the technical landscape.

    Weekly oscillators have turned up.

    Daily oscillators are now overbought (20-D Stochastic).

Based on this scenario, here was the proposed campaign. (See Figure 5.8.)

Trade: Short the S&P 500 (via Unit Investment Trust SPY) in August–September 2002

1. The rise off the July 23 low is so substantial that many are claiming this is *the* bottom. This is unlikely, given that economic fundamentals are rapidly deteriorating.
2. The overriding technical pattern is a long-term head and shoulders pattern, whose neckline was broken between $95 and $98. Price action has a tendency to return to the level of the breakout, and this is presently occurring.

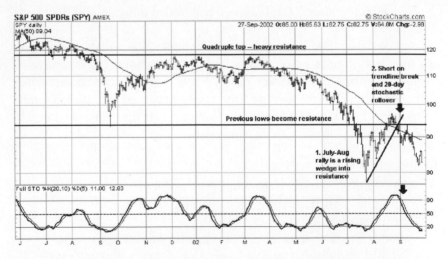

Figure 5.8   On August 23, 2001 Rhodes recommended a campaign to short the S&P 500 due to a combination of poor U.S. economic fundamentals and the potential for deteriorating technicals. He correctly forecast resistance in the $98 area, and the index quickly fell apart from there—rewarding short sellers.
Source: StockCharts.com.

3. The current formation incorporates a "rising wedge" pattern—whose ultimate resolution should be lower.

4. The short-term downtrend line off the June–July highs was broken to the upside, with price action subsequently breaking above the 50-day moving average. These are short-term bullish conditions.

5. Resistance between $95 and $98 is now under attack. Now look for price weakness in this area in conjunction with a turn lower in the 20-day stochastic.

6. If this occurs, sell short two units of SPY, or 10 percent of a portfolio, at the market price. The stop loss will be set about 15 percent above the entry price.

7. Look to add an additional unit, or 5 percent of a portfolio, upon a break lower through the "rising trendline," which crosses between $93 and $96. Lower the stop loss as prudent.

8. Look to add a fourth unit, or another 5 percent of the portfolio, upon a break lower through the early-August low of $83. Once again, adjust the stop loss to reflect the move lower.

9. Look to add two more units, or another 10 percent, upon a break of the July lows at $78. That should bring down the breakeven point substantially, and hence the stop-loss point.

10. Finally, I will look to exit our position upon fulfillment of the head and shoulders measurement at $65, but will play it by ear if prices are even weaker than expected.

Now that you know what Rhodes looks for and how he conducted three well-timed swing-trade battles, let's go a little further and see how his approach works against the backdrop of time.

In an online journal published at MSN Money, he pursued a successful campaign from 2001 through 2002, beating the market averages and five peers by a wide margin. Fifteen of twenty-two trades in a hypothetical $100,000 portfolio from December 3, 2001 through September 30, 2002 were successful, yielding a 56 percent return during a period when the S&P 500 was down 27 percent, the Nasdaq fell 36 percent, and the Russell 2000 fell 19 percent. (See Table 5.1.)

To learn how Rhodes' 2002 swing-trading campaign unfolded, let's look at excerpts from his comments on major trades during the year, along with annotations of the charts. The following are Rhodes' own words, which proved remarkably prescient. (Some entries have been combined to condense the narrative.)

Table 5.1 Richard Rhodes' 2002 Campaign in Strategy Lab

Security	Long/Short	# Shares	Open Date	Open $	Close Date	Close $	Return
Rydex Ursa (bear fund)	Long	2,418	6-Dec-2001	$10.34	4-Feb-2002	$11.01	6.48%
ProFunds UltraShort OTC	Long	693	6-Dec-2001	$36.08	4-Feb-2002	$43.28	19.96%
Cheesecake Factory	Short	500	15-Jan-2002	$35.20	4-Feb-2002	$37.25	-5.82%
Hot Topic	Short	750	15-Jan-2002	$22.53	4-Feb-2002	$22.31	0.99%
Schlumberger	Long	500	4-Feb-2002	$55.21	13-Mar-2002	$61.50	11.39%
Genentech	Long	431	4-Feb-2002	$49.75	7-Feb-2002	$46.95	-5.63%
Nasdaq-100 Trust	Short	500	14-Feb-2002	$37.15	13-Mar-2002	$37.41	-0.70%
Genentech	Short	500	14-Feb-2002	$49.45	15-Apr-2002	$39.80	19.51%
Micron Technology	Short	500	14-Feb-2002	$30.00	1-May-2002	$24.50	18.33%
BorgWarner Inc.	Short	500	13-Mar-2002	$64.00	22-May-2002	$64.96	-1.50%
Phelps Dodge	Short	500	13-Mar-2002	$40.90	2-May-2002	$36.05	11.86%
Delta and Pine Land	Long	500	28-Mar-2002	$19.15	3-Jun-2002	$19.35	1.04%
American Woodmark	Short	500	15-Apr-2002	$62.88	16-Aug-2002	$48.00	23.66%
MAXIMUS	Long	500	1-May-2002	$31.00	22-May-2002	$30.40	-1.94%
Williams-Sonoma	Short	1,000	1-May-2002	$28.71	16-Aug-2002	$25.05	12.73%
Newmont Mining	Short	1,000	22-May-2002	$31.05	3-Jun-2002	$31.18	-0.42%
Airborne	Short	1,000	22-May-2002	$21.58	16-Aug-2002	$13.39	37.95%
Whole Foods Market	Short	500	3-Jun-2002	$50.90	16-Aug-2002	$48.37	4.97%
Hot Topic	Short	500	3-Jun-2002	$25.60	16-Aug-2002	$16.43	35.82%
Coach	Short	1,000	30-Aug-2002	$24.02	*	$27.11	-12.86%
QLogic	Short	1,000	30-Aug-2002	$34.82	*	$26.96	22.57%
Manhattan Associates	Short	1,000	30-Aug-2002	$23.11	*	$13.90	39.85%

*Not closed on 9/28/02T

JOURNAL ENTRIES

Journal: **Dec. 6, 2002**

Buy $25,000 of Rydex Ursa, a bear fund that returns the inverse of the S&P 500.

"As we move forward into the New Year, I see several very specific themes that will dominate the economic landscape—chiefly, that international economic growth will be less than expected and thus will contribute little in the way of economic stimulus for 2002. Europe continues to falter as it lags the United States by up to six months in terms of lowering interest rates. On the other hand, Asia is faltering more so than at any other time in recent history, but the prevailing view is that a return to vigorous growth will occur. I shall politely disagree and look for tepid growth as the Tiger years of the 1990s come to a belated close. In essence, incremental world growth is slowing dramatically.

"On the domestic economic front, I believe the drivers will be consumer spending and corporate capital spending. Currently, I believe the consumer is in the process of retrenching and that corporate America will continue to lower business capital spending investment even more than expected. Consumer spending will falter, given real salary and wage decreases, thus leaving consumers with no incremental discretionary funding options.

"Corporate America has yet to see a return on investment from previous years' profligate spending and will continue to retrench as it seeks to use positive cash flow to service debt—something that didn't seem important when cheap bond and equity financing were available. For the year to work as bulls hope, several things must occur: Revenues must increase, SG&A (selling, general, and administrative) expenditures must decrease, and/or capital expenditures must decrease. My belief is that revenue will not increase sufficiently to mitigate still bloated cost structures, and thus SG&A and capital expenditures must move lower to accomplish this goal—hurting suppliers.

"On the domestic front, we continue to hear of additional cases of corporate America declining to offer employees pay raises of any sort for 2002. This encompasses current year-end bonuses, cost-of-living pay raises, and stock options, which will serve to limit the amount of fuel necessary to stimulate an increase in consumer spending above current levels. This is being borne out in stagnation of the personal income figures, and we suspect they will continue to worsen over the course of the next year, and will rightly affect consumer spending with a lag. Consumers will spend until it begins to hurt, and this point of pain is rapidly approaching.

"Given this view, I feel that all rallies should be sold and will buy $25,000 worth of the bear fund Rydex Ursa, which returns the inverse of the S&P 500 Index. [See Figure 5.9.]

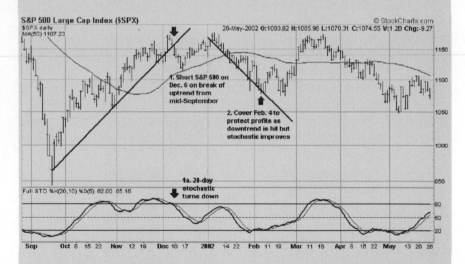

Figure 5.9   On December 6, Rhodes put 25 percent of his portfolio into a mutual fund that returns the inverse of the S&P 500 to leverage his belief that the rally that had started in late September following the terrorist attacks would be reversed as investors soured on prospects for the world economy. He sold the fund in early February for a profit when the market showed signs of reversing.
Source: StockCharts.com.

Journal: Jan. 15, 2002

**Short 500 shares of Hot Topic. Place stop at a trade above $38.
Short 500 shares of Cheesecake Factory. Place stop at a trade
above $38.**

"On Friday, we heard Fed Chairman Alan Greenspan speak on the
economy, and I believe the message was clear—the economy is going
to expand at a slower growth rate than which many are now basing
their market viewpoints upon.

"What I found interesting is that he warned the economy would not
recover if sustained business demand for investment did not materialize as expected. And he appeared to be quite worried in regards to this
fact, whereas, market participants are only too sure of this. While it
may be his job to worry, I believe his message was that one should
view the current market rally with a healthy dose of skepticism. He
was so worried that he continues to suggest future rate cuts will be necessary—a nod to the notion that this recession is worse than those in
the past.

"To wit, we saw that during the 1990–1991 recession there was a
slow V-shaped recovery, but this is the exception and not the norm.
Since the 1960s, many of the recessions were punctuated with a quarter or two of economic growth between quarters of economic decline,
giving a chart of the GDP the shape of a "W." This is where I believe
the economy is currently sitting, and quite possibly it could be sitting
in a worse position—that of a "U." If this is the case, the markets
aren't prepared for this, for the recent rally implies a "V" recovery,
and therefore I believe an adjustment is likely over the course of the
next several months.

"To profit from this potential decline, we believe that consumer
spending is finally going to falter, as consumer balance sheets are in poor
shape. From an employer's perspective, the tough business environment
is going to keep a lid on pay increases for the coming year, or if given at
all, they will be small indeed. And, when one adds to this the fact that
health-care insurance premiums are rising for employees, as well as co-
payments and deductibles, this will serve to decrease real wages, which
in turn would crimp consumer spending. This will be especially true in

the restaurant and teen clothing areas. As such, I offer the following short positions on the opening of trading Tuesday morning:

"Short 500 shares of Hot Topic. This retailer caters to teenagers, and we think that an economic decline will hit teens hard as job growth reverses and turns into job decline. Discretionary spending will be impacted. While teenagers should continue to spend, they will not spend as much—and this shall serve to keep profit margins slim as sale items become more prevalent. Place the stop loss at a trade above $38.

"Short 500 shares of Cheesecake Factory. Restaurants will suffer, as the public will eat out perhaps one less time per week, but it is precisely this one time per week that will hurt novelty restaurant chains. Place the stop loss at a trade above $38.

Journal: Feb. 4, 2002

- Sell position in Rydex Ursa Fund at the close.
- Sell position in ProFunds Ultra Short OTC Fund at the close.
- Cover short position on 500 shares of Hot Topic at the open.
- Cover short position on 500 shares of Cheesecake Factory at the open.
- Buy 500 shares of Schlumberger at the open. Place stop loss on a trade below $49.
- Buy 500 shares of Genentech at the open. Place stop loss on a trade below $47.

Fundamentally Bearish; Technically Bullish

"The trading action of the past week has been volatile indeed, but the market has ended essentially flat. The manner in which we arrived at this level is quite important—that is, we move lower through support in most of the major indices, but then return back through to trade at the levels that existed before support had been violated.

"I find that bullish, for when markets do not act as one thinks they should given the technical evidence, then there are other dynamics present. And given that I am currently short the indices and other equities, I believe the time has arrived in which to cover my entire position for the risk of holding them has increased.

"To gauge this, I simply use the 20-day stochastic, which has served me quite well in the past. For all the major indices, it has turned higher—in some cases before it was able to trade in oversold territory.

Thus, there is strength in the market, and I learned long ago that the markets are able to trade illogically and irrationally for far longer than I can remain solvent.

"I shall be closing out my long mutual fund positions related to being short the Nasdaq 100 and S&P 500; and, I shall cover my short equity positions in Cheesecake Factory and Hot Topic.

While I continue to be bearish on retail, the mental capital spent holding and watching these positions is clouding my trading judgment. Good riddance. Having said that, I feel there are several issues from a technical point of view that I would like to be—namely Schlumberger and Genentech.

"I feel that the current rally in Schlumberger is in the process of breaking out, given [that] the 200-day moving average at $53.25 has been violated to the upside. Additionally, as price action moves through $56, this would break through the neckline of a well-defined inverted head & shoulders pattern, and would then project to upwards [of] the high $60s. Furthermore, the 20-day stochastic has turned higher, and in combination with the bullish fundamental factors, clearly offers reason for a trade. [See Figure 5.10.]

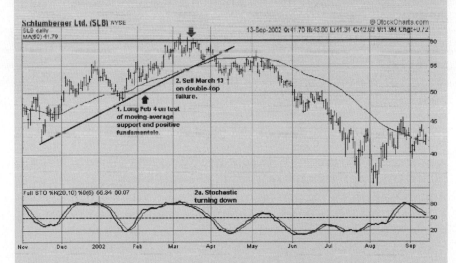

Figure 5.10 On February 4, Rhodes went long Schlumberger based on mild bullishness for the oil sector and technical strength. He closed the trade for a profit a month later, just in time, after it failed to punch through a double top.
Source: StockCharts.com.

"In Genentech, current price action has been quite bullish—support at $47 has been successfully retested, and yesterday's price action formed what is known as an "outside reversal day." I put great heed in this formation, and given that it occurred while testing previous low support, and [is] consequently breaking above its 200-day moving average—I feel this trade could materialize in large trade—my target over the next two months is $68 to $70.

"My current overall view of the equity markets has not changed. I am fundamentally bearish, but technically bullish. While as a rule, I don't trade in such circumstances, I feel compelled to do so at this time given the compelling technical arguments that can be made for the above issues.

Journal: Feb. 14, 2002

- Short 500 shares of the Nasdaq 100 Trust (QQQ) at the market open.
- Short 500 shares of Micron Technology (MU) at the market.
- Short 500 shares of Genentech (DNA) at the market.

"The current technical rally in the U.S. equity markets has come as expected, but its wherewithal is quite suspect. I expect overhead resistance levels to keep a lid on price action, and would look [to] sell, not buy, now.

"The economic evidence to date has stabilized, but there is no compelling evidence to suggest that a strong economic rebound is in order for the second half of this year. In fact, I believe the economy will do the "double dip," as consumer spending will falter in the months ahead. If one takes the retail sales figures, absolute level seen in January 2002 was identical to that seen in July 2001—and when one adds inflation to the equation, as small as it might be—then one sees that real spending is falling. I further believe this will become further engrained in the months ahead as "paycheck shock" filters its way through the spending habits of Americans. Paychecks aren't increasing, and real purchasing power has been lost—thus the future for a continued increase in consumer spending is quite dim from our perspective.

"On the capital-spending front, I believe current levels reflect inventory build due to depleted stocks, and the adding of additional stuff on shelves in response to the terrorist attack. In essence, just-in-time inventory systems have shown their weakness, and that must be compensated for as part of a disaster recovery plan. As the year moves forward, I expect capital spending to fall even further as revenue growth plans fall over and above those projected at this time. Therefore, in combination with slower consumer spending and slower capital spending, the world and in particular the equity markets are not prepared for this—especially in light of the retail sales data released on Wednesday.

"Thus, timing is critical. In the Dow Industrials, I see that on a technical basis a "double bottom" has formed as the 9,900 level was succinctly broken, and this would presage a move higher into measured resistance at 10,200. This would have the effect of breaking above the 200-day moving average, and may bring further buying to the Dow. However, I do not expect that to happen and would expect resistance at this important moving average to continue providing untenable resistance.

"As for the Nasdaq Composite, I would expect the potential for the current rally to continue into its confluence of resistance between 1,900 and 1,950—previous support turned resistance and the 200-day moving average reside in this area. However, given [that] the engrained downtrend should begin to exert itself soon, I find it hard to want to be long during this rally, and would prefer to sell into it.

"Having said this, I offer up the following recommendations to be executed as follows:

Short 500 shares of the Nasdaq 100 tracking stock (QQQ) at the market on the opening of trading. Given [that] the current rally has little in the way of legs, and the fact that the intermediate-term stochastics are falling, lead us to believe this rally will falter—and fairly quickly at that. Upon execution, I would place the stop loss at $42.

"Short 500 shares of Micron Technology (MU) at the market on the opening of trading. MU is trading up into resistance in the $39.00 to $41.00 area—which is the "apex" of a longer-term triangle formation—this generally denotes resistance, and given MU has risen from the $18 level to [the] current level, I believe this discounts a "V" shaped recovery in the memory market. Nothing could be further from the truth—business remains weak, and this shall become more apparent in the weeks ahead. [See Figure 5.11.]

"Short 500 shares of Genentech (DNA) at the market on the open-

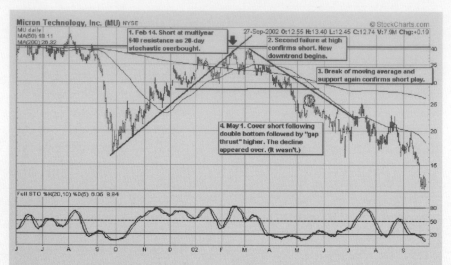

Figure 5.11   On February 14, Rhodes went short semiconductor maker Micron Technology to exploit his belief that the economy was rolling over and that the winter Nasdaq rally would not last. He took the position at a multiyear resistance level— $40—and hung on for an 18 percent gain over three months.
Source: StockCharts.com.

ing of trading. DNA has had every opportunity to move higher with the broader market over the past several days—but has not to the degree with which I would expect. In fact, resistance in the $50.00 to $51.00 area has proven untenable, and a reversal appears to have occurred to the downside on Wednesday. Thus, I shall sell weakness—and DNA is weak.

Journal: March 28, 2002

• Buy 500 shares of Delta & Pine Land at the open.

Anticipating Another Long Decline

"The current decline has moderated, and is showing a propensity to move higher from support in conjunction with the 20-day stochastic. I like this price action, and since I'm quite short in my portfolio, I will even it out just a bit.

"The current trading pattern can only be characterized as a topping process; one that takes time to accomplish, and with a good many fits and starts. At present we are in a fit, and I suspect this shall continue for several more weeks.

"The Dow Industrials and S&P 500 are unable to break above resistance set several weeks ago, and are undergoing a bit of technical regrouping for another possible assault on these levels given the near inexorable rise since September 2001. However, with benefit of time, it may turn out to be more than just a small fit—it's still too early to say definitively.

"Currently, I'm comfortable being short the market. I'm getting some leg room in several of the positions, and I'm able to sit tight and allow the market to see what I see—equity prices moving lower over the course of the next several months.

"However, I would like to add one long position in Delta & Pine Land (DLP). This is a defensive move since Delta Pine has no propensity to follow the ups and downs of the major indices. Instead, it nicely follows my simple technical discipline of trading with a rising 20-day stochastic. If anything, the stock's recent decline has been quite bearish. It's had nearly three straight months of bearish action, and is showing signs of moderating and turning higher—and it is doing so from daily support at the $17.50 level. Thus, I would expect to see short covering and value players look to enter Delta Pine on any decline from current levels, but I don't believe that will occur. I believe the price action of the past several days augurs well for a bottom and subsequent rise in Delta Pine.

"The consensus on interest rates is that the easing period now appears to be over, and a tightening round is about to begin in the months ahead. I have never seen such an aggressive campaign by the Federal Reserve not have an effect on the equity markets. All of the major averages are lower since the onset of the campaign to lower interest rates—with the obvious exception of the S&P 400 Mid Cap and S&P 600 Small Cap Indices. This isn't the stuff normal interest rate cycles are made of. I can only surmise several factors are at work that are restraining or impeding the major averages from moving higher in such an accommodating environment.

"First, I believe the profits recession is far from over given the fact revenues are not growing as expected, and pricing power has yet to return. Second, I believe that price-to-earnings ratios were quite high to begin with at the start of the FOMC's campaign, and thus the effect of lower rates only sought to validate such high P/Es in the first place. Thus, I feel that the expansion accorded a positive interest rate environment is already embedded in stock prices, but that of higher rates is not. Given the lofty valuation levels where stocks are currently trading—a contraction in P/Es combined with less than expected growth in revenue and earnings does not spell higher equity prices, but lower, and I fear *much lower* prices.

Journal: April 15, 2002

- Cover the short of 500 shares of Genentech at the open.
- Sell short 500 shares of American Woodmark at the open.

"The current market environment is treacherous: One day the market rallies violently, only to have the next day decline violently. This can only serve to confuse.

"At times such as these, it is best to step back and survey the landscape—and when we do, we can clearly see the Dow Industrials declining, the Nasdaq declining, the S&P 500 declining. The exceptions are the S&P 400 and 600, which continue to attract a good deal of the available capital to the detriment of the larger cap indices. However, we believe the bullish run seen by these indices is quickly coming to an end.

"Thursday's price action traced out what we would consider to be an ominous and extremely negative formation—the outside reversal day. Thus, if this formation holds true to form, then we can expect the strongest of the strong to falter, and if this occurs, we would expect the other indices to falter even further than currently seen.

"On the economic and earnings front, I believe the recent economic reports regarding retail sales are suspect. In fact, when we look at this report, we see that if one takes out the volatile auto and gas sectors, spending has risen at a 0.1% rate for February and March. And given that the auto sector fell even further during March, the rate of spending going forward is moderating, and it is doing so at a rate that is not and will not be friendly toward the equity markets.

"From an earnings perspective, General Electric's recent release left quite a bit to be desired given it is truly representative of the entire economy, for its subsidiaries cut a wide swath. If GE cannot match revenue figures, how can we, and why should we believe other less well-managed companies will be able to do so. Although the economy is growing due to an inventory buildup, it is not producing the profits necessary for companies to continue their capital investment programs. Therefore, where the growth is going to come from, we honestly don't know.

"Thus, we offer the following changes to our portfolio:

"Buy to cover the short of 500 shares of Genentech (DNA) at the market. This shall close out our position. We were fortunate to have been short of Genentech, for the decline in this issue has been substantial. Thus, our current propensity is to exit this position, for clearly the risk–reward ratio is tilted towards risk.

"Sell short 500 shares of American Woodmark (AMWD) at the open. American Woodmark has traded violently over the past several weeks, but not as violently as seen on Thursday, when prices moved to $67.50 only to close at $62.50. This formed the ominous "outside reversal day" as described above, but it did so against the backdrop of a consolidation within a larger downtrend. This is extremely bearish, and lower prices will result. [See Figure 5.12.]

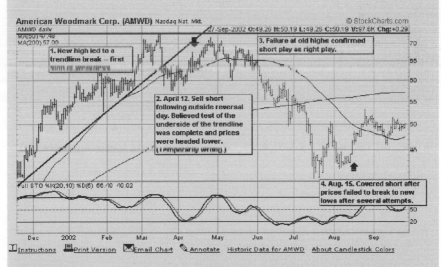

Figure 5.12 On April 15, Rhodes went short home products maker American Woodmark following an outside reversal day. This was temporarily a bad move, as prices turned higher. But the stock soon ran into resistance at old highs and collapsed. It was covered four months later for a 24 percent gain.
Source: StockCharts.com.

Journal: **May 1, 2002**

- Buy 500 shares to cover short position in Micron Technology.
- Buy 500 shares to cover short in Phelps Dodge.
- Sell short 500 shares of Williams-Sonoma.
- Buy 500 shares of Maximus (MMS) .

"Beware the rubber-band rally. The current rally off the new reactionary lows in all the major indices can only be characterized as a countertrend rally within the context of a much larger downturn. Given that the indices have moved steadily lower for the past several weeks, a period of brief rally is to be expected. In fact, it is warranted, as it shall bring the market back to technical health. In essence, it is relieving an extremely oversold condition.

"But the rally is of the "rubber-band" variety—quick, sharp and quite bearish. It brings those who are afraid of missing the beginning of the next leg higher in the equity markets. However, we don't believe this shall materialize, and those initiating long positions at this time will soon be underwater.

"And thus the angst will continue. The frustration of being long in this current environment outside of the mid-to-small cap area is wreaking havoc on the investing psyche, which of course is quite negative.

"I feel it necessary to revisit my current positions and adjust them to take advantage of the upcoming move lower. While a majority of my positions are short, I have interspersed several long positions amongst them, for although I feel the indices are moving lower, I also feel that this is a stock picker's market. Consequently, this provides a modicum of a hedged position for me. I like the thinking behind this tactic and am very comfortable in doing so.

"Today I wish to buy to cover 500 shares of Micron Technology (MU) at the market at the opening of trading. Micron has thus far worked extremely well for me, and therefore I believe the time is nigh where the propensity of traders will be to buy at depressed levels. While I believe it will move lower, the bang for the buck isn't there any longer, so I shall exit.

"Buy to cover 500 shares of Phelps Dodge (PD) at the market at the opening of trading. In much the same manner as MU, I believe I have gotten enough from PD, and feel other issues will give the bang for the buck I am seeking.

"Sell short 500 shares of Williams Sonoma (WSM) at the market at the opening of trading. The stock has risen approximately 200% off its September 2001 lows, and this near-parabolic move is showing signs of moderating, as it has yet to participate at the major indices are moving higher. This relative weakness should be sold. And further, the previous highs in 1999 are in the proximate area. Resistance shall be stiff indeed. [See Figure 5.13.]

"Buy 500 shares of Maximus (MMS) at the market at the opening of trading. Maximus formed a low in late March. It has since formed what would appear to be a consolidation, and is now moving higher with an outside reversal day on Tuesday. This is quite bullish, and thus our propensity is to own that which is showing strength . . . and Maximus is.

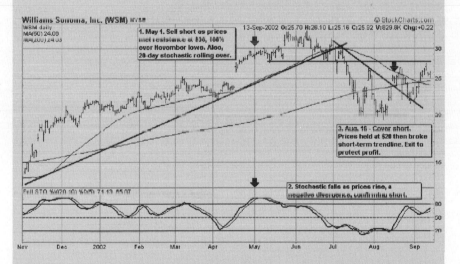

Figure 5.13 On May 1, Rhodes went short home retailer Williams Sonoma amid relative weakness following a 100 percent gain from terrorist-attack lows. The trade temporarily went against him, but declining stochastics at highs kept him in the trade. Exit for profit came three months later following rebound from July lows and break of downtrend.
Source: StockCharts.com.

Journal: **May 22, 2002**

- Cover short position in BorgWarner at the market.
- Sell long position in Maximus at the market.
- Sell short 1,000 shares of Airborne (ABF) at the market.
- Sell short 1,000 shares of Newmont Mining (NEM) at the market.

It's time to sell the small caps.

"The rally off the lows in the Dow Industrials and the Nasdaq Composite are countertrend rallies, which upon their completion should be sold—and sold quite hard.

"I don't believe we have seen the end of the current rally, and at a minimum I would expect to see prices move higher to test their recent highs. From my perspective, the current decline within the rally is nothing more than traders and investors alike selling upon the first sign of a rally. They have now become trained to do so, and thus will likely keep a lid upon any substantial price rally.

"This is a[n] 180 degree turn from previous times, when "buy the dips" was the mantra. However, if we turn towards the S&P Midcap 400 Index ($MID.X) and S&P Smallcap 600 ($SML.X), it is very clear that tops are formed and prices are now moving lower.

"I attribute this to sector rotation. These indices have benefited substantially since 1999 from the rotational effects from large caps to small caps. But I believe this effect has come to an end. Therefore, on a relative basis, if one were to own stocks, one would want large caps. And, if one were to be selling stocks—short or otherwise—one would sell the small-cap sector.

"I expect this phenomenon to continue for many months. Quite simply, the small-cap sector has been the beneficiary of nearly all the new money invested into the market. In essence, participants were chasing momentum. Now that momentum has shifted, I too shall shift. I offer the following changes to my portfolio:

"Cover entire short position in BorgWarner (BWA) at the market at the opening of trading. This short position has yet to work in my favor. It hasn't acted as I had expected; and it is doing nothing more than wasting precious mental trading capital. Clearly, there are other areas in which I would feel more comfortable.

"Sell entire long position in Maximus (MMS) at the market at the opening of trading. Once again, I have waited patiently for this position to bear fruit. It has not, and thus I am required by my trading rules to jettison this position immediately. The mental capital tied up in this position doesn't warrant hoping that it shall work as the current rally materializes. Enough said.

"Sell short 1,000 shares of Airborne (ABF) at the market on the opening of trading. My interest lies purely from a technical perspective in which Tuesday's trading pattern was nothing other than an outside reversal day lower, and I tend to want to trade on these type patterns for they indicate trend exhaustion. The recent rally off the April 2002 low was quite substantial on the order of 50%—and I believe the "rubberband" effect will snap ABF back lower. Also, oil prices continue to trade at recent high levels, and this will impact the cost structure of ABF moving forward. [See Figure 5.14.]

"Sell short 1,000 shares of Newmont Mining (NEM) at the market

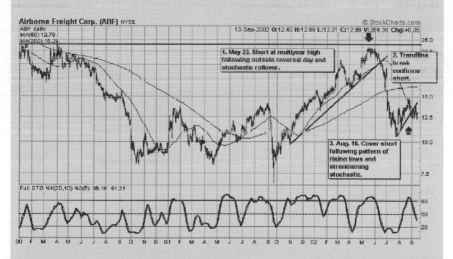

Figure 5.14 On May 14, Rhodes went short home retailer shipper Airborne Freight after it hit multiyear highs on weakening momentum and an outside reversal day. Although he did not cover at the lows, it was his second biggest win of the year at a gain of 38 percent.
Source: StockCharts.com.

on the opening of trading. Gold is now glittering, and it is glittering simply because there is a plethora of buying. This is hardly the stuff bull markets are made of, and given my belief that gold is nothing more than an industrial metal subject to the ebbs and flows of economic growth, I believe short positions are well warranted.

"While prices are hitting new highs, I believe the current rally will be the final rally. Therefore, I want to be short. I understand the risk of becoming short too early, but believe the upside will be quite well contained.

Journal: June 3, 2002

- Place order to sell 500 shares in Delta and Pine Land. Coat the market.
- Place order to cover position in Newmont Mining at the market.
- Place order to cover half of position in Williams Sonoma at the market.
- Place order to sell short 500 shares of Whole Foods Market at the market.
- Place order to sell short 500 shares of Hot Topic at the market.

In Position for the Summer Doldrums

"The summer doldrums have arrived: Volume has diminished, as interest is now directed at other more pressing matters, such [as] vacations, family events, and so forth. We wouldn't expect this pattern of low volume to dissipate anytime soon, and while many ascribe low volume trading sessions with a continued decline, we don't necessarily do so.

"History has shown that during the summer doldrums of May through August that rallies do in fact occur, and in many cases August turns out to be the high trade watermark for the year. Therefore, while the major indices have declined against our short-term beliefs that a rally would materialize, it would appear that the correction has garnered an inordinate amount of support over the course of the past several trading sessions. But I believe this correction is nothing more than just that—a correction—and that Thursday's rally off early-May support may have been enough to satisfy market participants as a successful test of support.

"What we do know is that although we are short-term bullish, we are extremely concerned by the nature of the developing technical patterns if in fact we are not correct, and I will seek to change my position very quickly as conditions warrant. Thursday's reversal off support at the lows pulled the major indices out of the throes of what could be a potentially disastrous decline back to the September lows in many of the indices. Quite obviously, this remains a very large concern for us, for we clearly want to become even shorter than we currently are into market rallies, and thus we are going to rearrange our portfolio to capture this move.

"Sell our long position of 500 shares in Delta and Pine Land Co. (DLP). Delta has returned to support and has shown very little in the way of rallying in the manner in which we thought it would, and thus does not bear out participation any longer. It is just that simple. Cover 1,000 shares, or all our position in Newmont Mining (NEM). To date, Newmont has yet to work for us, and thus I will sell half. There is no other reason—but it is a good reason, for mental capital is tied up in a position that has clearly not worked—thus our reluctance to continue participating, but nonetheless we shall be patient with our other half a while longer.

"Cover 500 shares, or 50% of our position, in Williams Sonoma (WSM). Given our large position, and the fact that earnings were a blowout, I am prepared to remain short only a 50% position and would rather diversify into other positions to mitigate the increased risk in holding this position.

"Sell short 500 shares of Whole Foods Market (WFMI). The rally seen in Whole Foods Market is faltering—losing momentum, and thus my propensity to become short that which is losing momentum—especially in the mid- to small-cap area—has been great[ly] increased. We would look for prices to move toward the $40 to $44 level over the course of the next several months.

"Sell short 500 shares of Hot Topic (HOTT). The decline in Hot Topic after reaching new highs is suggestive of a topping process, of which our 20-day stochastic has turned lower and has formed a "negative divergence" with price action. We feel this indicates "the top" is in—thus we want to be short—and once again, we want to do so in the mid- to small-cap area.

Journal: **July 3, 2002**

• No new trades. Do nothing—absolutely nothing. Sit tight, be patient—my positions are working well.

"The pendulum has swung—from that of aggressive accounting tactics to that of extreme conservatism. This will have the effect of clearing the decks, so to speak, but in doing so will cause earnings projections to fall, and more importantly, investor expectations of earnings to fall.

"In addition to these earnings revisions, we shall have the parallel process of "valuation" compression. This provides investors with a backdrop that is not conducive to purchasing equities. In fact, it is downright bearish given the high level of earnings expectations and the current level of valuations. Therefore, the current decline could become very nasty, perhaps on the order of 8% to 10% in all the major averages, and this may require only several weeks to accomplish.

"However, this slew of selling is likely to form an intermediate-term bottom, upon which a sharp rally will materialize. If I had my druthers, I would expect the low to arrive in the next several weeks and I would look to become long during that period. It will be followed by a rally into the late August to late September time frame, when I would then look to become very short once again. But until then, do absolutely nothing.

Journal: **July 26, 2002**

• No new trades. Do nothing—absolutely nothing.

Still can't see bottom.

"Investors and traders alike face a dilemma: Do they listen to the economists who say the economy is going to move higher in the future by virtue of it rising today, i.e., "trending growth," which will push supposedly undervalued stocks higher? Or, do they listen to price action, which clearly signifies (at least in my mind) that stocks continue to be relatively expensive, and that the economy may in fact hit a soft spot once again, or even a hard patch? Now, I must admit, price action is far from foolproof, but I prefer to listen to it, for it is the collective knowledge of all market participants at that point in time.

"Economists will point to a growing economy to lead share prices higher as earnings growth abounds, and the labor picture will "turn the corner" as companies find themselves too lean for their own good and then must begin hiring. This is the paint-by-numbers schematic. However, this is not the present case, so where is the growth? Unfortunately, companies find themselves with no pricing power whatsoever, and no commensurate revenue growth. Therefore, profitability has faltered, business capital spending remains tepid and employment growth is stagnating. Given the fact that the economy is expected to rise by 3%-4%, why aren't earnings growing? Why aren't companies more constructive in their outlooks? Are they setting the bar lower? I don't think so. I think they are being frank, and quite literally, business isn't all that good—especially in relation to the current level of interest rates and equity valuations. Ultimately, the share indice valuations are predicated upon the potential for net free cash flow of a company. If that company cannot earn a commensurate return through its invested capital or equity stock, then that company simply should not be valued at 25 times earnings when revenue growth is 2%-5%.

"This begs the question, "When will the market bottom?" And to that I answer, I honestly don't know. I thought a counter-trend rally was in the process of developing last week; it did not. I listened, and I have stayed short. My positions are working extremely well and I will change nothing for the time being, for nothing is compelling enough for me to do so. So keep your eye on the ball and once again do nothing—absolutely nothing

Journal: **Aug. 16, 2002**

• Exit all short positions immediately.

"The rally over the past several weeks was substantial and the manner in which it occurred leads many to believe that this is *the* bottom. However, I believe this is not the case. I believe that while this rally, quite likely [a] very sharp rally, will continue for several more weeks, I do not believe the final low has been seen.

"In essence, short-covering rallies are powerful, and destructive in nature if one is short. And given that I am short, I am obviously concerned with my positions, since they are wildly profitable. Thus, in the spirit of prudence, I am exiting all of my short positions immediately.

"I am moving to cash in lieu of further market data upon which to trade. I have been fortunate to be profitable during the recent downturn and even through a majority of the upturn. But the evidence is shaping up to support a rise in the near future, and if this is the case, my next move may be to move selectively to [the] long side of the market.

"I would do so with great trepidation. My reasoning is simple: The 10-year note yield has fallen to levels not seen in many a year. Given that a majority of institutions and hedge funds have been long the U.S. bond market for quite some time, they are about to take a good deal of those profits. The ability to earn large gains in the bond market appears to have passed.

"Thus, these institutions will simply redeploy these funds toward stocks. In essence, a pool of available liquidity for share prices is increasing over and above the loss seen at the retail level. As share prices rise further, there will be less of a propensity on the part of institutions to hold cash, or buy bonds. However, this, too, shall end—but not likely before a rally of proportion has occurred. Therefore, in the days ahead, I will be plotting the future—and this includes analysis regarding the long as well as the short perspective.

Journal: Aug. 30, 2002

- Sell short 1,000 shares of Coach at the market.
- Sell short 1,000 shares of Manhattan Associates at the market.
- Sell short 1,000 shares of QLogic at the market.

The rally is over; I'm going short.

"Just two weeks ago, I issued a call to move out of all short positions and head to the sidelines. This was obviously the prudent thing to do, as prices continued higher while my confidence in the downward move had been shaken.

"However, the time has arrived in which I believe the fundamentals and technicals are back in sync, and thus would augur for a return to the short perspective.

"Given that Tuesday's durable goods report was outstanding, it would appear at first blush that prices should have headed higher.

They did not to any significant degree. And, when consumer confidence was released later that morning, it showed that the ill effects of the continued equity market swoon, coupled with the tepid employment picture, have now come home to roost. The effect is to cause consumers who were once thought bulletproof to hunker down for the storm, for the downturn has gone on a good deal longer than many had ever expected.

"Thus, spending patterns must be adjusted—and the readily available evidence points to a substantial slowing of spending. If one takes RadioShack's words literally, August sales were "plunging," while Wal-Mart's sales were nothing short of weak. Both were weak during a[n] historically strong period. When we see events such as this engrain themselves in the economic fabric, it cannot and will not be conducive to the purchasing of equities. It is conducive to the selling short of equities.

"However, I should note that given the extreme move up off the lows, the potential exists for prices to be merely correcting. If that is the case, higher prices are obviously ahead. I don't believe that to be the case, but I understand the arguments behind it. Enough said.

"My first move today is with luxury good retailer Coach. The continued slowdown in consumer spending per GDP figures, per retail sales figures, per RadioShack, per Best Buy, per Wal-Mart, etc., will not bode well for the upper-end retailers. Consumers have taken substantial sums out of their homes over the past several months and have yet to deploy that money. This shift in spending characteristics bodes ill for this sector. And further—the technicals are deteriorating rapidly.

"I also want to be short Manhattan Associates. Although capital spending appears to have stabilized, it has done so at levels commensurate with March 2001. Hardly strong, but nonetheless, the levels have stabilized. Given the large price-to-sales valuation on Manhattan, I believe prices will move significantly lower with the course of time. And, given that the technical picture has failed at key resistance levels, the time to participate is now. [See Figure 5.15.]

"And I also wish to be short network storage device maker QLogic. In much the same vein as Manhattan, I believe that on a valuation basis, QLogic is significantly overvalued relative to its peer group and the market. And the relative price action of the past several weeks is poor indeed—so poor, that it is leading me to become short.

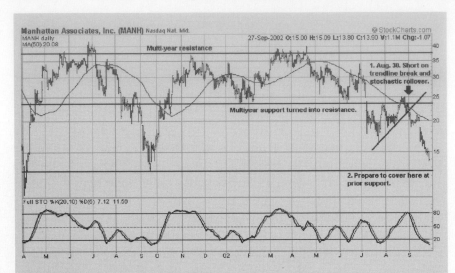

Figure 5.15　On August 30, Rhodes went short shares of supply-chain management software maker Manhattan Associates following a trendline break and failure to break through prior resistance. The trade netted a 40 percent return in a couple of weeks as the shares sank toward their post 9/11 low after a peer pre-announced weak results for the quarter.
Source: StockCharts.com.

As you can see, Rhodes' combination of fundamental beliefs about the economy combined with a limited number of technical analysis tools netted substantial gains in a year when so many other traders were constantly confused and off balance. Every play was not successful, but his trading rules help him exit failed positions with a minimum of loss. The lesson here is to formulate a strong set of convictions about the global economy, and then look for ways to exploit those notions with specific trading vehicles that show specific sorts of price strength or weakness.

Chapter 6

PHIL ERLANGER
Dr. Sentiment and Mr. Strength

Phil Erlanger is all about pain. He has built a sterling reputation among Wall Street insiders as one of the few analysts of any stripe who can definitively determine whether bulls or bears have made the biggest bet for or against any individual stock or sector, and would feel the most distress if the current trend were suddenly to go in the opposite direction. In industry argot, a gigantic move against short sellers is called a "short squeeze"—and accurately forecasting them can yield fantastic swing trades that last weeks or months.

Erlanger's studies of the market are really all about the study of human folly, for every important rise and decline in a stock is a reaction against the false beliefs of the biggest players in the previous move: The larger the mistake of those players, the larger and longer the following move.

It's pretty simple, if you think about it. When a stock goes up sharply after a fall, it is taking money away from bears who stay short too long. When a stock goes down sharply after a rise, it is taking money away from bulls who stay too long. The more bears who have to cover as the move goes against them, the more fuel for an upsurge. The more bulls who have to sell as the move goes against them, the more fuel for a decline.

Another way to see the market from Erlanger's viewpoint: Every stock and index constantly cycles through a series of advance phases followed by decline phases, and the magnitude of each phase is dictated by the size of the mistaken crowd as the phase turns from one direction to another. The more people who have committed the wrong way, the larger the subsequent move. This is due to one fact: The greatest single factor affecting investor psychology is price action. The more price moves in one direction, the more the crowd accepts this trend as status quo—and believes it will never change.

Of course, there are many gauges of market sentiment: margin debt, short selling, opinions of analysts or market letter writers, mutual fund cash levels, and odd-lot short selling to name just a few. Rather than ask questions of traders or newsletter publishers, as some simplistic senti-ment-analysts do, Erlanger instead studies their actions, for he believes actual trading commitments are more powerful measures of sentiment than opinion. The most telling and quantifiable display of sentiment, he has determined, has been the level of short selling. That's in part because the greatest number of short sales are historically made at exactly the wrong time, when a stock is the most likely to reverse and move up. A bearish newsletter publisher may not react to a suddenly strong price ad-vance in quite the same way as a trader who is carrying a major short po-sition. "Short selling is the quintessential sentiment indicator," he says. It can be associated with specific stocks, industry groups, sectors, mar-kets, and index derivatives. It is perfect because short sellers must buy back the stock they have sold short to get out of their positions so they not only represent opinion, they also represent future potential demand for a stock.

Erlanger didn't come by his views easily, or in any books. He has pa-tiently and creatively built his model of the market by pioneering com-puter-based research techniques well ahead of the crowd. Before we get to those techniques, let's see where they came from.

Education of a Sentimentarian

Erlanger's upbringing was rather genteel. He grew up in a handsome brownstone on the tiny Upper East Side of New York City, around Sixty-eighth Street and Second Avenue, where neighbors included entertainers Tony Bennett and Soupy Sales. His father owned a textile design and manufacturing company that wove fabrics in Massachusetts factories and sold them around the world. The business afforded young Philip the opportunity to attend Trinity School, a Manhattan prep academy known for having kicked out Humphrey Bogart and for having helped to launch the career of tennis star John McEnroe.

After graduating in 1972, Erlanger went to Boston University and studied economics and law. He didn't want to become a lawyer and debate people the rest of his life, so as he mulled a career he became entranced with the idea of becoming a stockbroker. His stepbrother's cousin, who in this case was not a distant relation, worked at Merrill Lynch and took him around the trading floor. He became enamored with the glamour even though the visit came during the great bear market of the mid-1970s—when the market was just emerging from crash levels and about to enter into a rather dull sideways crawl. With gathering belief that he would head for Wall Street, the university student threw himself into econometrics courses, which he described as mostly about finding 50-cent words for 5-cent ideas.

It wasn't easy to get a job at a brokerage firm after graduation, since so many brokers had been thrown out of work. He canvassed every brokerage office he could find in phone books up and down the East Coast, and ultimately found his first job as an account executive at a cheesy commodity options-trading firm. Frustrated with that role, he went to a personnel agency for help. The guy he interviewed with had previously been a broker, and in two weeks had left the agency for a new job at Reynolds Securities. Never one to pass up an opportunity, Erlanger took the interviewer's place at the personnel agency. Then he took a page from his interviewer's playbook, and pestered that guy to give him an interview with his boss. Ultimately he got the job at the company that would soon become Dean Witter Reynolds, and he was up and running with a desk, a telephone, and a stack of leads after a six-month training course. "The one thing I didn't understand about a broker's job is that it's more of a sales job than anything else. Your understanding of the markets is secondary to your ability to sell," he recalls. At first, it was hard to get people interested because they had never heard of his firm. "I'd cold-call people and say, 'Hi, I'm Phil Erlanger from Dean Witter Reynolds,' and people would say, 'What do you want me to rent?' They thought it was *Rentals*."

Before long, the young broker moved on to Merrill Lynch to build his book, or list of clients, as an account exec. He learned at both places the limitations of fundamental analysis: It's great at getting you into situations, but useless for getting you out. "The greatest crime on

Wall Street is the idea that you will do well with any great company in the long term if you buy shares when they've been kicked down," he says. "It's like a casino telling a losing bettor, 'Keep betting, you'll get it back.' " With an increasingly cynical eye, Erlanger began to notice that when everyone loved a stock, it would always go down. If you faded the best idea on the Street by selling short, it would almost always work. One example from the era was the case of Eastern Airlines. The last thing anyone could imagine at the time was that this popular airline, headed by astronaut Frank Borman, with new planes and excellent service, could go belly up—even in a recession. Erlanger bought the bonds, not stock, for clients—and when they started to drop in price and looked like they offered a terrific yield, analysts continued to recommend them. He recalls feeling so strongly about the bonds that he bought some for his family, and they ended up completely worthless—leaving him with a distinctly sour feeling about the ability of fundamental analysis to comprehend the worth of a mismanaged company.

Erlanger says he was never a top producer at Merrill, as he enjoyed the analysis part of his job more than the sales. Bosses criticized him for doing more research than marketing, but he couldn't help wanting to find ways to time trades better. "The market is a living, breathing organism where timing is of the essence," he says. "But they weren't interested in me learning to quantify that."

At nights and on the weekends, he gravitated increasingly toward the study of technical analysis as he saw other brokers study and adopt hand-charting techniques. He read a new book on the moving balance indicator, by Humphrey E. D. Lloyd, and many of the classics of the field. By the late 1970s, he moved to a brokerage that actually had an Apple II-Plus computer he could use to run the only charting software at the time—sold by the notorious newsletter publisher Joseph Granville—and learned to program it himself in Apple Basic. Working with his brother, his first effort produced the industry's first index-charting software that offered a picture of the market with a 10-day moving average of volume. "It is nothing wild by these days' standards—but back then it was fantastic! We called it The King of Wall Street," he recalls. Soon other brokers wanted his program, which ran straight from code with no client-side application. It started at $200, and Erlanger kept raising the price until he was charging $1,000 a pop and brokers were buying thousands of dollars worth of computer hardware to run it. That gave him his first reputation as an analyst. "As pathetically simple as it sounds now, it wasn't then," he says.

Technical analysts at the time were still outsiders on the Street, and gathered in "research clubs" to swap ideas with luminaries like Walter Murphy at Merrill Lynch. Sure, their practice was considered voodoo by fundamental analysts. But even then, if you had a room full of fundamental analysts and one technician, everyone wanted to talk to the technician—as they were so much less vague, even if they were not correct. Erlanger recalls making a presentation to his research club in 1982 that he was long-term bullish—a very contrarian view then—and a member of the audience, a top broker at the brokerage Advest, bought his program and recommended him for a job in the company's research department. The young broker was ecstatic about the opportunity they offered: He didn't have to do any more marketing or selling, just develop his own research and offer technical ideas to the brokers in the Advest system. "To me, that was nirvana," he says.

He made a lot of good calls at Advest. One came after the Dow Jones Industrials had risen to 1,200, and he was quoted in the *Wall Street Journal* and *USA Today* as stating that the Dow would never move below 1,000 again. "That may seem easy to say now, but at 1,200 it was a ballsy thing to declare," he says. "Granville picked it up and in his letter he said it was an example of the enthusiasm you see at the top."

In the late 1970s and early 1980s, Granville could move the market by breathing a few words. But from 1982 on, he fought the market all the way up and people stopped listening. The same happened with renowned Elliott Wave theoretician Robert Prechter. Their demise led Erlanger, who was bullish, to look upon Gann theory and Elliot Wave work as having too many rules that were subject to interpretation.

> One of my core beliefs is that your concepts have to be simple and your applications have to be simple—the more complex, the more opportunities to fool you. Things like the Relative Strength Indicator, or RSI, which many technicians swear by, work great half the time—but the rest of the time they don't. You need to use tools that add value consistently and improve your trading performance.

At Advest, Erlanger developed what he calls his "big, big" philosophy: When you enter a trade, the more you feel like you are putting your hand in a flame, the more successful it will be. "The more offbeat, the more painful the decision is to make, the better your odds are," he says. "My knees knock with every trade I make. It's when I feel cocky that my trades blow up." There's something in the human brain, he likes to say, a psychological widget, that makes us think the wrong way as a trader— that makes us feel comfortable with making terrible mistakes in the market and that makes us feel nervous when acting correctly. And we must work assiduously to sense when that widget is turned on. As an example, if you ask most people if they'd rather buy a stock at a new high or a new low, most will say they'd rather buy the new low. In the view that Erlanger was developing, that was a product of the evil widget—for in buying the new low, you are trying to catch the proverbial falling dagger, while in buying the new high you are buying strength, all other things being equal.

At Advest, Erlanger began to test every computer program the first day it came down the pike—including the first Tradestation, which is now a mainstay on the Street. But the breakthrough for the trading style that would come to characterize him came quite by accident. Journalists used to call him regularly for a quote—he was virtually the voice of Advest—and one asked him for the short interest ratio in a certain month. That information was not readily available, but he figured it out—it's the current short interest divided by average daily volume. Short interest in stocks was reported by the exchanges, but average daily volume wasn't easily found. Pretty soon, the *Wall Street Journal* stopped calling everyone else and from 1982 to 1988, almost every month the short-interest column featured data and a quote from Erlanger.

The final boost, however, came in 1984 when a *Journal* columnist asked him to factor out arbitrage-related short selling, which had become prevalent at the time. He figured it would take a couple of weeks, but was worth the risk if she followed through on her promise to write a "Heard on the Street" column about it. He went down to the stock exchange, and with a guard looking over his shoulder, made copies of the New York Stock Exchange short-interest data for the past five years. Then he had to keypunch the data into his computer for each stock and each month— more than 100,000 entries.

After many sleepless nights, he ended up with more than a "Heard" column on his new arbitrage-free, short-selling indicator, which he called the At Risk Short Interest Ratio. He had the world's only database of individual stocks' short interest ratios for the prior five years.

So, being a data geek, he couldn't help but study it—and his jaw dropped when he determined that, time after time, when a stock went down in price over months you could see the short interest rise to a peak, then plateau. The stock would then bottom for a while, then rally and all the shorts would disappear. "It was like the holy grail," he said, "so I started to look at all the stocks in an industry, like computers or copper, and I would see it again and again: Whenever there was a big jump in short interest, it would not signal the exact low—but the greatest part of the decline would end when short selling got to extremely high levels."

Moreover, Erlanger learned that in the five years of data you could see short interest in stocks oscillate from high to low and back again as a forward mirror of stock prices. So he homed in on the concept of a two-factor model for forecasting prices that combined price action (relative strength) and sentiment (short selling).

Philosophically, the concept made sense: When short selling is light, margin buying is heavy and bulls are really excited about the stock. Then if you wait for the stock's strength relative to the market to diminish as it sinks in price, you have a scenario where the market is inflicting great pain on a large number of people. And it's on those distressed people, who must then begin to sell in bulk, whom you wish to focus on hurting as a short seller.

Erlanger ironically calls the two-factor model, which he uses to this day, "painfully simple"—though it requires a lot of data crunching. The path to success, in his view, is "strewn with the bodies of lazy people—you have to do the work to get at something that works."

He stayed at Advest for five years, and left on good terms when mutual fund giant Fidelity Investments hired him as a senior technical analyst in the chart room at their headquarters on Devonshire Street in Boston. He jumped at the high-paying chance to work with Fidelity's great portfolio managers and legendary leaders Ned Johnson, Peter Lynch, and Jeff Vinik; the only thing he'd have to give up was his relationship with the press. (Fidelity rarely allows its analysts to talk to reporters.) He soon began to develop his Type 1-4 screens for longs and shorts, which we examine in a moment, and as appreciation of his accuracy grew he became the company fireman—putting out blazes in areas as diverse as junk bonds and overseas markets. "Portfolio managers would come by my office before they made half-billion-dollar trades—it was an amazing time," he said. Among his more prescient calls were a sell on the bonds of the soon-to-be-controversial Taj Ma-hal casino in Atlantic City, which not long after dropped by 70 percent, and a sell on the Japanese stock market, the Nikkei, which he forecast correctly would fall to less than 10,000 from its perch at the time around 30,000.

While at Fidelity, Erlanger worked with a lot of advanced mathematicians who were increasingly fond of developing nonlinear models of the market. But at the same time his own work was tending more toward simplification. He tried and tested a plethora of indicators for forecasting stock movement, and settled essentially on just his favorite two: relative strength for price action and short selling for sentiment. His goal in the mid- to late-1990s then narrowed to a hunt for ways to systematically improve his understanding of relative strength. The result was a nonlinear pattern-recognition computer program that categorized the 10 most common types of price-slope chart patterns by their return expectations. (See Figure 6.1.) Now he could feed the data for thousands and thousands of charts into his computer, and it would sort them into one of 10 patterns, which were normalized from 10 percent to 100 percent likelihood of an up move. He sells this stock-specific relative-strength data as a "factor" to quantitative analysts and institutions around the world. But more importantly, for this discussion, it is also one-half the equation he uses to find strong stocks to buy and weak stocks to short.

Erlanger stayed at Fidelity for over five years, but in 1994 hooked up with some institutional salespeople and decided to start his own company. That was a tough time in the market, but tough times are Erlanger's favorite times—as that is when his price/sentiment model shines. Indeed, he had his best years in 2000–2002, as he made one successful call after another, mostly from the short side, for both institutional clients who get regular publications and data feeds, and for more than 11,000 private investors, who subscribe to his daily Erlanger Squeeze Play website and newsletter. (See Figure 6.2.)

Leaving Fidelity also gave him an opportunity to spend more time at home with his wife, Judith, and to pursue his love for golf. He regularly shoots in the mid- to high-80s, which is excellent, and travels with his clubs when he visits clients around the country—preferably in places like Pebble Beach, California. He also trains hunting dogs as a hobby, which allows him to indulge his passion for the outdoors and animals.

Now let's see exactly how he hunts for swing-trading setups for two-week to six-month trades.

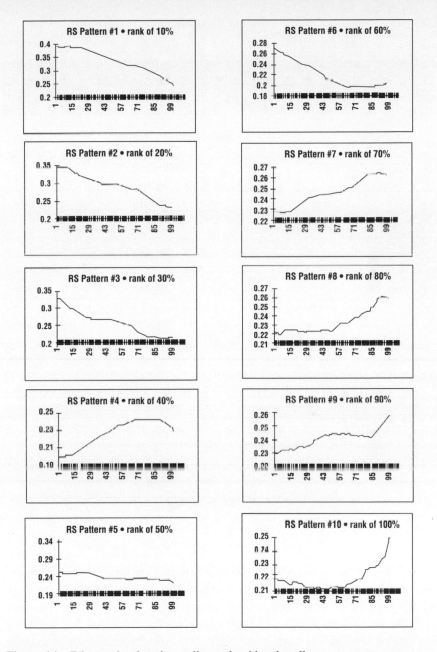

Figure 6.1 Erlanger developed a nonlinear algorithm that allows a computer to sort through thousands of stock charts at a time and sort them into 10 patterns by the relative strength shown in their slopes. In this figure, the first column shows relative-strength types 1–5, from top to bottom, ranked by the likelihood that the next move is up. The second column shows relative strength types 6–10. Relative strength is a key component of the "technical rank" that Erlanger's computers give each stock.

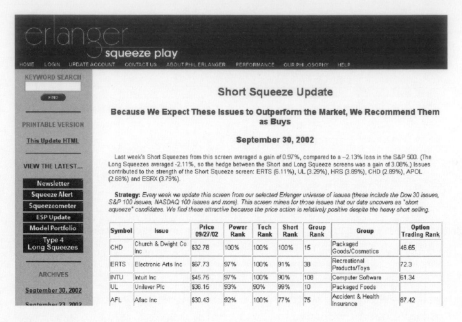

Figure 6.2   At his ErlangerSqueezePlay.com website, Phil Erlanger provides a list of long and short candidates every week, as well as a daily newsletter on market timing. His Short Squeeze Update of proposed longs and shorts appears every Monday morning. *Source:* ErlangerSqueezePlay.com.

Erlanger's Setups

At the end of the day, Erlanger's work is all about finding stocks to go long or short. He starts with the big picture, a philosophical point of view about whether the market is in a secular bull or bear phase. He then determines which broad market sectors and industry groups are individually in their own bull or bear phases by studying both their technical strength and the short-selling ratios of their components. (He does the same for the major market averages—the S&P 500, the Nasdaq 100, and Dow 30—by adding the short interest for each of the component issues.) And then he uses the data to determine whether bulls or bears have made the most extreme bets against the prevailing trend, and are thus the most likely to be squeezed in an explosion of buying or selling that will make a terrific swing-trade opportunity.

As an overlay, to assist his timing, he also pays attention to historic seasonality of stock prices—believing that history shows the market tends to regularly rise or fall in particular months, in years of the decade, during the U.S. presidential campaign cycle, and over a 20-year cycle. Erlanger particularly pays attention to whether the market behaves as expected during these turns of the wheel. For instance, in the first half of 2002, typically strong months like January and April were weak. Some observers said that the discordance with history suggested either that seasonality is unimportant—or that the seasons had flipped allegiances. But Erlanger's take was that if the market did poorly in historically strong periods, it's going to do extremely poorly in seasonally weak periods. "It's all about clues," he said. "When a market does poorly at a time when it typically does well, that's a clue that, wow, all is not well. Don't expect it to turn around and do well in a seasonally weak period— it doesn't work that way."

Erlanger is always thinking up ways to create a new market microscope. One of his favorite lenses is the Volatility Index of the Chicago Board Options Exchange, widely referred to by its symbol, VIX. It essentially measures the amount by which options traders, who are believed to be sophisticated, are overpaying for puts, which are leveraged bets against the market, or calls, which are leveraged bets in favor of the market. When the VIX is high and trending up, stocks are typically trending down. But when the VIX crosses a certain threshold on the up side— around 30 or 40—it means that put buyers are the ones who are overpaying as the market goes lower and lower. When the VIX crosses a certain threshold on the down side—usually around 20—it means that call buyers are overpaying as the market goes higher and higher.

Erlanger likes the VIX as a timing indicator because it is a measure of sentiment that generally cannot be fudged, and it helps organize his thinking about the short-term and medium-term direction of the market. As a result, he has invented a measurement he calls the Squeezeometer, which normalizes and detrends the VIX and gives him and subscribers an easy way to understand when sentiment has reached such excessive levels that traders can begin to look for a setup in the opposite direction of the trend. (See Figure 6.3.) In the early spring of 2002, when the Dow Jones Industrials crested the 10,500 level and all seemed well in the world again, the VIX dropped to around 20 and many analysts opined that it had lost its significance; they said market volatility was diminishing and the VIX would fall into a range around the 10 level as it was in

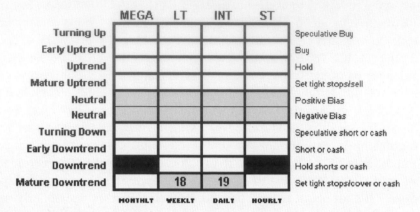

S&P 500 SQUEEZEOMETER 09/30/02

Closing Data

	MEGA	LT	INT	ST	
Turning Up					Speculative Buy
Early Uptrend					Buy
Uptrend					Hold
Mature Uptrend					Set tight stops/sell
Neutral					Positive Bias
Neutral					Negative Bias
Turning Down					Speculative short or cash
Early Downtrend					Short or cash
Downtrend					Hold shorts or cash
Mature Downtrend		18	19		Set tight stops/cover or cash
	MONTHLT	WEEKLT	DAILT	HOURLT	

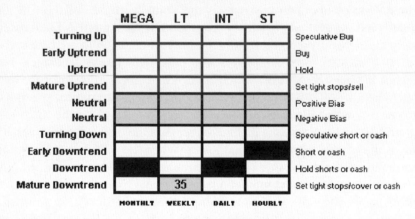

NASDAQ 100 SQUEEZEOMETER 09/30/02

Closing Data

	MEGA	LT	INT	ST	
Turning Up					Speculative Buy
Early Uptrend					Buy
Uptrend					Hold
Mature Uptrend					Set tight stops/sell
Neutral					Positive Bias
Neutral					Negative Bias
Turning Down					Speculative short or cash
Early Downtrend					Short or cash
Downtrend					Hold shorts or cash
Mature Downtrend		35			Set tight stops/cover or cash
	MONTHLT	WEEKLT	DAILT	HOURLT	

Figure 6.3 Erlanger's Squeezeometers for the S&P 500 and Nasdaq are a normalized, detrended version of the VIX with lipstick. They convert high and low VIX numbers into 10 deciles, or buckets, of price action from Turning Up, on the buy side, to Mature Downtrend on the sell side in four time dimensions: monthly (megatrend), weekly (long-term trend), daily (intermediate trend), and hourly (short-term trend). He sees the periods as similar to waves, and investors as surfers. Trying to trade on hourly information, he says, is like trying to surf on a raindrop, while monthly waves are more like the big surf in Maui. When indicators in the weekly and daily columns move into the top two squares, fear in the market is at its apex, and it is time to buy. On the day shown in this figure, September 30, 2002, the two intermediate trends were at the bottom—meaning that it was time to cover shorts. Good timing: The S&P 500 moved up 4 percent the next day in a massive rally.

the mid-1990s. Erlanger dismisssed that view at the time, calling it "the mantra of the undead." He added:

> Those are the last words you utter before entering the great void—when you say things will be different now. Sentiment is never different. Many seemingly smart people said the same thing in 1994 when short-interest ratios were high and people said they didn't mean a thing, and that the market would never go up again. I said they were wrong—that a big squeeze was coming. And the disbelievers got their lungs ripped out in one of the sharpest rises in history.

The bottom line is that no matter what measure you follow, it's key to remember that sentiment is fuel for the next phase. The more bearish the sentiment, the more people who can become buyers. If everyone has already bought and mutual funds have low cash positions, after all, where is the money going to come from to push stocks up? It's a representation of market physics, in a way—the market equivalent of Newton's Third Law of Motion: Every action has an equal and opposite reaction. In this case, every major move occurs when people who weren't thinking one way before change their minds and suddenly go the other way. Furthermore, the more people who need to change their minds, the more extreme the following move. "Bearishness is fuel for an advance; bullishness is fuel for a decline," Erlanger repeats. "If you fight this, you will fail. And if you don't organize your thinking in this direction, you will fail."

To determine the extreme levels of bearishness and bullishness, Erlanger normalizes the VIX into what he calls "confidence indexes" for the Nasdaq and the S&P 500 that stretch from 0 to 100. When his Buy Confidence Index is high, fear is so high as expressed in the VIX that he believes traders can buy with confidence. Conversely, when the Sell Confidence Index is high, fear is so low as expressed in the VIX that traders can short with confidence. (See Figure 6.4.)

Generally speaking, in the early fall of 2002, Erlanger said he believed the big picture was overwhelmingly negative. "The charts are pretty scary—you have to hide the children." Even though the Nasdaq 100 was 85 percent off its peak, he said his short-interest ratios showed nowhere near the level of short selling that has been historically required to call an excess of fear. Sentiment was still bullish, as investors hoped

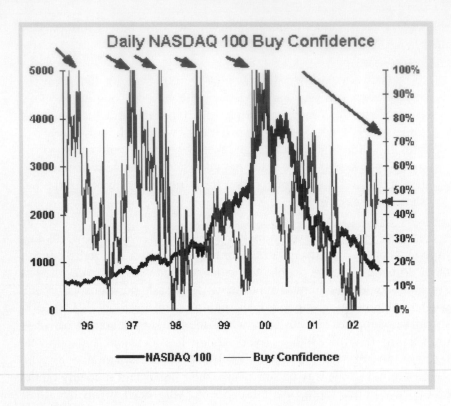

Figure 6.4   Buy Confidence chart of Nasdaq 100, 1995–2002.

that every rally would be the one to start a new bull market. To achieve a lasting bottom and an end to the secular bear market, he said, there needs to be a complete shift toward hatred of stocks and massive amounts of short selling to prove it. Then, as the market begins to rise, the common wisdom must be that the rise is false and will never last—as was the case in the early 1980s and in 1995. "A good bull market is a generally rising market that is perpetuated by short, sharp, scary selloffs, like October 1987 and August 1998. Bear markets, on the other hand, are declines peppered with a whole bunch of one-day and one-month wonders that make people think the downtrend is over—little spiky rallies that make it tough for the bears to have conviction."

So how does he make these declarations with confidence? That two-factor model of price action and sentiment.

Ideally, in his world, you want to find stocks that are the most heavily bet against and yet are showing some relative strength that will cause the shorts to cover in a panic, and potentially even convert to buyers.

On the sentiment side, he looks at a five-year history of monthly data on individual stocks and calculates the short-interest ratio, or the current short interest divided by the 12-month average daily volume. (Just the level of short interest alone tells you nothing, as it continues to rise along with the increase in stock trading volume.) He then normalizes it into an oscillator that stretches from 0 to 100 for each stock. He calls that level of short intensity the Short Rank. On the price-action side, he computes a "technical rank" that rises in value as a stock performs increasingly better against the overall market. It's simply the price of a stock divided by the level of an index, plotted as a line as shown in Figure 6.1. He likes the technical rank so much, in fact, that he says that if he were on a desert island and could pick only one indicator, this would be it. "When a stock is outperforming the market," he says, "its relative strength is telling you something. It's saying: This is what's going up."

So now you have Short Rank measuring short-selling intensity for sentiment, and Technical Rank measuring relative strength for price action. Put those together and you get the Erlanger Power Rank: the higher the power rank, the greater the short-selling intensity and the greater the technical rank. So the perfect Erlanger setup is a stock experiencing its historical peak of short selling at the same time that the stock is moving up at a faster rate than the market. A high Power Rank means price is moving against the shorts, and they will ultimately be forced to cover in size. That is a short squeeze and can lead to tremendous, long-lasting swing trades.

On the other hand are "long squeezes," which are stocks with the lowest Power Ranks—meaning they are under-shorted, overloved, and acting terrible. The market is saying that all those votes in favor of these stocks are wrong—and they are headed down. Erlanger captured just about every disaster story of 2002 with this screen, including General Electric, Philip Morris, Brocade Communications, and Tyco International. Each of these was set up with a low Power Rank early in the meaty part of its declines.

Now if you go long the high Power Rank stocks and go short the low Power Rank stocks, you end up with a hedged portfolio that should beat the market—and Erlanger's did, both through the bullish late

1990s and through the bearish 2000–2002 period. In a bull market, the short squeezes should do well, and the long squeezes should muddle through; in a bear market, the short squeezes should perform in line with the market, while the long squeezes should outperform. In this strategy, all Erlanger needs is volatility. The only way someone following this strategy gets hurt is if the market goes sideways with low volatility—an unlikely scenario these days. This style isn't for everyone, but it works for traders who prefer clear signals for high-volume stocks that they can easily hit as they come right down the center of the plate. "If you follow a strategy like this," Erlanger says, "you don't have to be overly aggressive worrying that you may miss a move. You will make a lot of money every day in the market, and when you die you will have a very shiny casket."

Erlanger publishes a list of the week's top short-squeeze and long-squeeze candidates every week on his website; institutional investors who take his service receive daily feeds containing every stock's Technical Rank, Short Rank, Short Ratio, and Power Rank. A trader who subscribes to his $29.95 per month service can use the lists either as a launching pad for further research of stocks to go long or short, or could just buy all the short-squeeze candidates and short all the long-squeeze candidates as a basket. The latter technique would have worked out quite well from March through September 2002, as shown in the following tables. In Table 6.1 are the absolute returns for each over that time. In Table 6.2 are the cumulative returns for a holder and shorter of all the stocks each week. As you can see, going long the short squeezes allowed a trader to do a little better than the S&P 500, but when combined with shorts of the long squeezes, a trader would have been up 52 percent over the period, versus the 32 percent decline in the S&P 500.

To understand how a few of these trades worked in practice, we will take a look at their charts and see how the short selling and relative strength combined as a setup. First let's pan back a bit and look at the moves of the Dow Jones Industrials and S&P 500 in the mid-1990s, as well as chip stock Micron Technology.

In Figure 6.5, note the heavy short selling of the indexes through the mid-1990s. Most investors, Erlanger says, were worried that the markets were about to fall apart. Mainstream Wall Street fundamental analysts had difficulty in finding value and spurred negative sentiment despite rising prices. Moreover, Alan Greenspan's "irrational exuberance" comments added additional support for the wall of worry that allowed for a subsequent sharp advance of the market averages. The market's historic

Table 6.1 Absolute Returns—March to September 2002

Date	Short Squeeze Screen	Long Squeeze Screen	Combo	S&P 500
3/8/02	−2.26%	−1.89%	−0.37%	−0.88%
3/14/02	−0.86%	−2.54%	1.68%	0.05%
3/21/02	0.65%	−3.20%	3.85%	−0.49%
3/28/02	−2.02%	−3.29%	1.27%	−1.83%
4/4/02	0.26%	−6.08%	6.34%	−2.00%
4/11/02	1.80%	5.72%	−3.92%	1.88%
4/18/02	−2.67%	−8.70%	6.03%	−1.11%
4/25/02	0.68%	−5.26%	5.94%	−0.63%
5/2/02	−2.23%	−0.79%	−1.44%	−1.06%
5/9/02	2.30%	5.18%	−2.88%	2.35%
5/16/02	−2.81%	−3.09%	0.28%	−1.31%
5/24/02	−1.80%	−2.89%	1.09%	−1.72%
5/30/02	−1.62%	−10.22%	8.60%	−3.54%
6/7/02	−1.53%	−2.71%	1.18%	−2.13%
6/14/02	0.93%	−7.34%	8.27%	−1.80%
6/21/02	−1.71%	−0.81%	−0.90%	−0.15%
6/27/02	−3.00%	−0.61%	−2.39%	−0.16%
7/5/02	6.60%	7.41%	0.81%	6.84%
7/12/02	−3.00%	−7.79%	4.79%	−7.99%
7/19/02	5.10%	0.81%	−4.29%	0.60%
7/26/02	0.37%	−4.46%	4.83%	1.34%
8/2/02	5.80%	5.78%	0.02%	5.14%
8/9/02	1.04%	5.77%	4.73%	2.22%
8/16/02	0.72%	1.20%	−0.48%	1.30%
8/23/02	−3.05%	−5.19%	2.14%	−2.63%
8/30/02	−0.62%	−5.27%	4.65%	−2.42%
9/6/02	1.77%	−2.91%	4.68%	−0.46%
9/13/02	−2.71%	−5.77%	3.06%	−4.99%
9/20/02	0.97%	−2.11%	3.08%	−2.13%

rise ultimately wiped out the short positions of the mid-1990s. No doubt the unwinding of these massive shorts added fuel to the advance, as the shorts were squeezed into buying back the shares they had shorted. Understanding the posture of short sellers was the single greatest factor that kept Erlanger bullish on the way up. Levels of short selling reached multiple decade lows by the end of the 1990s, which was a signal that the market was especially vulnerable.

Short selling as a measure of sentiment can be viewed most vividly in

Table 6.2 Cumulative Returns—March to December 2002

Date	Short Squeeze Screen	Long Squeeze Screen	Hedge Combo	S&P 500	Diff. over S&P
3/8/02	−2.26%	−1.89%	−0.37%	−0.88%	0.51%
3/14/02	−3.12%	−4.43%	1.31%	−0.83%	2.14%
3/21/02	−2.47%	−7.63%	5.16%	−1.32%	6.48%
3/28/02	−4.49%	−10.92%	6.43%	−3.15%	9.58%
4/4/02	−4.23%	−17.00%	12.77%	−5.15%	17.92%
4/11/02	−2.43%	−11.28%	8.85%	−3.27%	12.12%
4/18/02	−5.10%	−19.98%	14.88%	−4.38%	19.26%
4/25/02	−4.42%	−25.24%	20.82%	−5.01%	25.83%
5/2/02	−6.65%	−26.03%	19.38%	−6.07%	25.45%
5/9/02	−4.35%	−20.85%	16.50%	−3.72%	20.22%
5/16/02	−7.16%	−23.94%	16.78%	−5.03%	21.81%
5/24/02	−8.96%	−26.83%	17.87%	−6.75%	24.62%
5/30/02	−10.58%	−37.05%	26.47%	−10.29%	36.76%
6/7/02	−12.11%	−39.76%	27.65%	−12.42%	40.07%
6/14/02	−11.18%	−47.10%	35.92%	−14.22%	50.14%
6/21/02	−12.89%	−47.91%	35.02%	−14.37%	49.39%
6/27/02	−15.89%	−48.52%	32.63%	−14.53%	47.16%
7/5/02	−22.49%	−55.93%	33.44%	−21.37%	54.81%
7/12/02	−25.49%	−63.72%	38.23%	−29.36%	67.59%
7/19/02	−30.59%	−64.53%	33.94%	−28.76%	62.70%
7/26/02	−30.22%	−68.99%	38.77%	−27.42%	66.19%
8/2/02	−24.42%	−63.21%	38.79%	−22.28%	61.07%
8/9/02	−23.38%	−57.44%	34.06%	−20.06%	54.12%
8/16/02	−22.66%	−56.24%	33.58%	−18.76%	52.34%
8/23/02	−25.71%	−61.43%	35.72%	−21.39%	57.11%
8/30/02	−26.33%	−66.70%	40.37%	−23.81%	64.18%
9/6/02	−24.56%	−69.61%	45.05%	−24.27%	69.32%
9/13/02	−27.27%	−75.38%	48.11%	−29.26%	77.37%
9/20/02	−26.30%	−77.49%	51.19%	−31.39%	82.58%

the rise and fall of the shares of semiconductor maker Micron Technology. Back in 1995, short selling swelled in Micron Technology, as shown in Figure 6.6.

At the time, Erlanger recalls, fundamental analysts declared Micron overvalued. While it was just moving above $20, massive short selling was established despite rising relative strength. Micron then began a memorable advance that confounded the short sellers. It wasn't until the shorts were squeezed out that Micron topped out above $90. At this point

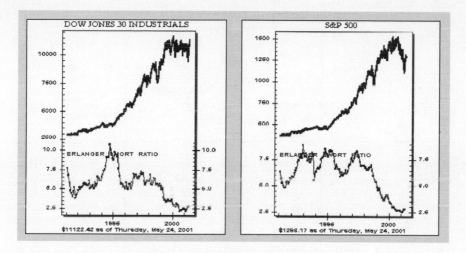

Figure 6.5 Dow 30 and S&P 500 indexes advanced from 1993–1999 in the face of high short-selling, as indicated in the chart of the Erlanger short rank.

the bears had capitulated, and late blooming bullishness became widespread. Micron Technology then went into a tailspin that didn't end until the shorts came back into the market, which helped establish another base for Micron's price recovery. The swings of sentiment set the stage for the next contrary phase. The lesson is plain: *The market tends to move against the majority at risk.*

Yet it is not enough to uncover an excess in sentiment. It is also necessary to judge the price action. To properly time a contrary opinion trade, you must see the market move against the majority. By waiting for the "squeeze play" to begin, the investor increases the odds of a favorable outcome. That is why price action must be added to the sentiment-player's arsenal.

Power Ranks, described previously, are where sentiment and price action intersect. Rather than simply using the numbers 1–100, Erlanger divides the universe into four types:

1. Type 1: Short Squeeze—Strong Technical with Heavy Shorting (Buy). *Technical strength > 70%; Short intensity > 50%; Short interest ratio > 1.5.*
2. Type 2: Recognized Strength—Strong Technical with Light Shorting (Hold). *Technical strength > 70%; Short intensity < 30%; Short interest ratio < 4.0.*

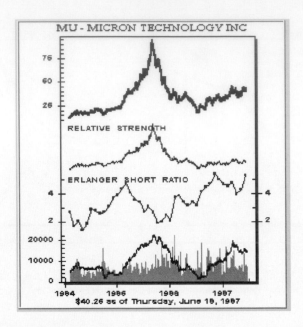

Figure 6.6 Micron Technology, Inc. Micron rose sharply 1994–1997 in the face of rising Erlanger short ratio, as short-sellers were squeezed.

---

3. Type 3: Shorts Are Right—Weak Technical with Heavy Shorting (Sell). *Technical strength < 40%; Short intensity > 50%; Short ratio > 1.5.*
4. Type 4: Long Squeeze—Weak Technical with Light Shorting (Short). *Technical strength < 40%; Short intensity < 30%; Short ratio < 4.0.*

Figure 6.7 shows type classifications in action during the big move in Micron Technology from 1993 to 1996. It's important to note how few changes there are in type classification. Erlanger says he told clients to hold on during the rocket shot from the $20s through $90. The type classifications simply make it easier to describe the action, he says.

To add to his arsenal of scientific measures of sentiment, Erlanger also examines options trading as a tool for shorter-term trading. Options are another superb expression of sentiment. Option buyers take risky bets that depend on immediate results, because options are *wasting assets* that expire within months (most options expire within four months). The underlying stock must begin to move in the desired

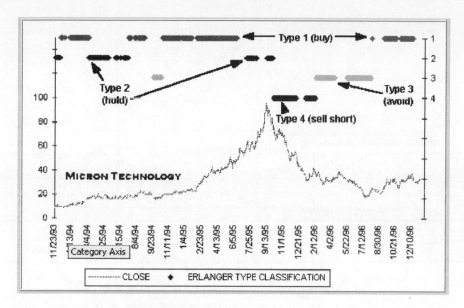

Figure 6.7   Erlanger type classification.

direction as time decay shrinks the time premium portion of an options value. So market direction and time work against the option player, who therefore must be strongly committed to the position taken—a measure of sentiment.

Call option buyers are betting that the price of the underlying stock or index will rise. Calls give you the right to buy a stock at a fixed price for a limited period of time. Puts are the reverse—a bet that the underlying stock or index will decline. Puts give you the right to sell at a fixed price for a limited period of time. Erlanger uses put/call ratios to measure the ebb and flow of *bearish* sentiment, and call/put ratios to better see the *bullish* sentiment swings.

In Figure 6.8, Erlanger points out that you can see a strong relationship between sentiment excess and future price direction in Microsoft stock in 1999 and 2000. Clearly, bearish sentiment increased into the fourth quarter of 1999. Microsoft exploded over 30 percent in just a few weeks of trading—and as a result, sentiment shifted from bearishness to an excess of bullishness. The explosion of call buying relative to put buying was a clear indication of the top for Microsoft in the beginning of

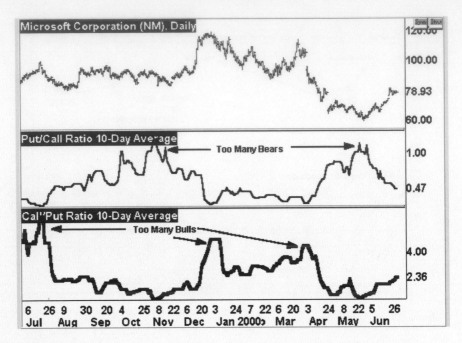

Figure 6.8 Sentiment excesses helped to augur the future path of Microsoft shares in 1999–2000.

2000. Moreover, this began a period where Microsoft's legal issues with the government came to a head; most people thought that traders were flat into the ruling regarding the split up of Microsoft. Erlanger told subscribers that prior to the decision there was so much bullish speculation that its technical underpinnings were weak. The stock gapped down in late April as the longs got squeezed.

Now let's look at his of stock picks from 2001–2002 (see Table 6.3) and see how Erlanger used his theories about sentiment and strength to make a remarkably accurate set of intermediate-term swing trades.

We can start with NVIDIA, which was one of the few technology stocks to sail through 2001 with barely a hiccup, ultimately soaring 300 percent. Its crowning moment came late in the year when it was added to the S&P 500. All the while, short sellers were squeezed and squeezed and squeezed, until at its apex in January 2002, as shown in Figure 6.9, the stock's Short Ratio (the bottom chart) fell to an all-time low of 1.48.

Table 6.3 June 2001 to September 2002 Erlanger Model Portfolio

Open Date	Company/Fund	Sym	Short/Long	Open Price	Close Price	Chg.	Days in Trade	Close Date	Diff. from S&P 500
6/26/2001	Apache	APA	Short	$51.98	$47.34	-4.14	84	9/17/2001	7.96%
6/26/2001	Noble Affiliate	NBL	Short	$37.01	$34.50	-2.41	84	9/17/2001	6.51%
6/26/2001	Stone Energy	SGY	Short	$43.51	$39.28	-4.23	84	9/17/2001	9.72%
7/16/2001	Converse Tech	CMVT	Short	$26.03	$24.25	-1.78	67	9/20/2001	6.84%
8/21/2001	IBM	IBM	Short	$102.80	$94.50	-8.3	31	9/20/2001	8.07%
8/1/2001	General Elec	GE	Short	$42.76	$33.60	-9.16	55	9/24/2001	21.42%
8/1/2001	United Tech	UTX	Short	$72.36	$44.00	-28.36	55	9/24/2001	39.19%
7/24/2001	Cisco	CSCO	Short	$18.27	$12.54	-5.73	72	10/3/2001	31.36%
7/24/2001	Microsoft	MSFT	Short	$67.09	$54.86	-12.23	72	10/3/2001	18.23%
10/8/2001	Bruker Daltonics	BDAL	Long	$16.85	$19.90	3.05	3	10/10/2001	18.10%
8/21/2001	Sony	SNE	Short	$47.25	$35.52	-11.73	51	10/10/2001	24.83%
7/24/2001	KLA–Tencor	KLAC	Short	$49.21	$31.81	-17.4	79	10/10/2001	35.36%
6/26/2001	Schlumberger	SLB	Short	$54.52	$45.86	-8.66	107	10/10/2001	15.88%
7/24/2001	Qualcomm	QCOM	Short	$60.85	$40.88	-19.97	79	10/10/2001	32.82%
10/11/2001	Micron Tech	MU	Long	$21.23	$22.60	1.37	7	10/17/2001	6.45%
10/11/2001	IBM	IBM	Long	$97.25	$106.90	9.65	22	11/1/2001	9.92%
10/17/2001	Pharm Res	PRX	Long	$36.71	$32.00	-4.71	21	11/6/2001	-12.83%
10/11/2001	Raytheon	RTN	Short	$33.80	$29.90	-3.9	37	11/16/2001	11.54%
11/29/2001	Disney	DIS	Short	$20.28	$22.28	2.0	8	12/6/2001	-9.86%
11/29/2001	Merrill Lynch	MER	Short	$49.10	$53.50	4.4	8	12/6/2001	-8.96%
11/29/2001	Molex	MOLX	Short	$29.08	$31.65	2.57	8	12/6/2001	-8.84%
10/17/2001	IBM	IBM	Long	$102.80	$121.08	18.28	58	12/13/2001	17.78%
12/13/2001	Amer. Express	AXP	Short	$32.78	$37.72	4.94	23	1/4/2002	-15.07%
1/11/2002	Textron	TXT	Short	$41.44	$45.83	4.39	22	2/1/2002	-10.59%
11/29/2001	Anadigics	ANAD	Short	$16.45	$12.21	-4.24	79	2/15/2002	25.78%
10/11/2001	US Cellular	USM	Short	$45.70	$41.35	-4.35	147	3/6/2002	9.52%
2/15/2002	Veritas	VRTS	Short	$36.99	$42.48	5.49	20	3/6/2002	-14.84%

(Continued)

295

Table 6.3 *(Continued)*

Open Date	Company/ Fund	Sym	Short/ Long	Open Price	Close Price	Chg.	Days in Trade	Close Date	Diff. from S&P 500
3/7/2002	Anheuser–Busch	BUD	Short	$49.90	$52.73	2.83	21	3/27/2002	–5.67%
11/1/2001	Agnico Eagle	AEM	Long	$9.81	$15.71	5.9	188	5/7/2002	60.14%
2/15/2002	Cisco	CSCO	Short	$17.32	$14.78	–2.54	82	5/7/2002	14.67%
11/29/2001	Exar Corp	EXAR	Short	$20.39	$21.50	1.11	161	5/8/2002	–5.44%
12/13/2001	Citigroup	C	Short	$47.30	$45.40	–1.9	153	5/14/2002	4.02%
2/15/2002	QLogic	QLGC	Short	$46.89	$52.70	5.81	89	5/14/2002	–12.39%
3/7/2002	Daiseytek	DZTK	Long	$15.85	$12.35	–3.5	93	6/7/2002	–22.08%
5/24/2002	Cleveland Cliffs	CLF	Long	$28.23	$25.30	–2.93	21	6/13/2002	–10.38%
5/24/2002	Microsoft	MSFT	Short	$53.75	$52.13	–1.62	34	6/26/2002	3.01%
5/24/2002	NVIDIA	NVDA	Short	$34.51	$17.11	–17.4	41	7/3/2002	50.42%
12/13/2001	Rydex Tempest	RYTPX	Long	$72.05	$98.07	26.02	211	7/11/2002	36.11%
5/24/2002	Starbucks	SBUX	Short	$22.57	$22.17	–0.4	49	7/11/2002	1.77%
7/12/2002	NASDAQ 100	QQQ	Long	$25.16	$24.85	–0.31	1	7/12/2002	–1.23%
7/12/2002	S&P 500	SPY	Short	$92.20	$91.10	–1.1	4	7/15/2002	1.19%
7/18/2002	BioTech Holders	BBH	Short	$74.07	$71.19	–2.88	2	7/19/2002	3.89%
7/18/2002	Diamonds Trust	DIA	Short	$85.60	$80.89	–4.71	2	7/19/2002	5.50%
7/22/2002	Qualcomm	QCOM	Long	$29.15	$26.00	–3.15	4	7/25/2002	–10.81%
7/25/2002	CDW Corp	CDWC	Long	$47.22	$50.66	3.44	6	7/30/2002	7.29%
7/22/2002	Cleveland Cliffs	CLF	Long	$22.90	$27.26	4.36	9	7/30/2002	19.04%
7/22/2002	Diamonds Trust	DIA	Long	$77.34	$86.56	9.22	10	7/31/2002	11.92%
7/22/2002	S&P 500	SPY	Long	$82.25	$90.31	8.06	10	7/31/2002	9.80%
7/25/2002	United Tech	UTX	Long	$63.87	$70.24	6.37	7	7/31/2002	9.97%
7/22/2002	Rydex Titan 500	RYTNX	Long	$6.45	$7.96	1.51	10	7/31/2002	23.41%
7/22/2002	IBM	IBM	Long	$68.53	$71.05	2.52	10	7/31/2002	3.68%
8/7/2002	S&P 500	SPY	Short	$86.25	$91.90	5.65	3	8/9/2002	–6.55%
9/12/2002	ADOBE	ADBE	Short	$18.96	$20.24	1.28	2	9/13/2002	–6.75%
9/13/2002	Genzyme	GENZ	Short	$18.75	$22.50	3.75	7	9/19/2002	–20.00%
8/15/2002	JP Morgan	JPM	Short	$24.80	$19.20	–5.6	40	9/23/2002	22.58%
9/12/2002	Maxim Integ.	MXIM	Short	$29.03	$23.39	–5.64	12	9/23/2002	19.43%
8/12/2002	Microsoft	MSFT	Short	$48.13	$45.00	–3.13	43	9/23/2002	6.50%

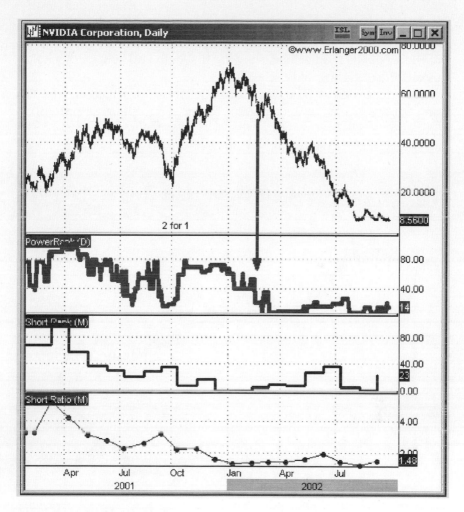

Figure 6.9 NVIDIA Short Ratio.

To qualify for inclusion as a short candidate in the weekly Type 4 Long Squeeze Screen or as a proposed trade in the Erlanger Model Portfolio, a stock's Technical Rank must sink below 40 percent, its Short Rank sink below 30 percent, and its Short Ratio sink beneath 4.0. More broadly, its Power Rank needs to fall below 40 percent. NVIDIA qualified as a Long Squeeze in late January 2002, at the time shown with the arrow, as short selling still failed to materialize with the stock fading fast. The stock later qualified as a portfolio pick on May 24, at $34.51; it

was sold short for a 50 percent profit 41 trading days later on July 3 at
$17.11. The stock went on to fall by 50 percent again with still little di-
minishment in its short selling, showing that bulls still held out hope that
this one-time leader would rise again.

Now let's look at General Electric, Figure 6.10, which entered the
Long Squeeze screen in mid-July 2001 after short selling dropped off a
cliff, with as relative strength of the stock was falling dramatically. Erlanger notes that he rarely trades on the basis of just one factor, such as a

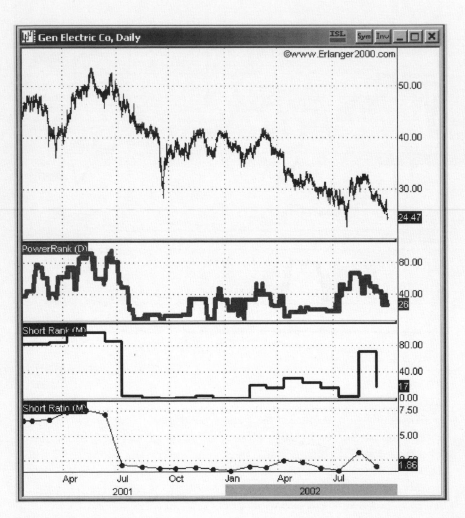

Figure 6.10   GE Long Squeeze.

low Short Ratio, but rather waits until all the indicators line up by producing a falling Power Rank. In this case, the Power Rank plunged in late July when the stock was at $40, well off its high in the $50s—but also well above the level it would go on to hit a few months later. Notice that the short ratio continued at low levels even as the stock fell and fell and fell, indicating that market players continued to hold in the false hope that it would rise again soon.

Agnico Eagle Mines, shown in Figure 6.11, represents the opposite

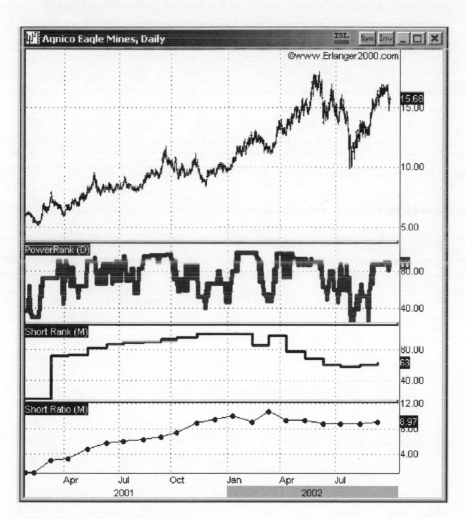

Figure 6.11   Agnico Eagle Mines long.

side of the coin. It was Erlanger's best model portfolio trade of the period, and it was a long. He recommended purchase in November 2001, at $9.81, well before most people had come to recognize that precious metals would constitute a strong sector in the coming months. It had the ideal setup for a purchase: a rising Power Rank, increasing technical strength, and increasing short intensity. The stock kept getting shorted more and more intensely as it rose, forcing more and more shorts ultimately to capitulate and cover—providing further fuel for the move. Erlanger held it in the portfolio for 188 days, until May 7, 2002 for a 60 percent profit. For him, it was more than a trade. For more than 20 years in his work as an analyst, he had never recommended gold or silver mining shares, but in the summer and fall, he came to believe they would make a major move in the face of tremendous skepticism. He told clients to put 15 percent of their assets in gold stocks. He recommended clients end the trade in May not because the stocks were breaking down but because, as he put it, "the cat was out of the bag" as the sector had suddenly become widely recognized as a big story. "At $15, AEM had gone parabolic, and I didn't want to wait for the last tick," he says.

Web security services firm VeriSign, shown in Figure 6.12, had a high level of short-selling intensity through most of 2001 and traded in a range between $35 and $65, but when it fell to $20 in January 2002, the short sellers covered, apparently believing the worst was over. The combination of a low Power Rank and low short interest made it an ideal shorting candidate for Erlanger in his Long Squeeze screen in May, and it did go on to plunge from $20 to the $5 area over the next few months. "Shorts apparently thought the stock had reached a low at $20—but what you were really seeing was complacency," Erlanger says. "So it fell another 75 percent from there. And the short interest is still light!"

The sad ambit of oil and gas distribution and marketing giant Williams Cos in 2001 and 2002 is another case of light short selling combined with low price strength leading to further weakness. (See Figure 6.13) From April 2002 through July, short interest was extremely light compared with the company's history, even as its Power Rank weakened below 25 percent. Erlanger put the stock on his Long Squeeze screen for shorting in the high teens and proposed holding it until it reached $3.50 after short-interest popped up. "When the short intensity advances sharply, that takes me out of the game," he says.

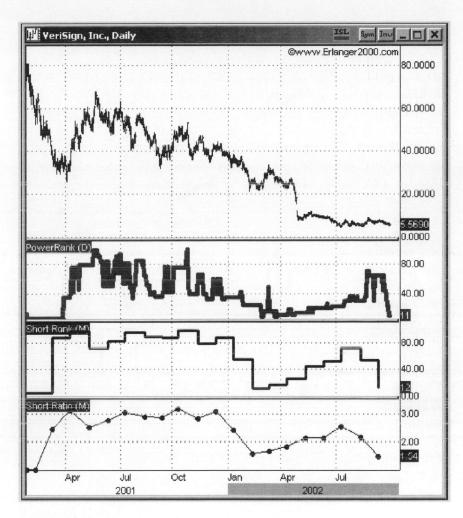

Figure 6.12 VeriSign, Inc.

Singapore-based contract manufacturing services specialist Flextronics International was a classic of the genre, as shown in Figure 6.14. As the price declined, its short intensity dropped to 25 percent. In a properly acting bull market, Erlanger points out, the short interest would rise as the stock gets cut in half with investors increasingly anticipating weaker prices—and that bearishness would itself provide fuel for the next leg up. Instead, the short interest rises as the psychology is one of

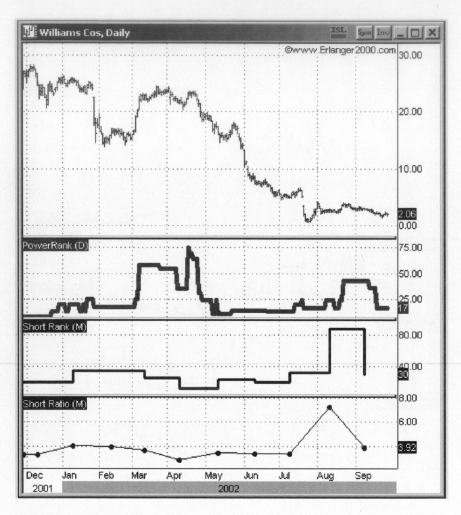

Figure 6.13   Williams Cos.

increased hope rather than increased fear. As the stock fell from $30 to $15, more and more traders covered their shorts and bought the stock, and the lower prices caused other sideline players to become more bullish. As it muddled along between $15 and $20 between February and May 2002, the short interest really fell off until it dropped to almost nothing. The lack of shorts to squeeze, or alternatively the increase in complacency, is in part what led the stock to get cut in half again to around $7 by September 2002.

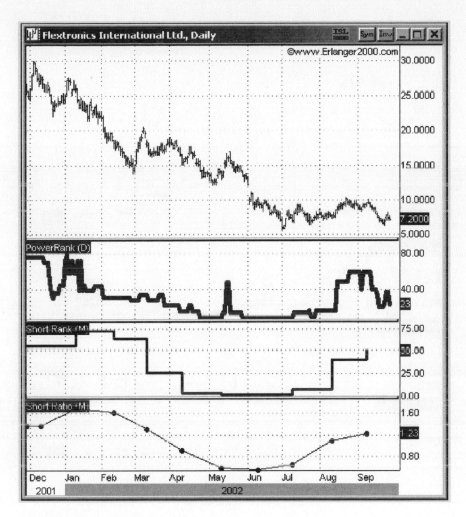

Figure 6.14 Flextronics International Ltd.

This chart shows exactly what was wrong with the entire stock market in 2002. There was an inability to generate a healthy wall of worry. The psychological widget was making people do the wrong thing at the wrong time. The stock looks like a safe bet for longs all the way down—it was a classic mistake. Here the investor would want to see the short interest at 3.0 before going long. "Pretty much everyone who owns shares now is a loser, which is not a good way to start a new bull run," Erlanger said.

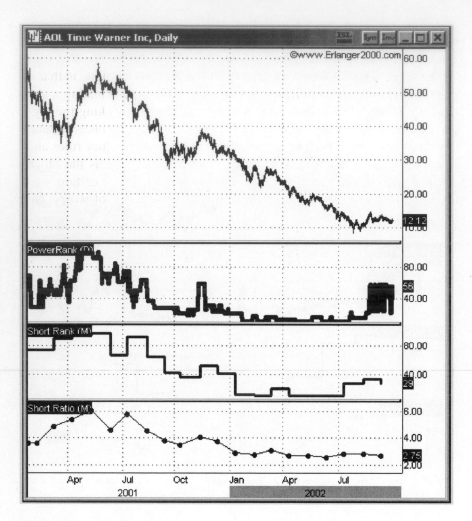

Figure 6.15   AOL Time Warner.

AOL Time Warner appeared to be a good short squeeze, or long candidate, momentarily in late April 2001, and Erlanger made a bit of money on the long side for a short while. (See Figure 6.15.) As the stock fell throughout 2001 the short interest also fell—another sign of complacency and a signal that more selling would follow. AOL was the archetypal overloved stock in its heyday. It became a good short candidate in January 2002. Its Power Rank slipped below 40 percent, as the short ratio sank below 4.0, and short intensity almost disappeared. Following the discipline of observing the low level of shorting combined with price weakness would have given traders confidence to stay short until the stock was in the $10–$12 range.

Erlanger's lesson for swing traders, if it isn't clear by now, is that it pays to focus on the sentiment surrounding a stock by formulating a statistically valid opinion about whether bulls or bears are making the bigger bet. If short selling declines as the stock price of a once-popular company weakens, it is an almost certain sign that complacency rules and more weakness lies ahead. And if short selling increases as the stock price of a once-hated company strengthens, it is an almost certain sign that it will benefit from the healthy construction of a wall of worry. No pain, no gain.

Index